PREFACE

Arguably the Germans invented the single seat fighter as we know it today… Despite numerous attempts by other countries to outfit an airplane with a forward-firing machine gun, including Roland Garros fitting his Morane-Saulnier Parasol with steel plates on the propeller blades, it was when Anthony Fokker introduced his famous Eindecker with a practical synchronization system that would allow him to fire a machine gun on the line of flight between the propeller rotating blades that the true fighter airplane was born, dedicated exclusively to fighting enemy machines in the air.

Throughout most of World War I, German fighter pilots fought against a numerically superior enemy, and yet, thanks to the technical superiority of many of their aircraft, to clever tactics, an immense courage, and an esprit de corps that bonded them in a band of brothers, they fought their enemy until the very end of the war. In the aftermath, many of them would bitterly but proudly declare that they did not lose their war.

Probably, due to a government-backed advertising campaign, with constant newspaper articles chronicling their exploits, collectible cards with their portraits (the famous Sanke Cards), and promotion and awards granted for their aerial victories, plus the flamboyant and colourl could say today that German fighter pilots were the rock stars of the Great War!

A wide range of German-built single seat fighter aircraft saw action during the Great War, from the first Fokker Eindeckern of the summer of 1915 to the revolutionary all-metal Junkers D-I monoplane of the last days of the war.

In preparing these artworks for publication, I decided not to elaborate much on a text, since everything I could say about these airplanes has already been written by historians and authors much more authorised than me, and since my forte is the profile artwork, and that's what the readers will be looking for when buying this book, I had come to the conclusion that what I should do is focus on my aircraft profiles, and try to display them in a size where the smallest details can be observed, with a few captions that provide the basic data and some comments when I deemed necessary.

All the profiles are illustrated in a constant style, so that it is possible to see the comparative size between each type of aircraft.

Ronny Bar

ABOUT RONNY BAR

Ronny Bar was born on February 11, 1951 in Buenos Aires, Argentina, and grew up near the El Palomar Air Force Base. He first flew aged 12 in the back seat of a T-34 Mentor trainer. He began drawing and craft and building models – first Spitfires and Messerschmitts, then Camels and Fokkers later...

He then became a bass player and singer in several rock bands and enjoyed a successful career in music.

Continuing to create aviation artworks, he then discovered the collection of WW1 aircraft at Hendon, near London, establishing his already growing interest in that period. Since 2005 he has illustrated works by writers including Greg VanWyngarden, Alan Toelle, Peter Kilduff, Colin Owers, George Haddow, Gregory Alegi, Paolo Varriale, Alan Carey, Terry Phillips, Josef Scott, Jim Wilberg, Bruno Schmaelling, Paul Hare, JS Alcorn and others. His art has appeared regularly in publications such as Windsock Datafile, Windsock Worldwide, Cross & Cockade International, Over the Front, Luftwaffe im Focus, WW1 Aero, etc. From 2005 he was part of Peter Jackson's team, doing all the profile artwork for the Wingnut Wings high quality injection moulded WW1 aircraft kits. He started pilot training in 2008.

> **Profile artwork is really a crazy art... There's no such thing as a profile in nature, there are no perspectives on a profile... And despite this I keep on looking for more and more realism in my profiles!**
>
> - Ronny Bar

CONTENTS

006 | FOKKER E-I TO E-IV ▶

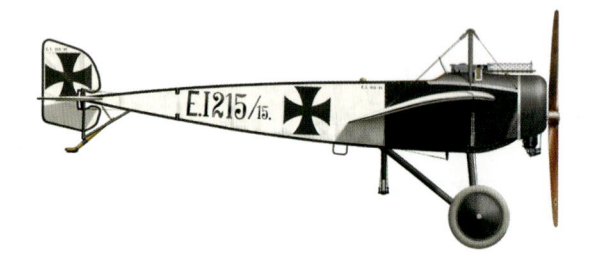

◀ **014** | PFALZ E-I TO E-IV

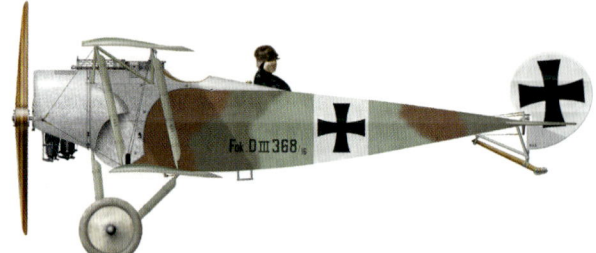

024 | FOKKER D-I TO D-III ▶

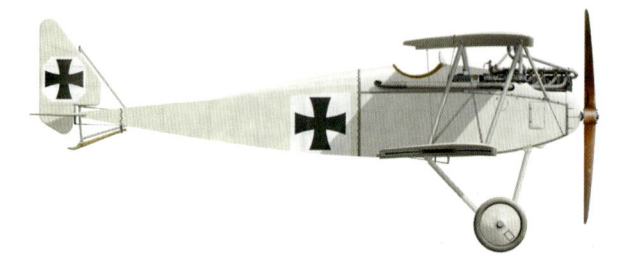

◀ **026** | HALBERSTADT D-II TO D-V

034 | ALBATROS D-I TO D-III ▶

◀ **050** | ROLAND D-II AND D-IIA

056 | SIEMENS-SCHUCKERT D-I ▶

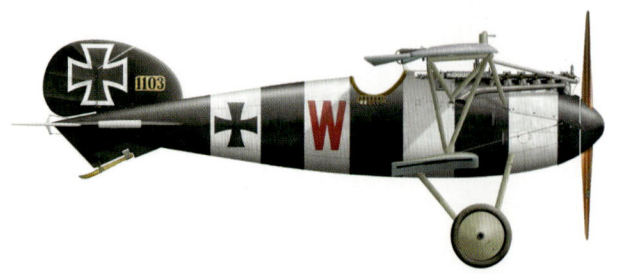

◀ **058** | ALBATROS D-V AND D-VA

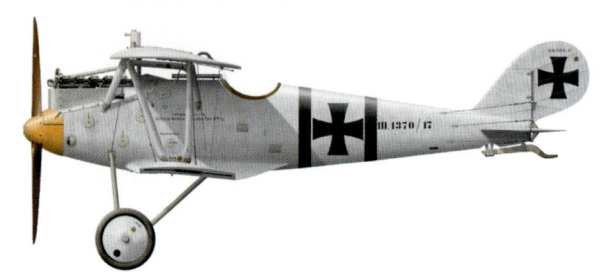

072 | PFALZ D-III AND D-IIIA ▶

086 | FOKKER F-I AND DR-I

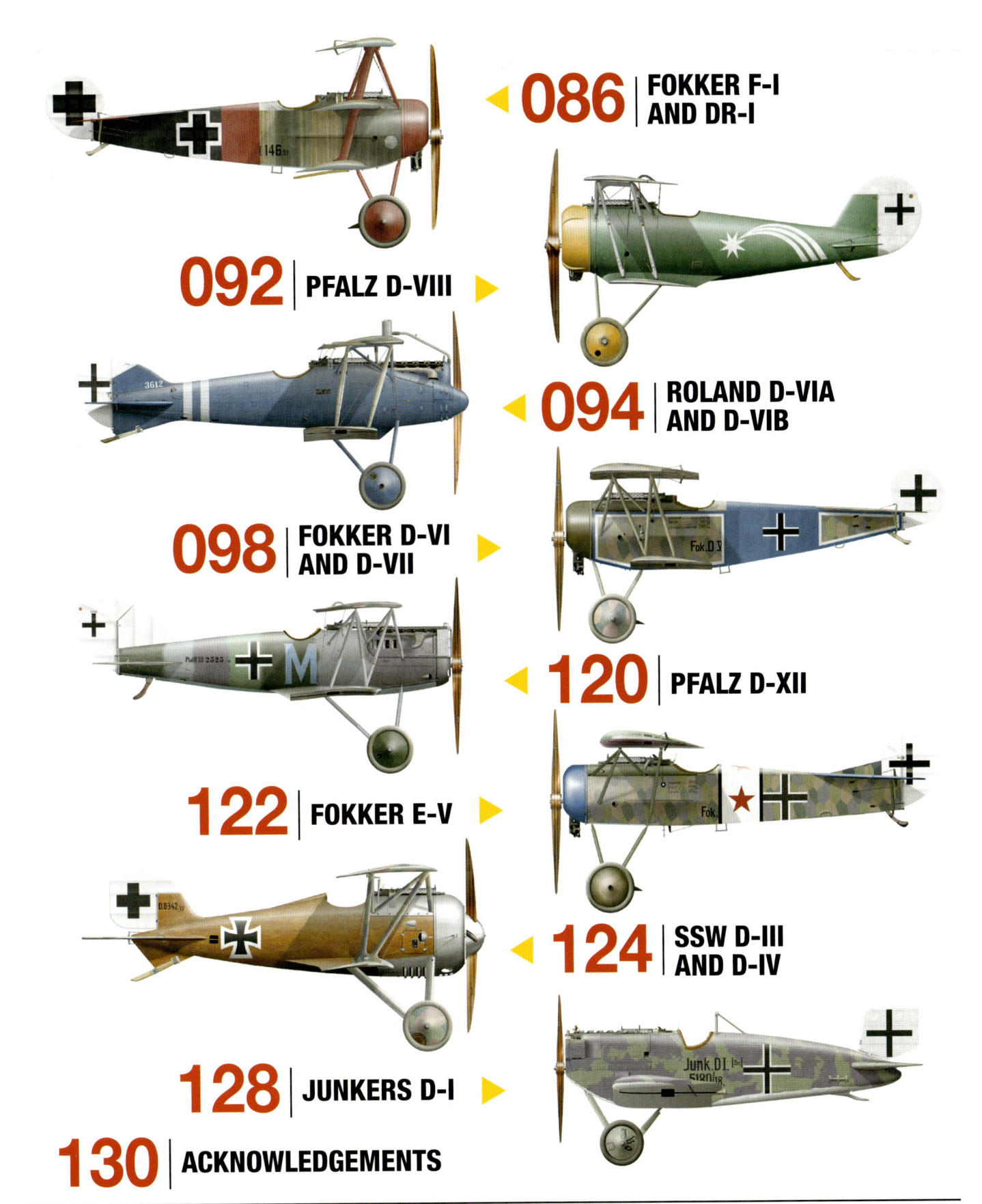

092 | PFALZ D-VIII

094 | ROLAND D-VIA AND D-VIB

098 | FOKKER D-VI AND D-VII

120 | PFALZ D-XII

122 | FOKKER E-V

124 | SSW D-III AND D-IV

128 | JUNKERS D-I

130 | ACKNOWLEDGEMENTS

All illustrations:
RONNY BAR
Design:
DRUCK MEDIA PVT. LTD.
Publisher:
STEVE O'HARA
Production editor:
DAN SHARP

Published by:
MORTONS MEDIA GROUP LTD, MEDIA CENTRE, MORTON WAY, HORNCASTLE, LINCOLNSHIRE LN9 6JR.
Tel. 01507 529529
ISBN: 978-1-911703-44-0

Mortons MEDIA GROUP LTD

© 2024 MORTONS MEDIA GROUP LTD. ALL RIGHTS RESERVED. NO PART OF THIS PUBLICATION MAY BE REPRODUCED OR TRANSMITTED IN ANY FORM OR BY ANY MEANS, ELECTRONIC OR MECHANICAL, INCLUDING PHOTOCOPYING, RECORDING, OR ANY INFORMATION STORAGE RETRIEVAL SYSTEM WITHOUT PRIOR PERMISSION IN WRITING FROM THE PUBLISHER.

FOKKER E.I

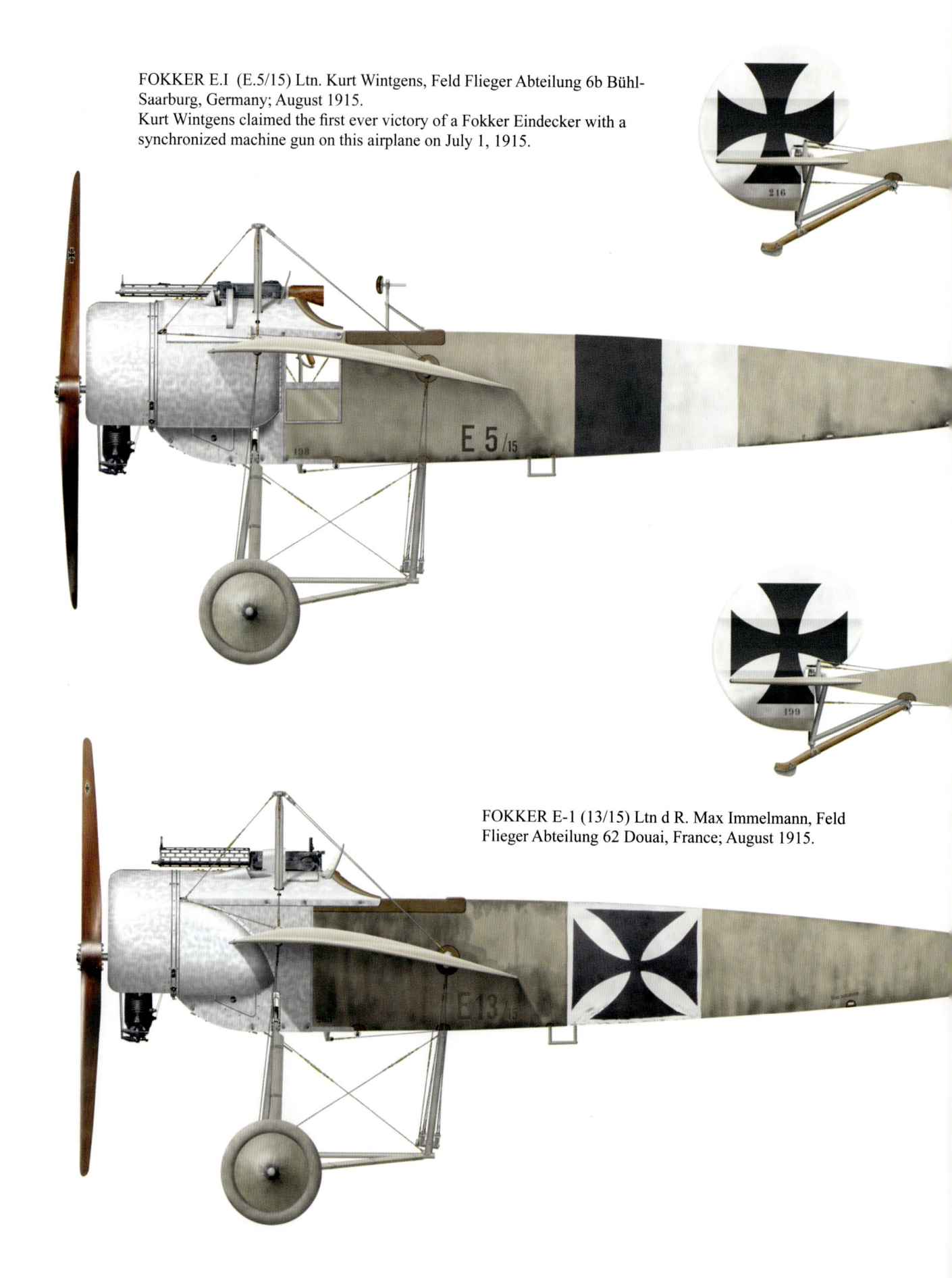

FOKKER E.I (E.5/15) Ltn. Kurt Wintgens, Feld Flieger Abteilung 6b Bühl-Saarburg, Germany; August 1915.
Kurt Wintgens claimed the first ever victory of a Fokker Eindecker with a synchronized machine gun on this airplane on July 1, 1915.

FOKKER E-1 (13/15) Ltn d R. Max Immelmann, Feld Flieger Abteilung 62 Douai, France; August 1915.

FOKKER A.III (A.16/15) Ltn. Otto Parschau, Feld Flieger Abteilung 62 Douai, France; July 1915.
Otto Parschau's personal airplane, this Fokker A-III, in late May 1915 was the first one to be fitted with a workable synchronization gear, becoming the Fokker Eindecker prototype.

FOKKER E-1 (6/15) Uffz. Richard Dietrich, Feld Flieger Abteilung 24 Lille, France; August 1915.

FOKKER E-II

FOKKER E-II (69/15) Ltn. Kurt von Crailsheim, Feldflieger Abteilung 53 Monthois, France; September 1915.

FOKKER E-II (33/15) Vzfw. Eduard Böhme, Kampfeinsitzer Kommando Ensisheim, Ensisheim, Germany; October 1915.

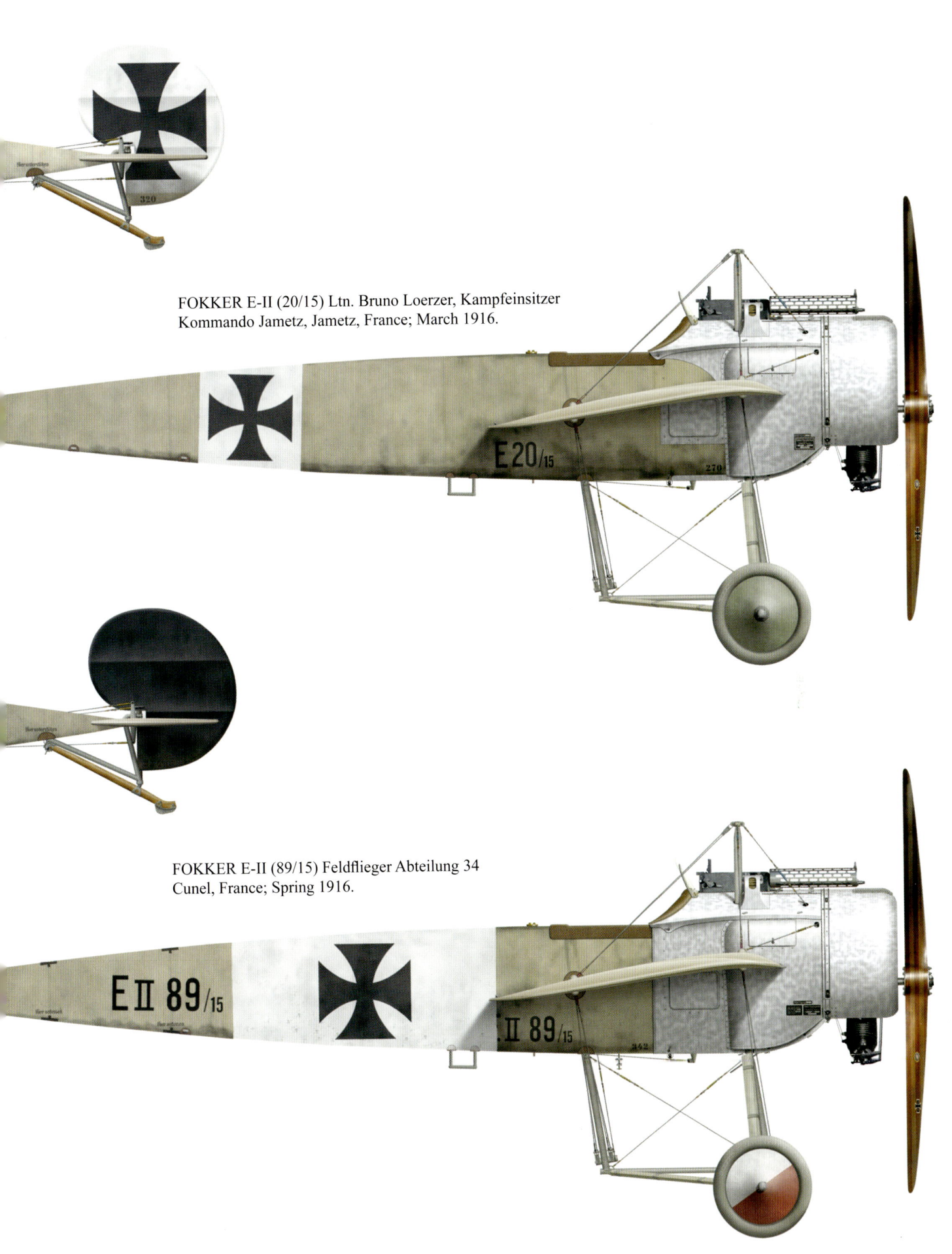

FOKKER E-II (20/15) Ltn. Bruno Loerzer, Kampfeinsitzer
Kommando Jametz, Jametz, France; March 1916.

FOKKER E-II (89/15) Feldflieger Abteilung 34
Cunel, France; Spring 1916.

FOKKER E-III

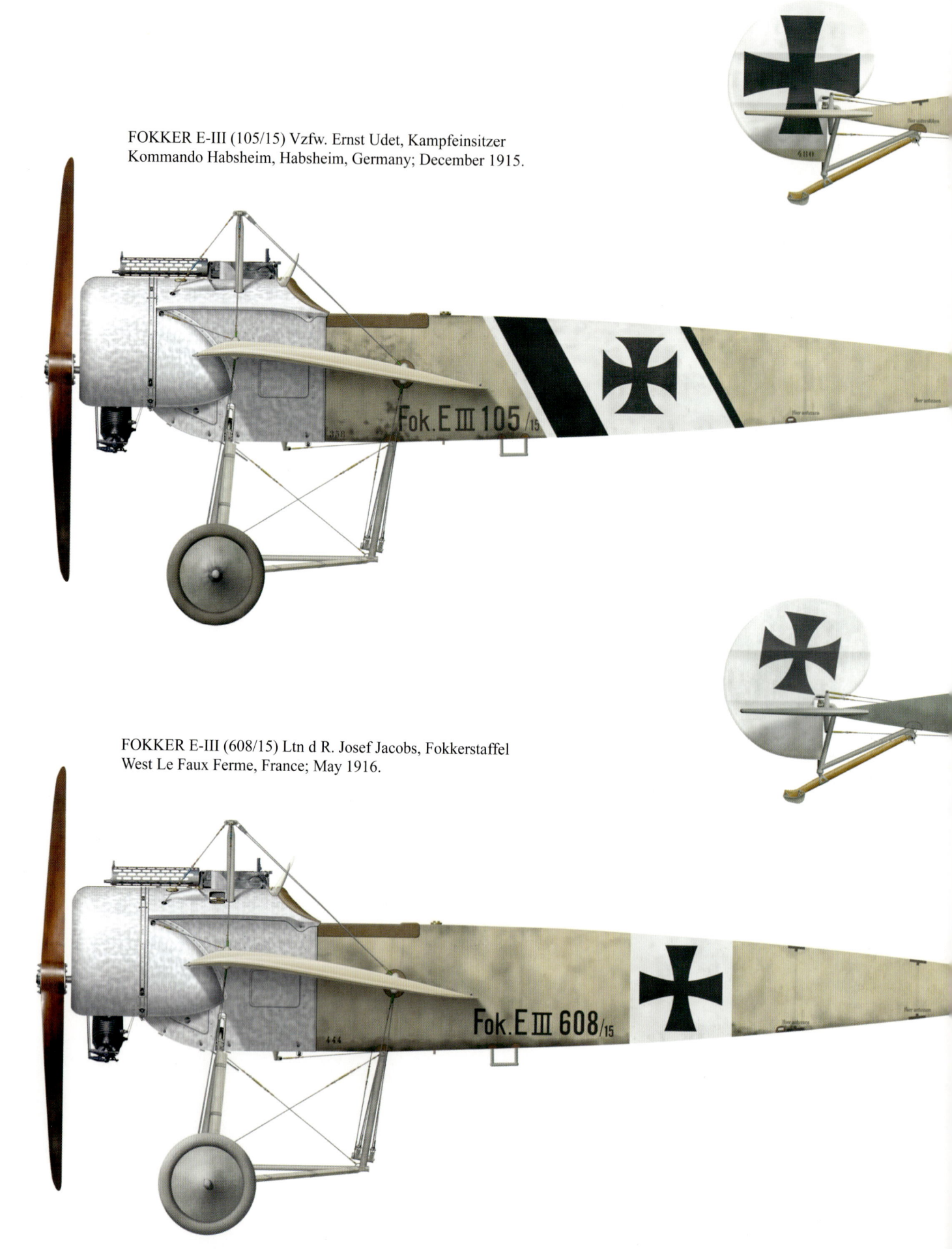

FOKKER E-III (105/15) Vzfw. Ernst Udet, Kampfeinsitzer Kommando Habsheim, Habsheim, Germany; December 1915.

FOKKER E-III (608/15) Ltn d R. Josef Jacobs, Fokkerstaffel West Le Faux Ferme, France; May 1916.

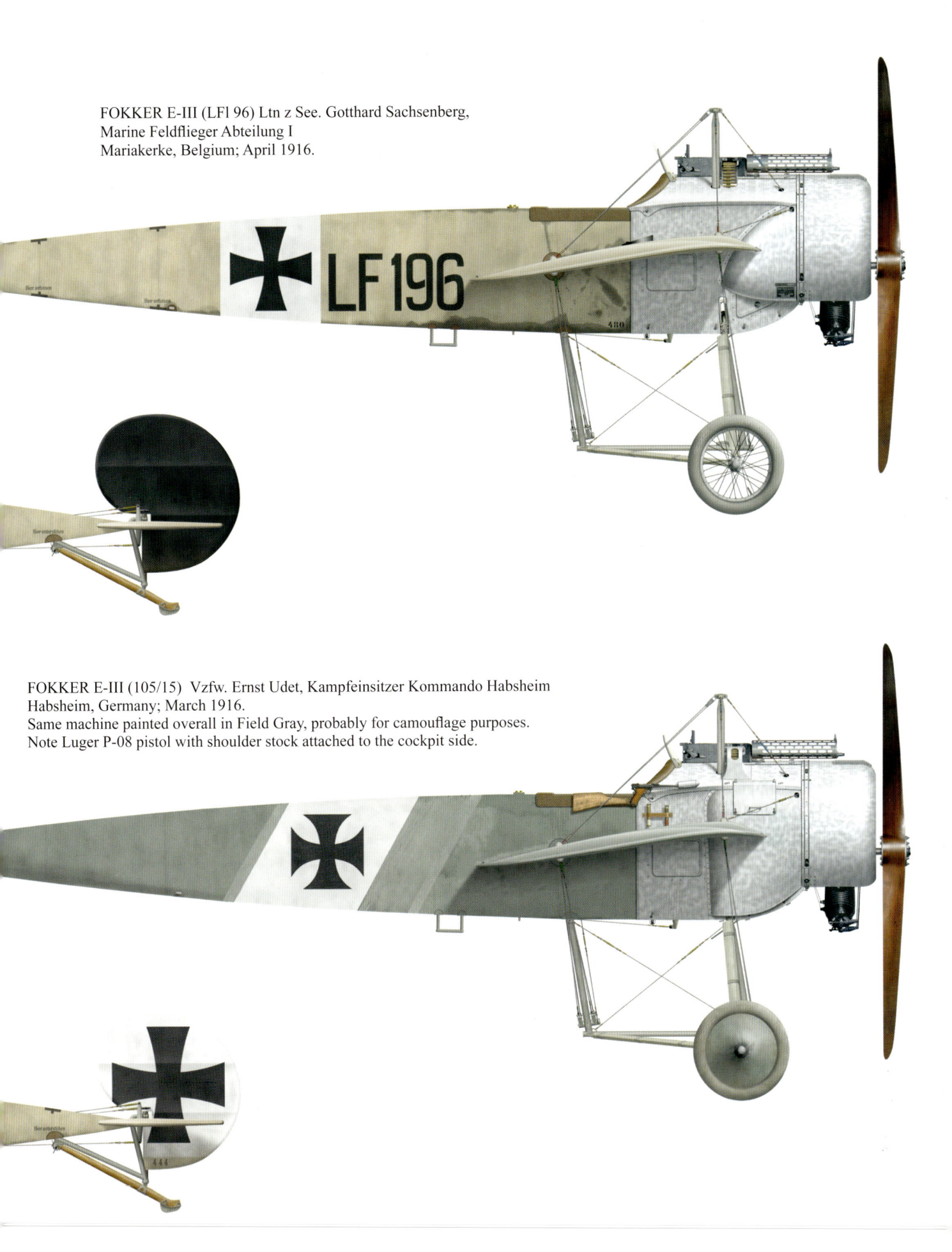

FOKKER E-III (LFl 96) Ltn z See. Gotthard Sachsenberg,
Marine Feldflieger Abteilung I
Mariakerke, Belgium; April 1916.

FOKKER E-III (105/15) Vzfw. Ernst Udet, Kampfeinsitzer Kommando Habsheim
Habsheim, Germany; March 1916.
Same machine painted overall in Field Gray, probably for camouflage purposes.
Note Luger P-08 pistol with shoulder stock attached to the cockpit side.

FOKKER E-IV

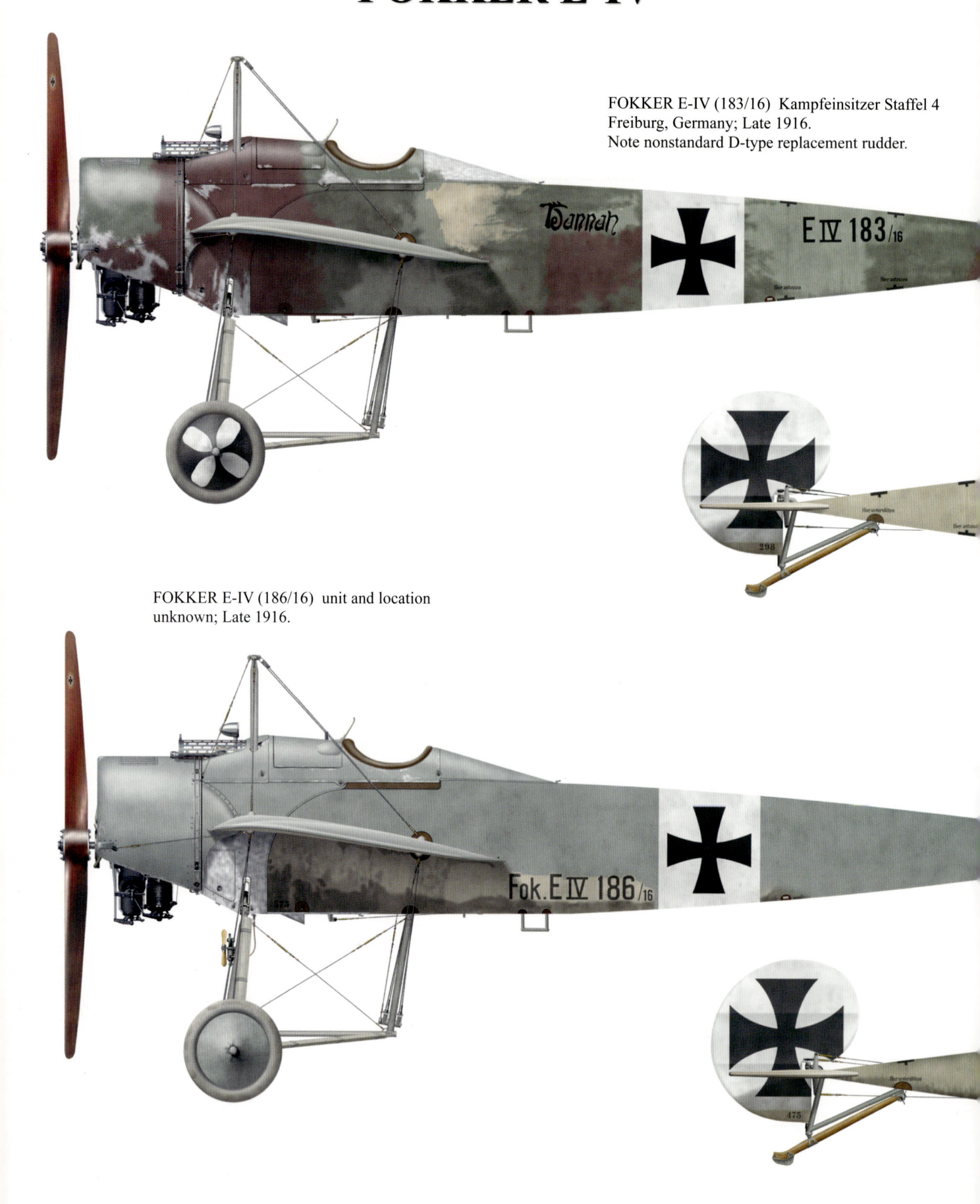

FOKKER E-IV (183/16) Kampfeinsitzer Staffel 4 Freiburg, Germany; Late 1916.
Note nonstandard D-type replacement rudder.

FOKKER E-IV (186/16) unit and location unknown; Late 1916.

12

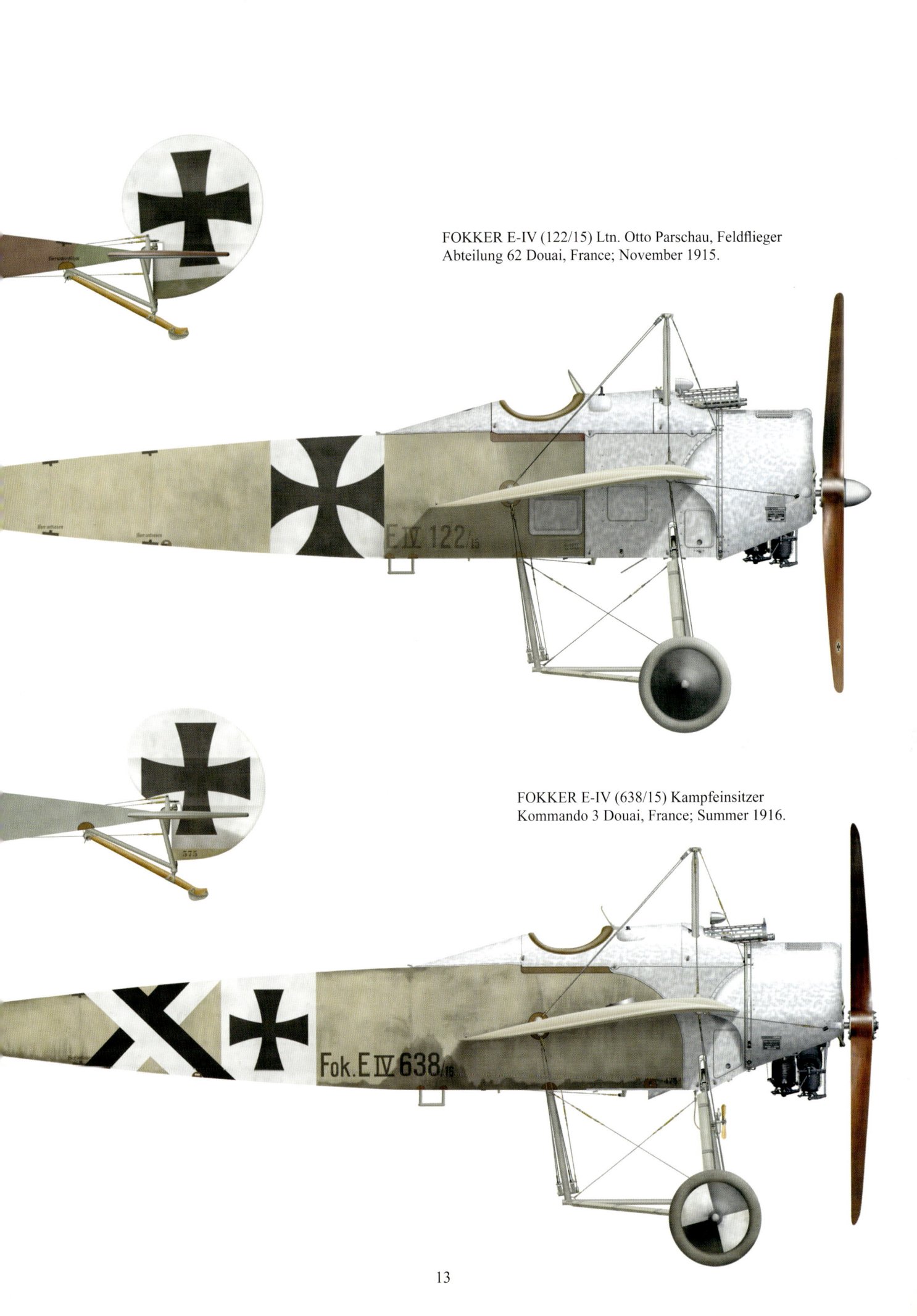

FOKKER E-IV (122/15) Ltn. Otto Parschau, Feldflieger Abteilung 62 Douai, France; November 1915.

FOKKER E-IV (638/15) Kampfeinsitzer Kommando 3 Douai, France; Summer 1916.

13

PFALZ E-I

PFALZ E-I (479/15) Feld Flieger Abteilung 51
Vilna, Russia; December 1915.

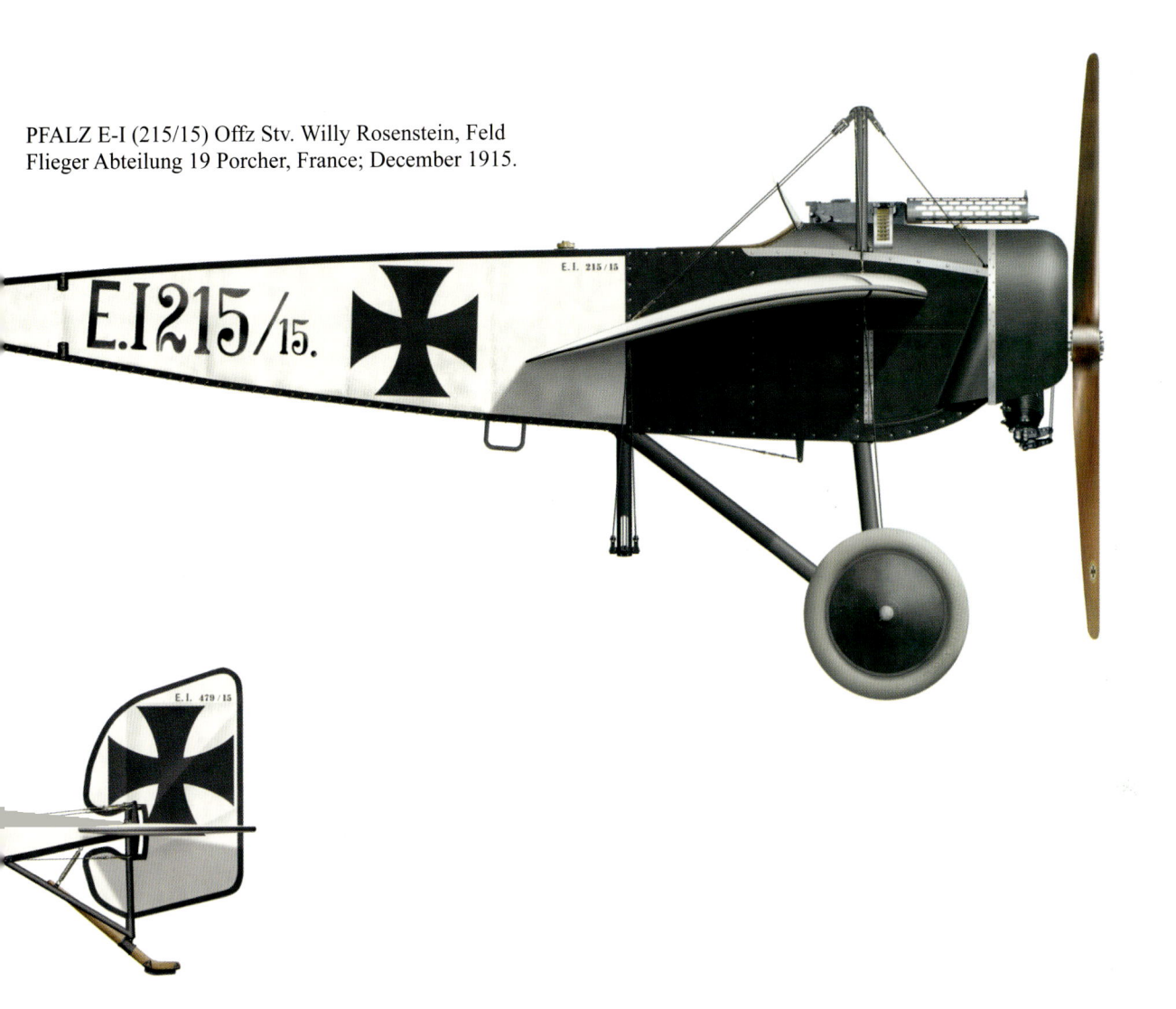

PFALZ E-I (215/15) Offz Stv. Willy Rosenstein, Feld Flieger Abteilung 19 Porcher, France; December 1915.

PFALZ E-I (205/15) Ltn d R. Ernst von Lössl, Feld-Flieger Abteilung 21 location unknown; Late 1915.

PFALZ E-II

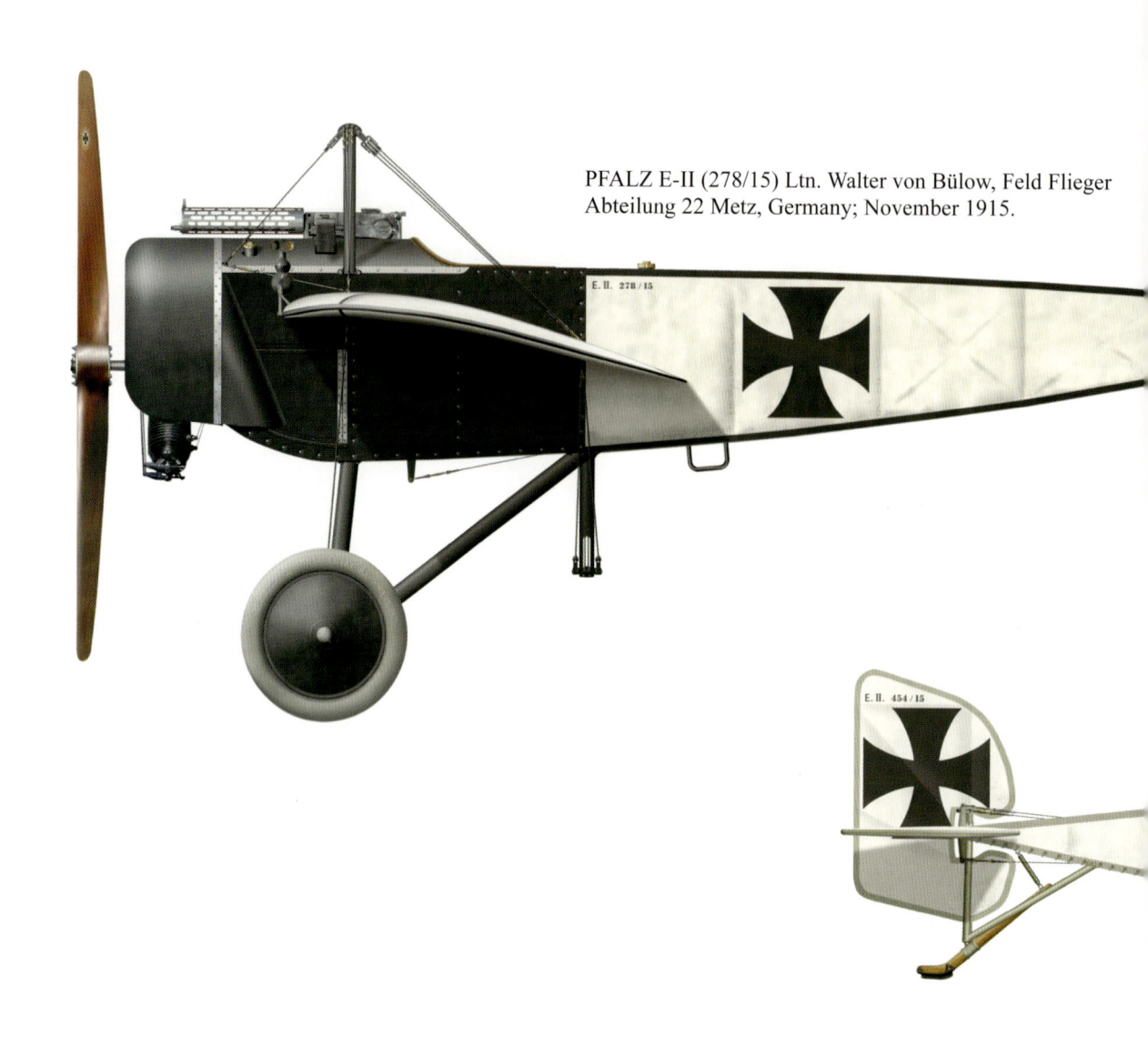

PFALZ E-II (278/15) Ltn. Walter von Bülow, Feld Flieger Abteilung 22 Metz, Germany; November 1915.

PFALZ E-II (serial, unit and location unknown) Early 1916.

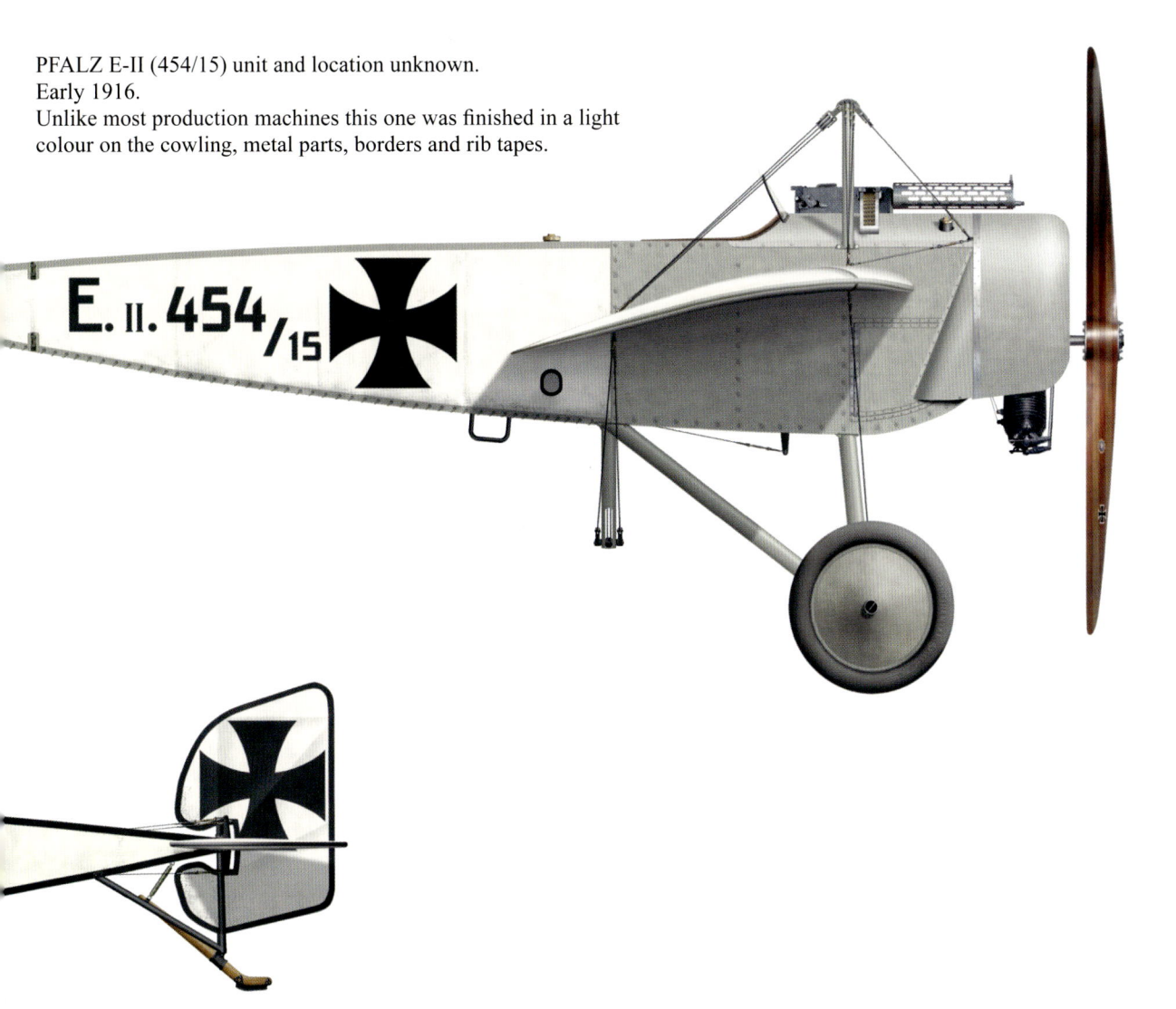

PFALZ E-II (454/15) unit and location unknown.
Early 1916.
Unlike most production machines this one was finished in a light colour on the cowling, metal parts, borders and rib tapes.

PFALZ E-IV

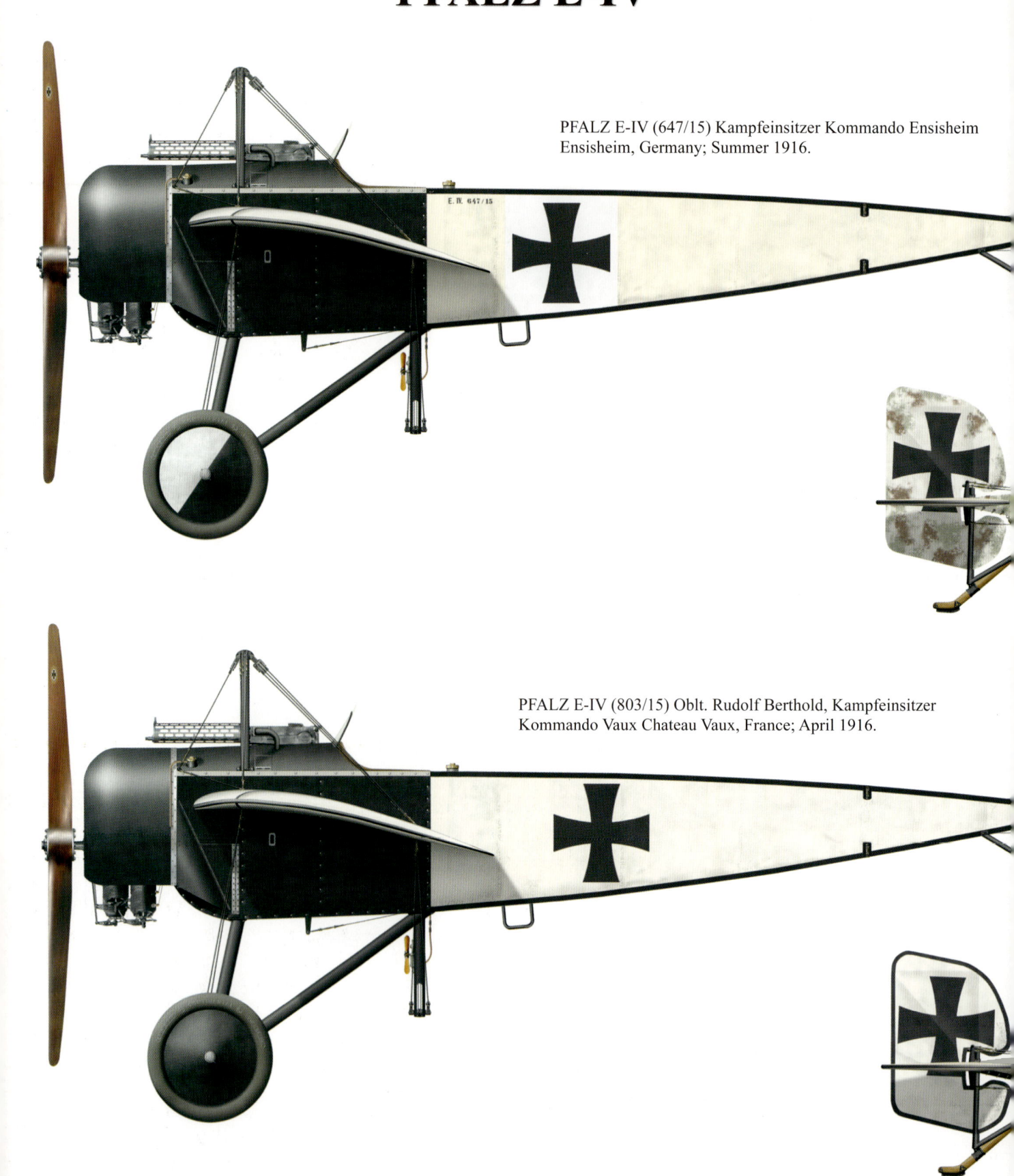

PFALZ E-IV (647/15) Kampfeinsitzer Kommando Ensisheim Ensisheim, Germany; Summer 1916.

PFALZ E-IV (803/15) Oblt. Rudolf Berthold, Kampfeinsitzer Kommando Vaux Chateau Vaux, France; April 1916.

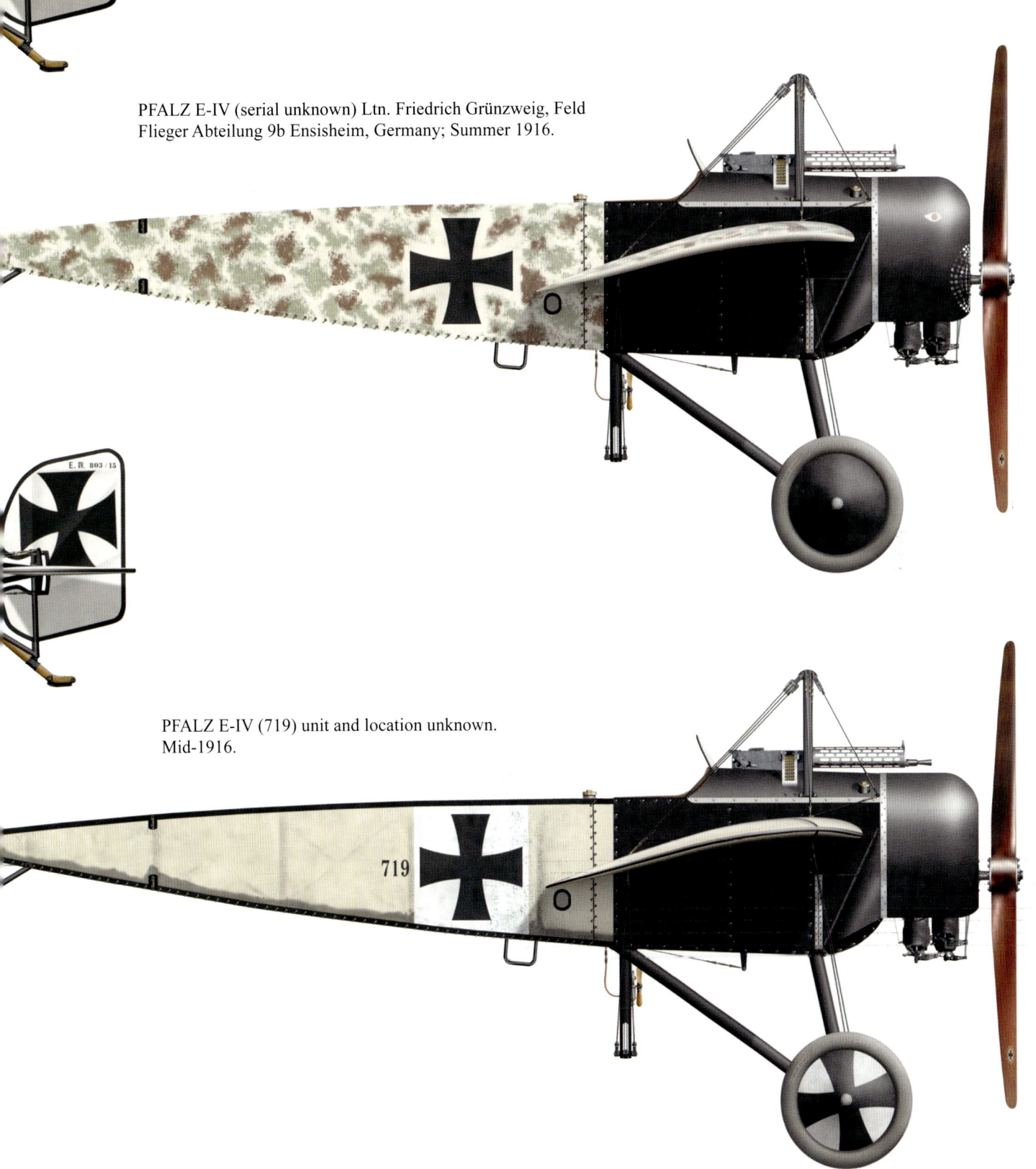

PFALZ E-IV (serial unknown) Ltn. Friedrich Grünzweig, Feld
Flieger Abteilung 9b Ensisheim, Germany; Summer 1916.

PFALZ E-IV (719) unit and location unknown.
Mid-1916.

FOKKER D-I

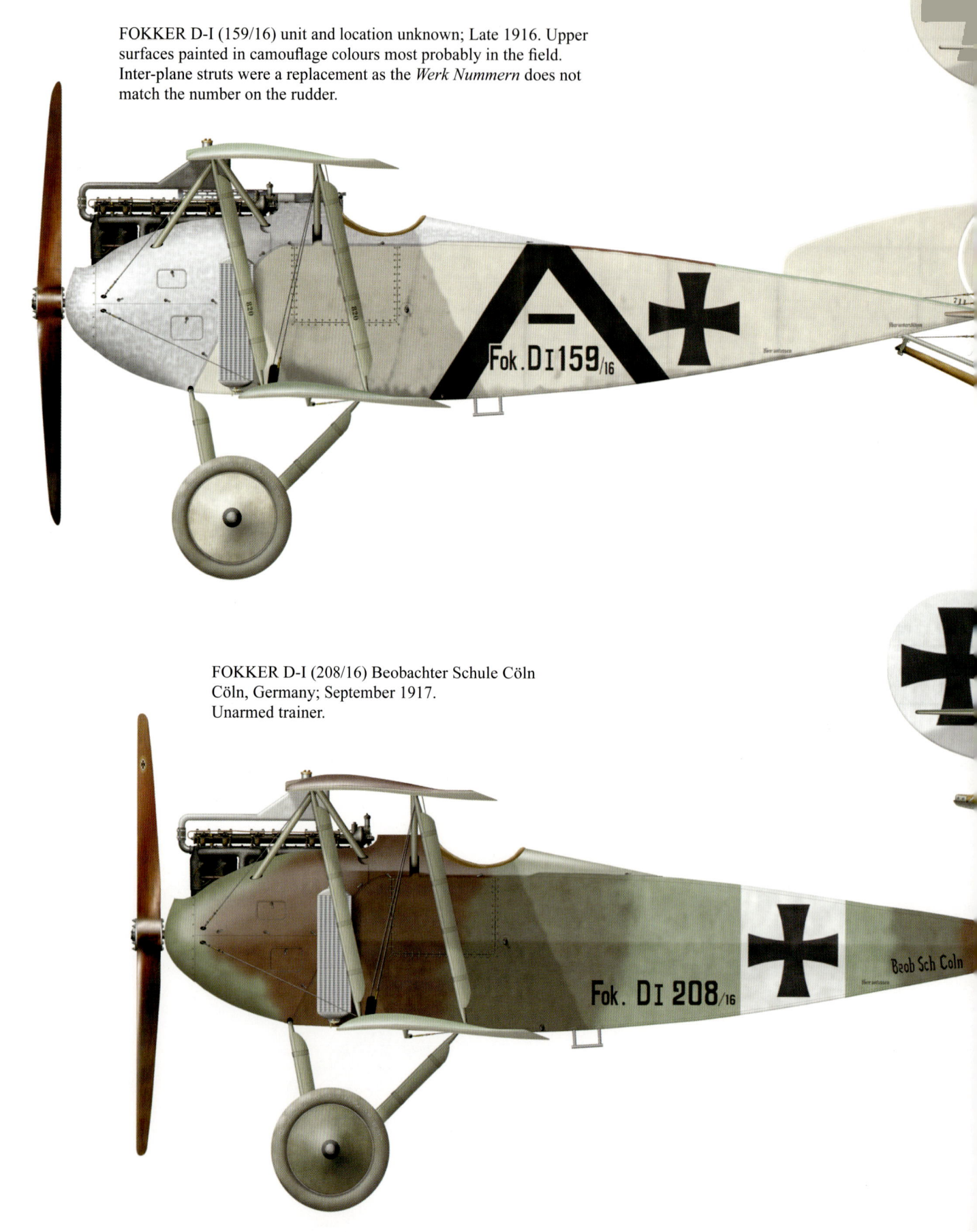

FOKKER D-I (159/16) unit and location unknown; Late 1916. Upper surfaces painted in camouflage colours most probably in the field. Inter-plane struts were a replacement as the *Werk Nummern* does not match the number on the rudder.

FOKKER D-I (208/16) Beobachter Schule Cöln
Cöln, Germany; September 1917.
Unarmed trainer.

FOKKER D-I (151/16) Jagdstaffel 1
Bertincourt, France; August 1916.

FOKKER D-I (190?/16) Ltn. Otto Kissenberth, Jagdstaffel 16
Ensishiem, Germany; Late 1916.
One of the ten machines from the second batch ordered in October 1916 and numbered 1900/16 to 1909/16.
Since its *Armee* Nr. unconfirmed it was speculatively depicted as 1900/16.

FOKKER D-II

FOKKER D-II (serial unknown) Ltn. Otto Kissenberth, Jagdstaffel 16 Ensisheim, Germany; November 1916.

FOKKER D-II (2393/16) Kampfeinsitzer Staffel 4 Freiburg, Germany; Late 1916.

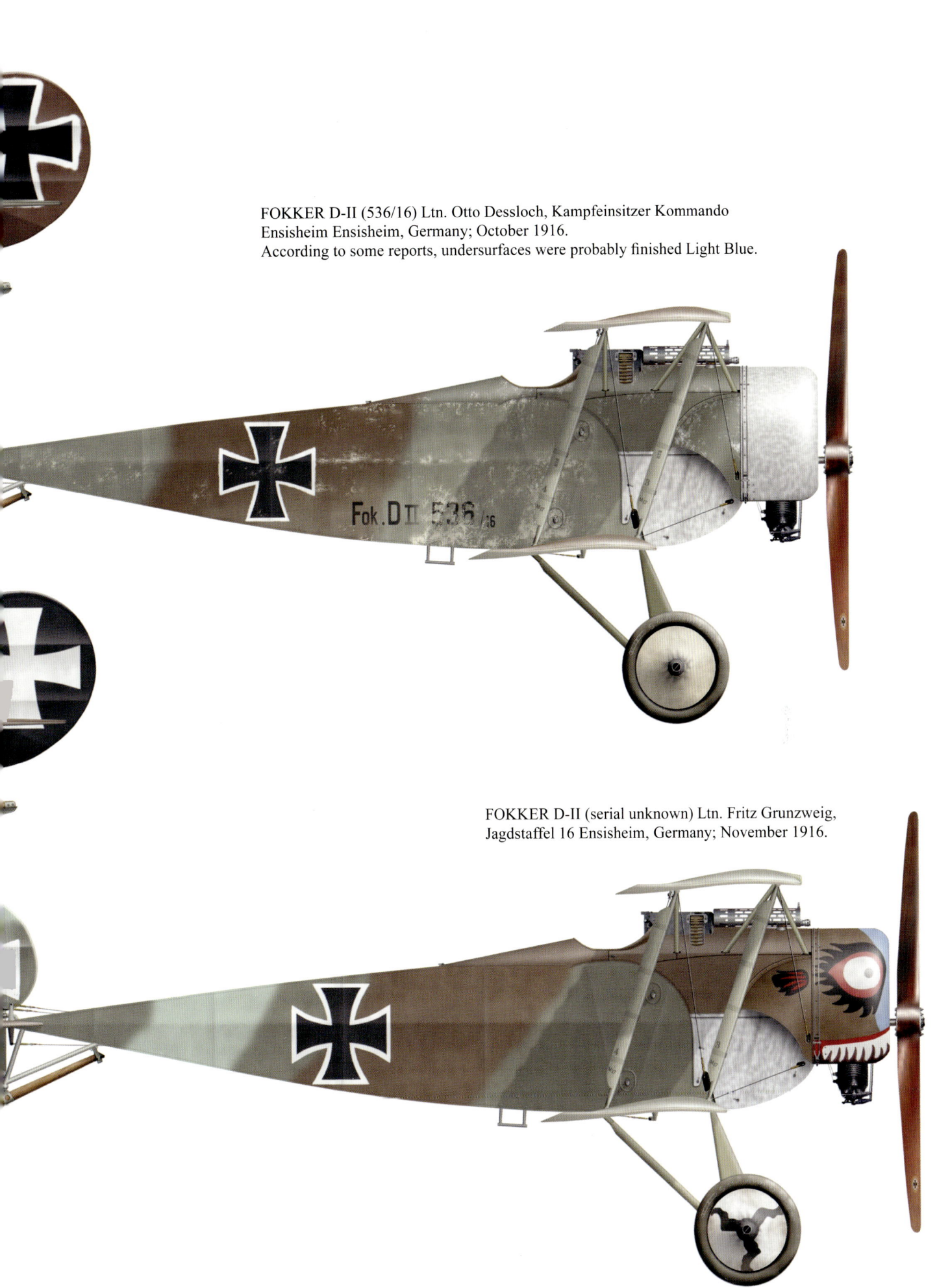

FOKKER D-II (536/16) Ltn. Otto Dessloch, Kampfeinsitzer Kommando
Ensisheim Ensisheim, Germany; October 1916.
According to some reports, undersurfaces were probably finished Light Blue.

FOKKER D-II (serial unknown) Ltn. Fritz Grunzweig,
Jagdstaffel 16 Ensisheim, Germany; November 1916.

FOKKER D-III

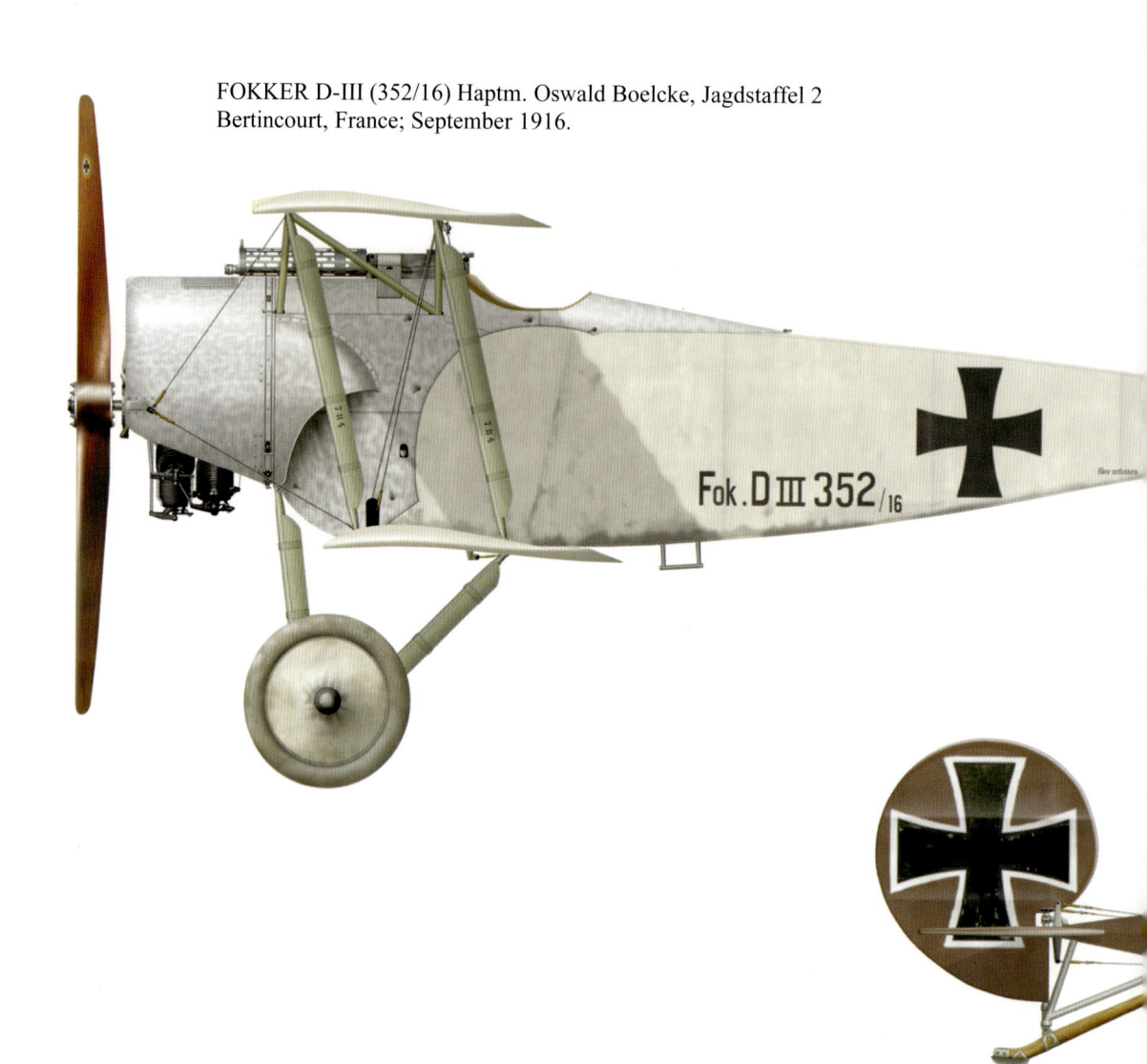

FOKKER D-III (352/16) Haptm. Oswald Boelcke, Jagdstaffel 2
Bertincourt, France; September 1916.

FOKKER D-III (368/16) Vzfw. Ernst Udet, Jagdstaffel 15
Habsheim, Germany; October 1916.
Notice the silhouette of an observer made of tin plate to deceive
the enemy pilots into thinking they were attacking a two-seater.

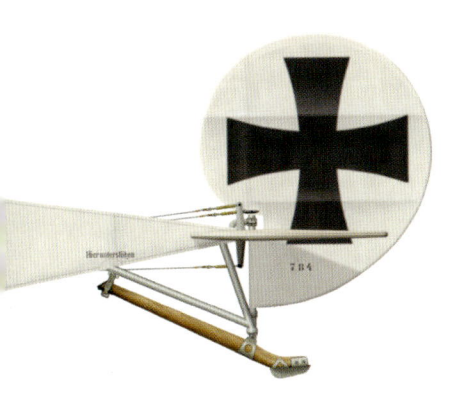

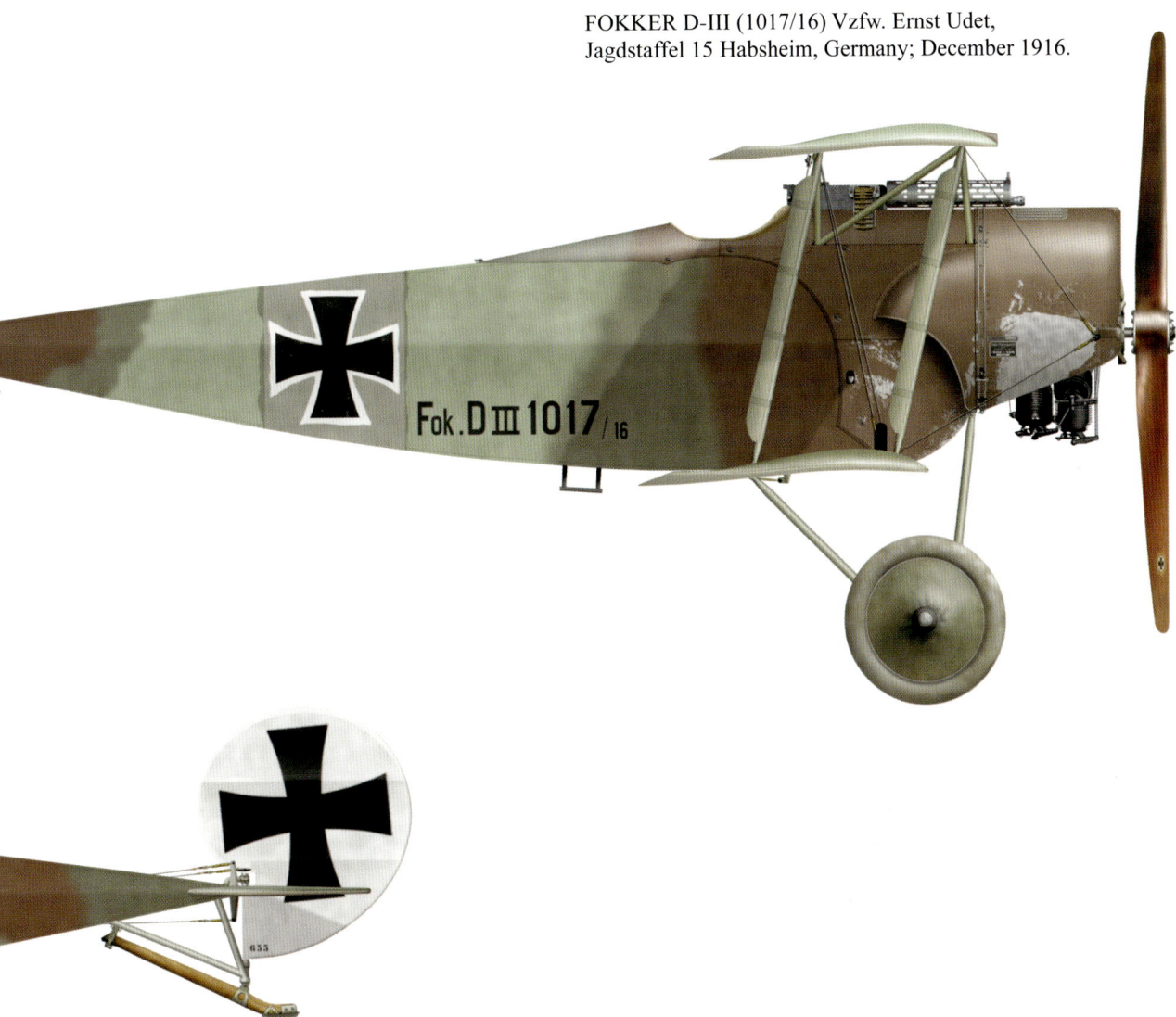

FOKKER D-III (1017/16) Vzfw. Ernst Udet,
Jagdstaffel 15 Habsheim, Germany; December 1916.

HALBERSTADT D-II

HALBERSTADT D-II (serial unknown) Offz Stv. Klein, Jagdstaffel 5
Gonnelieu, France; February 1917.

HALBERSTADT D-II (serial unknown) Kampfstaffel Metz
Metz-Frescaty, Germany; October 1916.
Notice replacement rudder from a camouflaged machine.

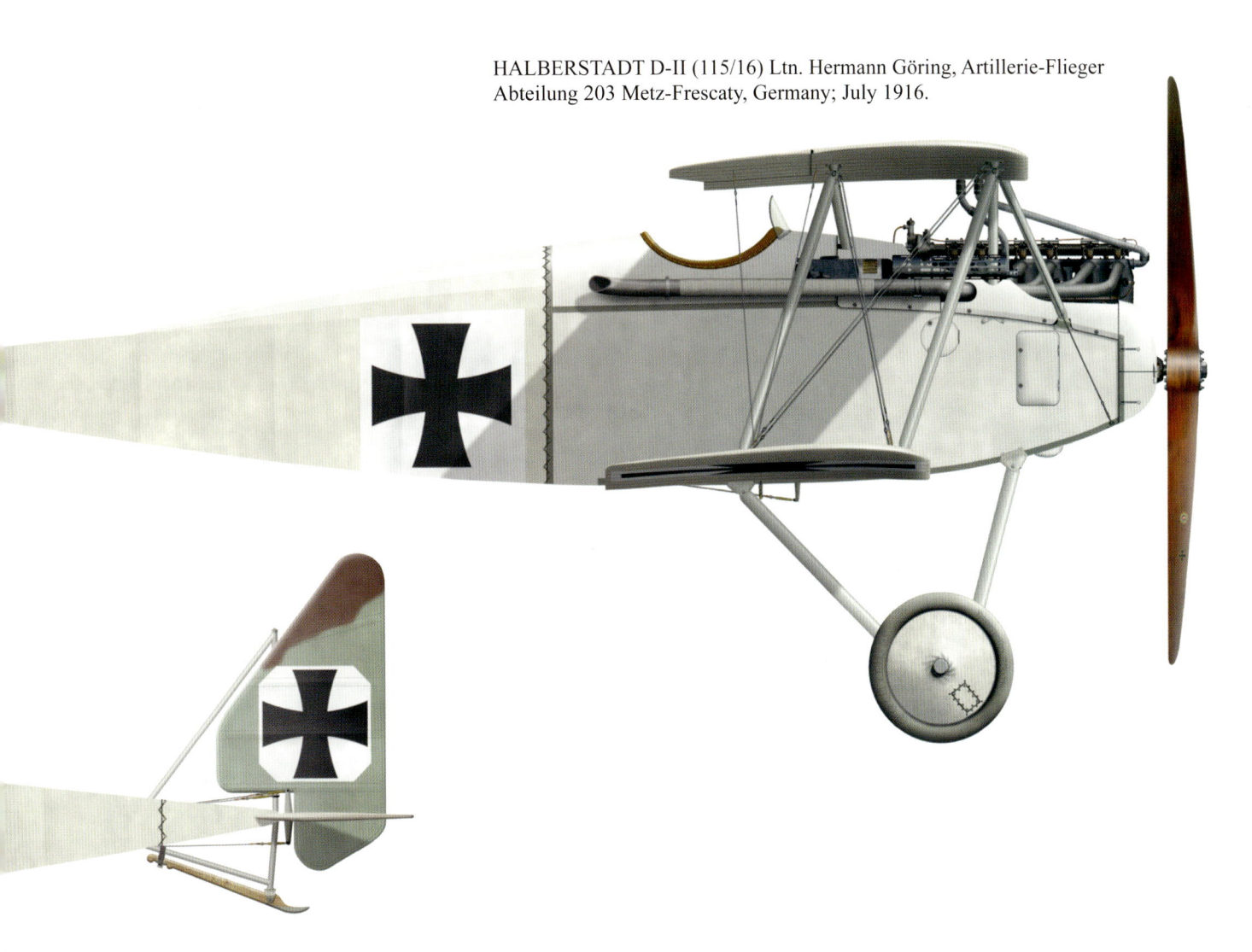

HALBERSTADT D-II (115/16) Ltn. Hermann Göring, Artillerie-Flieger Abteilung 203 Metz-Frescaty, Germany; July 1916.

HALBERSTADT D-II (HAN) & (AV)

HALBERSTADT D-II (Han) (810/16) Vzfw. Erich Schutze,
Jagdstaffel 25 Kanatrlarci, Macedonia; Early 1917.

HALBERSTADT D-II (Han) (813/16) Jagdstaffel 25
Kanatrlarci, Macedonia; Early 1917.

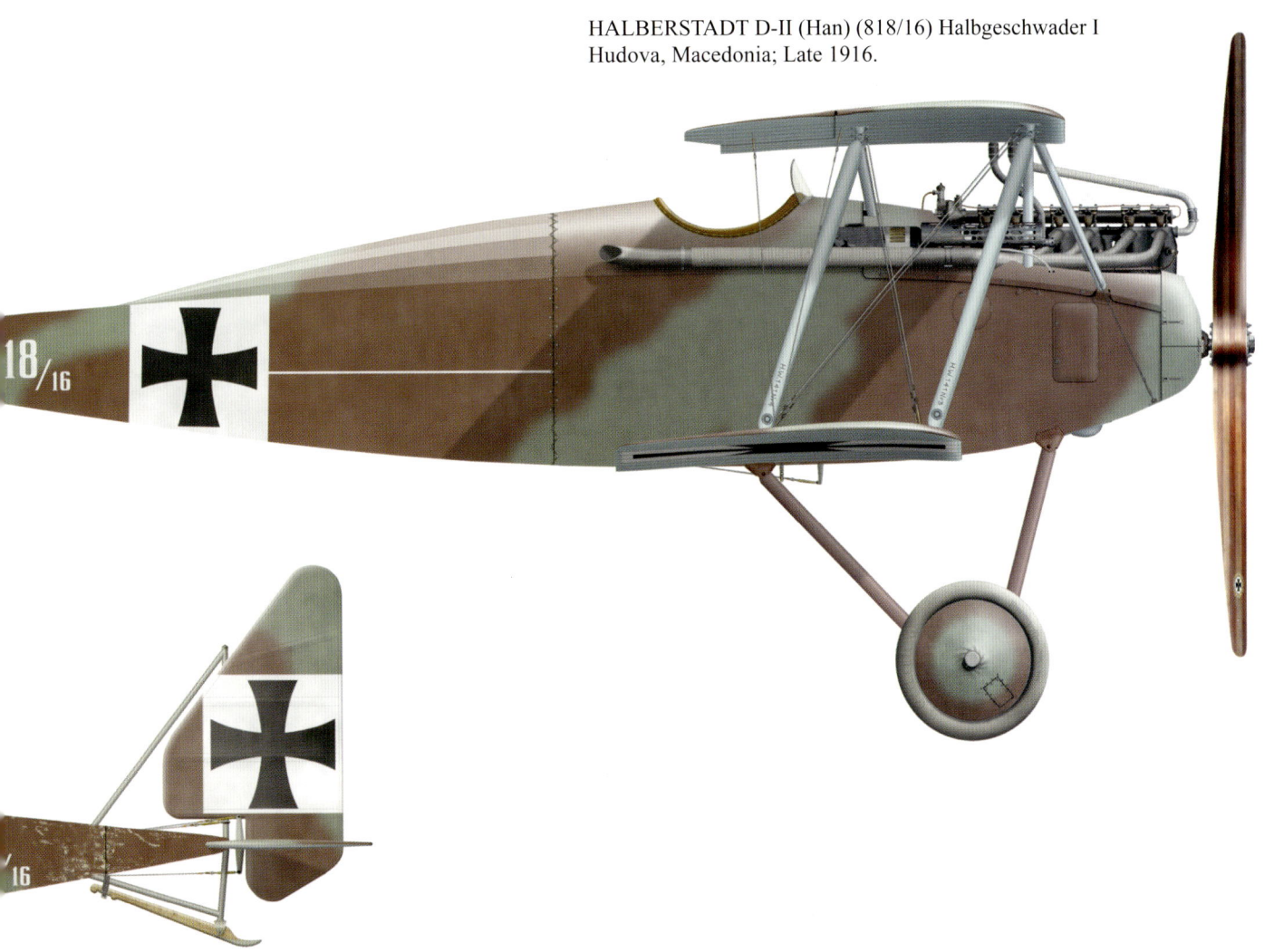

HALBERSTADT D-II (Han) (818/16) Halbgeschwader I
Hudova, Macedonia; Late 1916.

HALBERSTADT D-III

HALBERSTADT D-III (serial unknown) Kampfeinsitzer
Staffel 4 Freiburg, Germany; Late 1916.

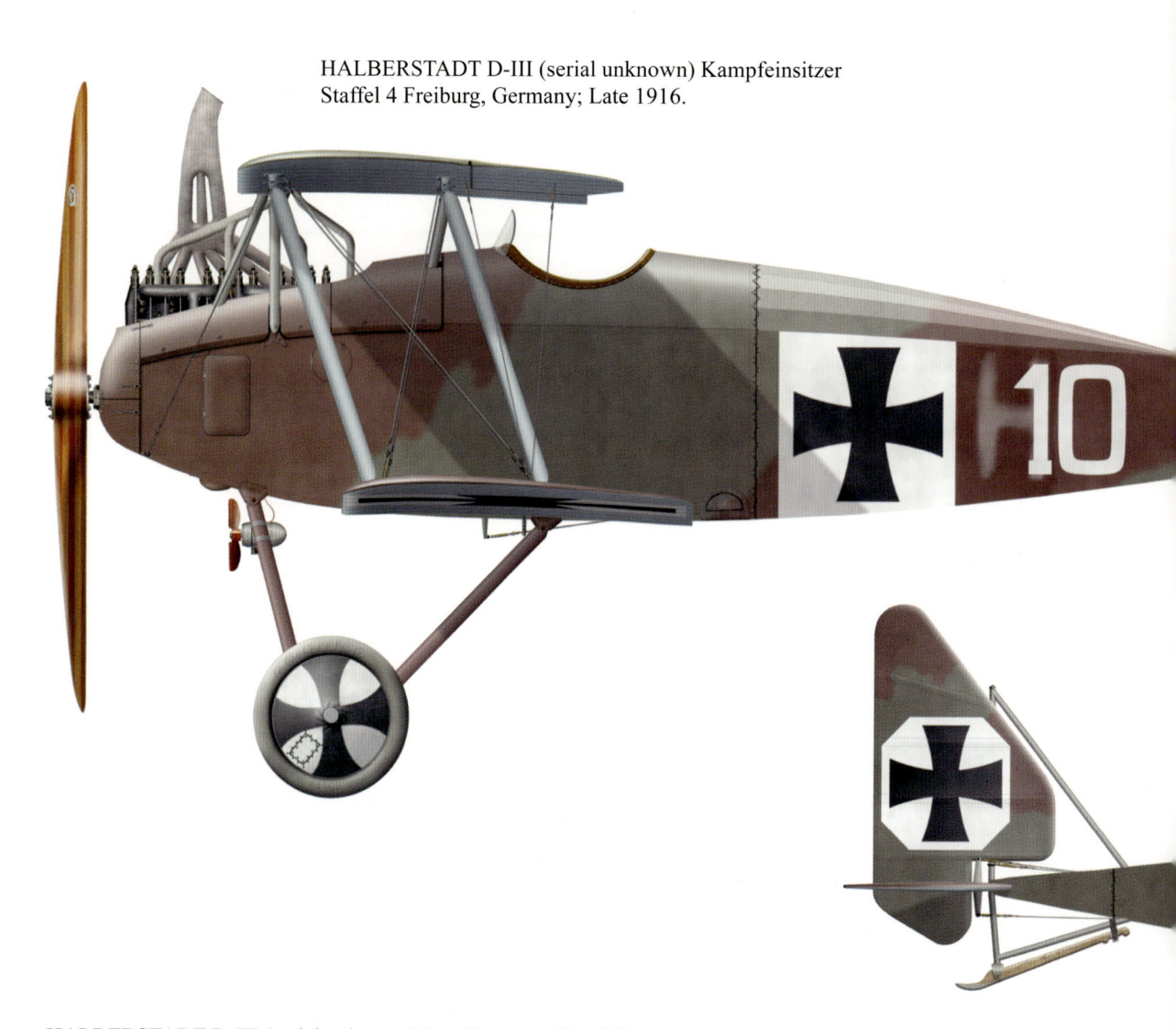

HALBERSTADT D-III (serial unknown) Ltn. Hans von Keudell,
Jagdstaffel 1 Bertincourt, France; September 1916.

HALBERSTADT D-III (serial unknown) Ltn. Ernst von Althaus, Jagdstaffel 4 Vaux, France; August 1916.

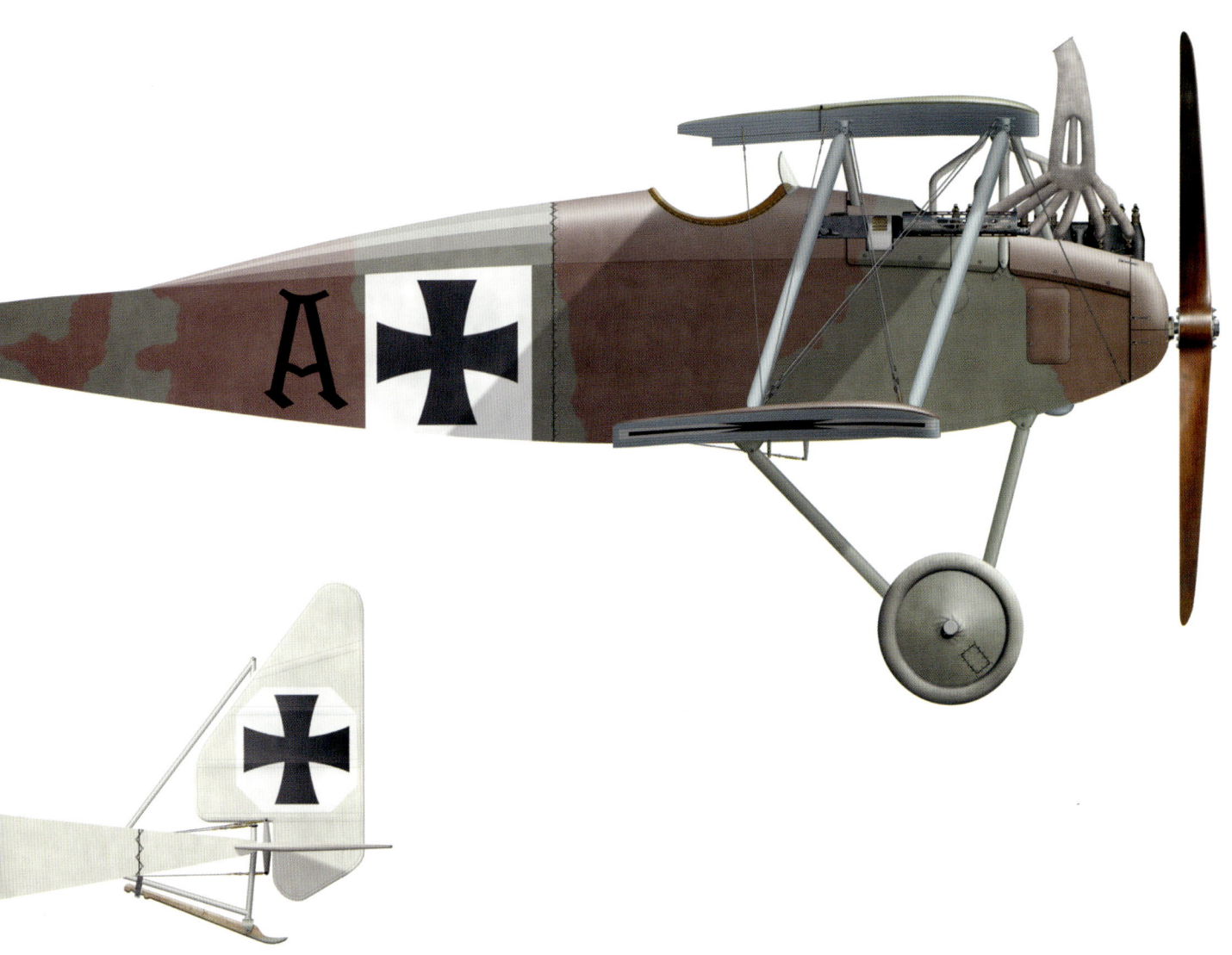

HALBERSTADT D-V

HALBERSTADT D-V (serial unknown) Ltn d R. Josef Jacobs,
Jagdstaffelschule I Valenciennes, France; December 1916

HALBERSTADT D-V (serial unknown unit unknown)
Tourmignies, France; circa 1917.

32

HALBERSTADT D-V (serial unknown) Oblt. Hans Berr, Jagdstaffel 5 Gonnelieu, France; October 1916.

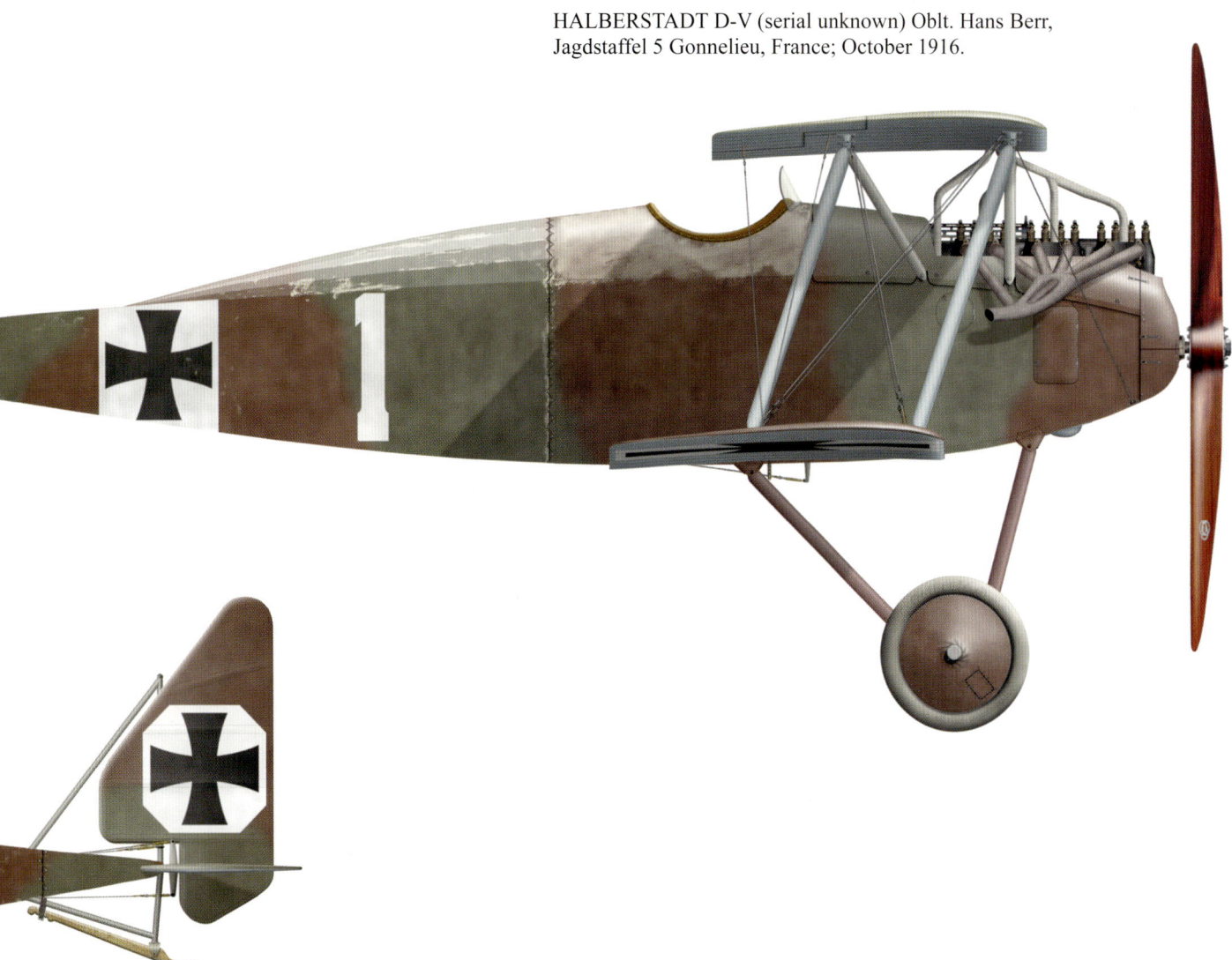

ALBATROS D-I

ALBATROS D-I (449/16) Jagdstaffel 10
Phalempin, France; October 1916.

ALBATROS D-I (serial unknown) Prinz Friedrich Karl von
Preussen, Jagdstaffel 2 Pronville, France; March 1917.
Same aircraft previously flown by Dieter Collin.

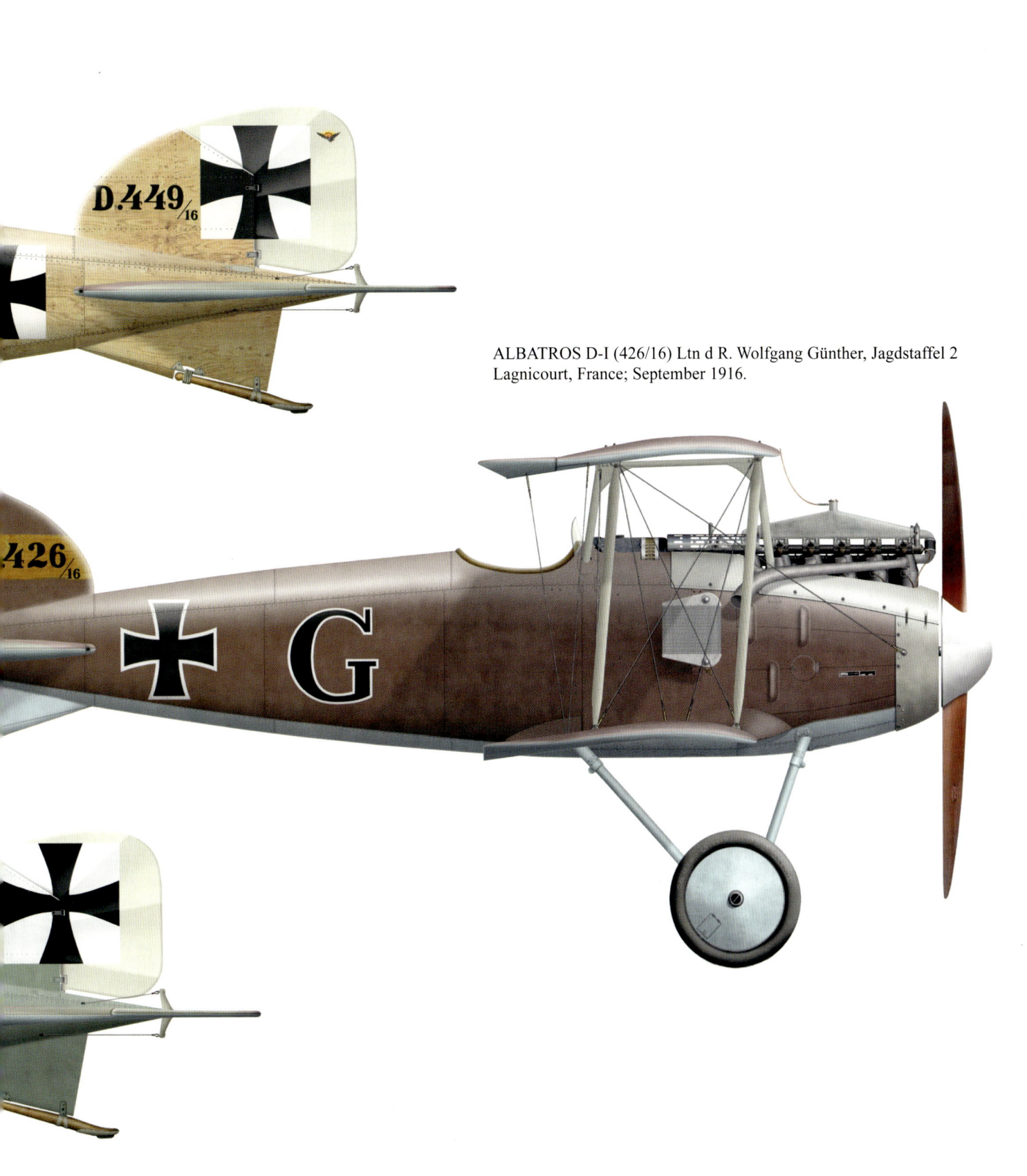

ALBATROS D-I (426/16) Ltn d R. Wolfgang Günther, Jagdstaffel 2 Lagnicourt, France; September 1916.

35

ALBATROS D-II

ALBATROS D-II (1727/16) Ltn d R. Wilhelm Gros, Jagdstaffel 17 Metz-Frescaty, Germany; December 1916.

ALBATROS D-II (1799/16) Ltn. Walter Neisen, Jagdstaffel 5 Boistrancourt, France; March 1917.

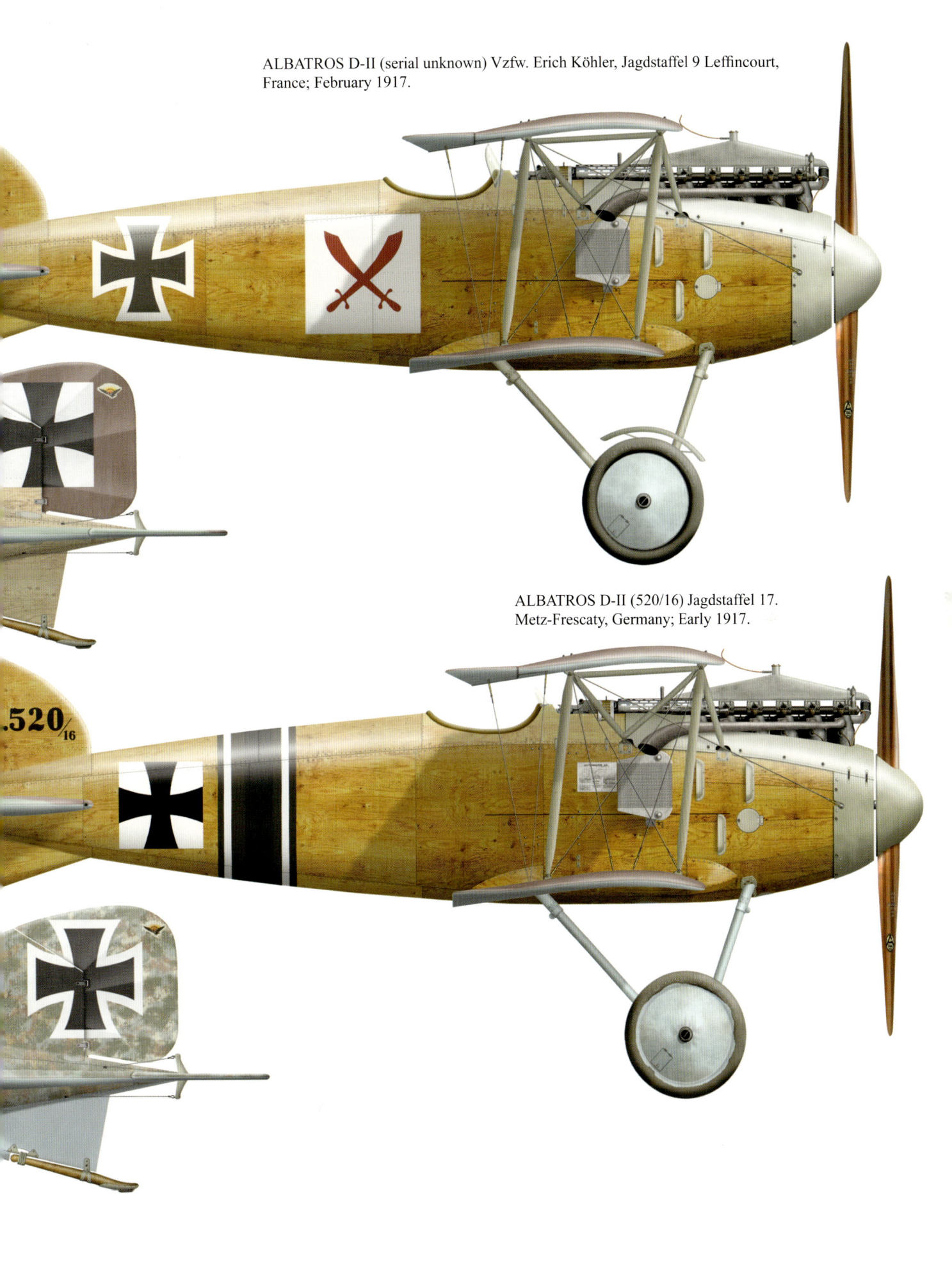

ALBATROS D-II (serial unknown) Vzfw. Erich Köhler, Jagdstaffel 9 Leffincourt, France; February 1917.

ALBATROS D-II (520/16) Jagdstaffel 17. Metz-Frescaty, Germany; Early 1917.

37

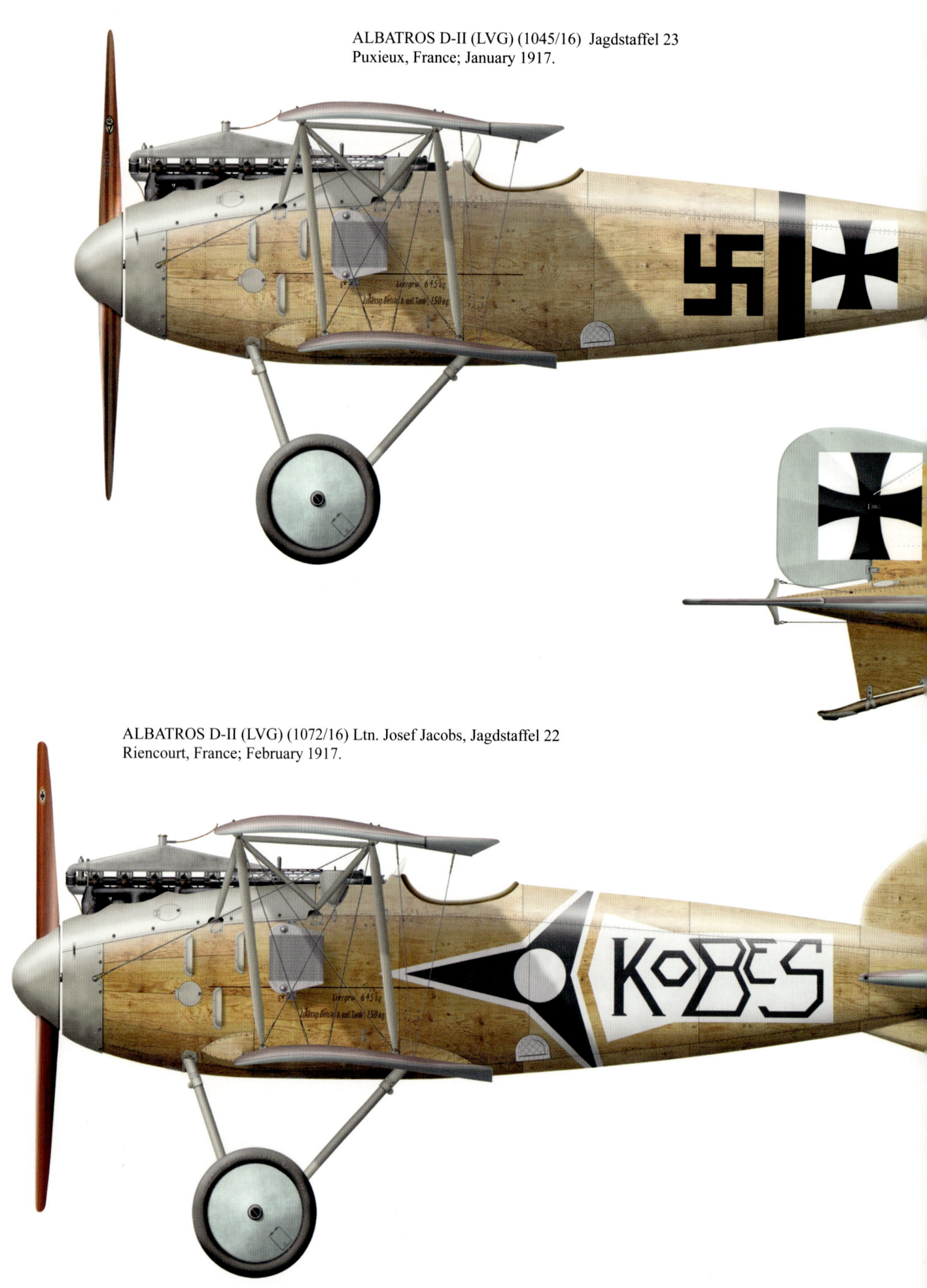

ALBATROS D-II (L.V.G.)

ALBATROS D-II (LVG) (1045/16) Jagdstaffel 23
Puxieux, France; January 1917.

ALBATROS D-II (LVG) (1072/16) Ltn. Josef Jacobs, Jagdstaffel 22
Riencourt, France; February 1917.

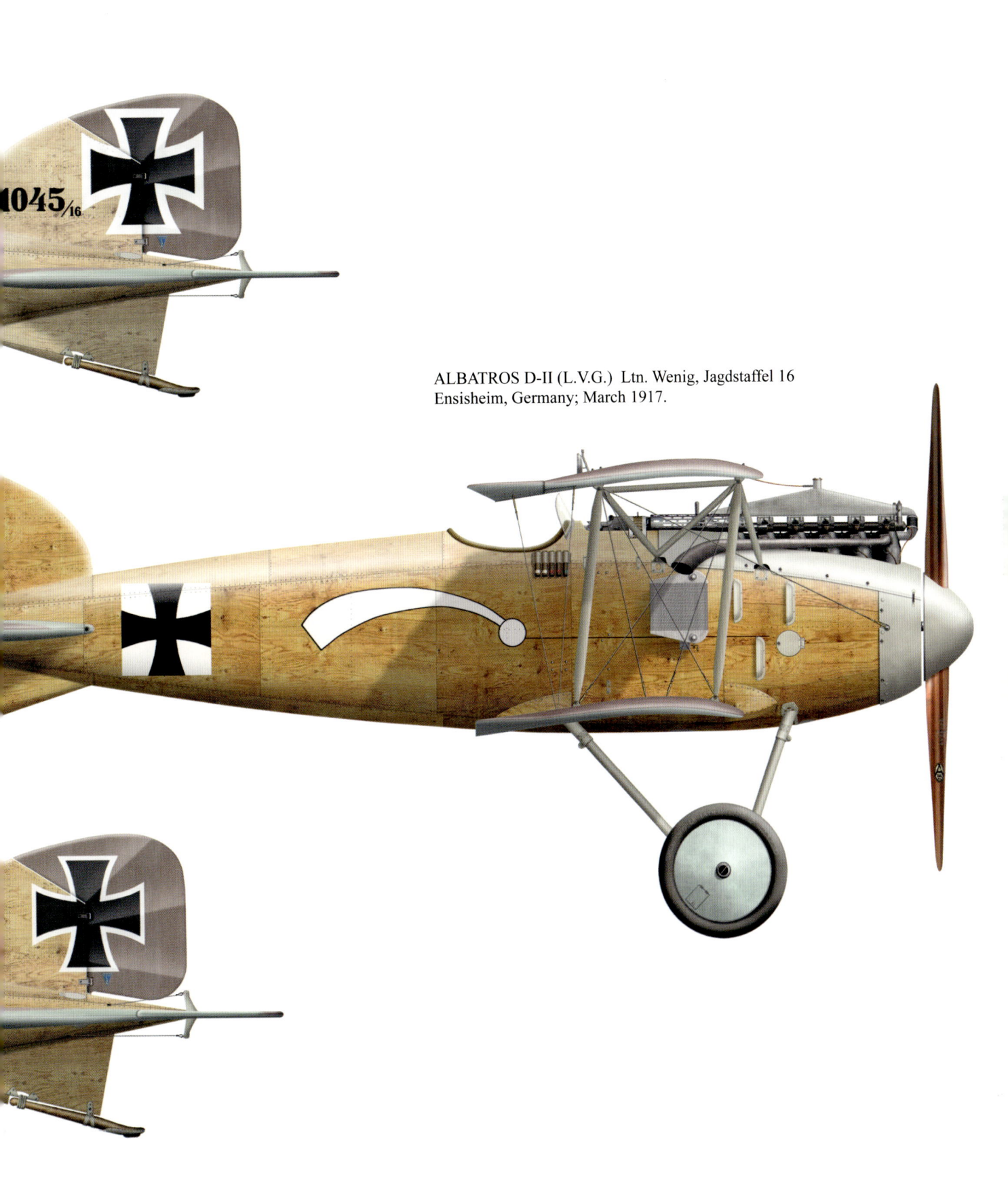

ALBATROS D-II (L.V.G.) Ltn. Wenig, Jagdstaffel 16
Ensisheim, Germany; March 1917.

ALBATROS D-II (O.A.W.)

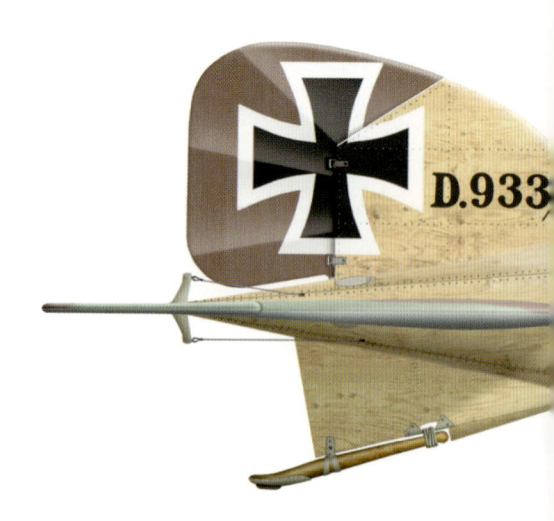

ALBATROS D-II (O.A.W.) (910/16) Ltn. Max Böhme, Jagdstaffel 5
Gonnelieu, France; March 1917.
Notice overpainted number 4 under the number 8 on the fuselage sides.

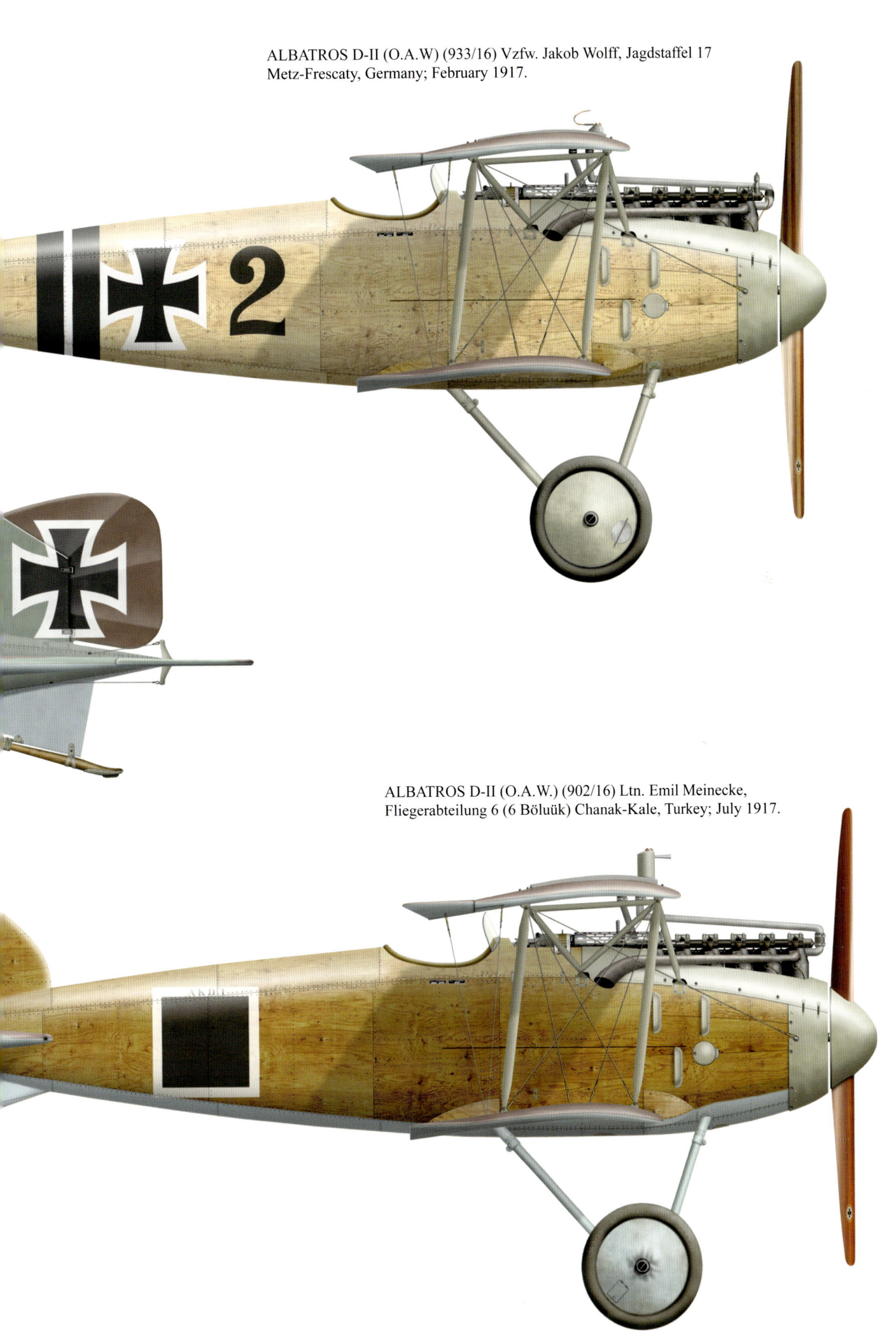

ALBATROS D-II (O.A.W) (933/16) Vzfw. Jakob Wolff, Jagdstaffel 17
Metz-Frescaty, Germany; February 1917.

ALBATROS D-II (O.A.W.) (902/16) Ltn. Emil Meinecke,
Fliegerabteilung 6 (6 Bölüük) Chanak-Kale, Turkey; July 1917.

41

ALBATROS D-III

ALBATROS D-III (serial unknown) Rittm. Manfred von Richthofen, Jagdstaffel 11
Roucourt, France; April 1917.
This particular airplane was famous in the trenches on both sides as *Le Petit Rouge.*

ALBATROS D-III (2016/16) Jagdstaffel 11
Roucourt, France; April 1917.

ALBATROS D-III (2125/16) Ltn. Ernst von Stenglin, Jagdstaffel 1
Vivaise, France; Spring 1917.

ALBATROS D-III (2274/16) Oblt. Adolf von Tutschek, Jagdstaffel 12
Roucourt, France; May 1917.

ALBATROS D-III (serial unknown) Ltn. Karl Wewer, Jagdstaffel 26
Iseghem, Belgium; June 1917.

ALBATROS D-III (2033/16) Vzfw. Julius Buckler, Jagdstaffel 17
St Quentin-le-Petit, France; April 1917.

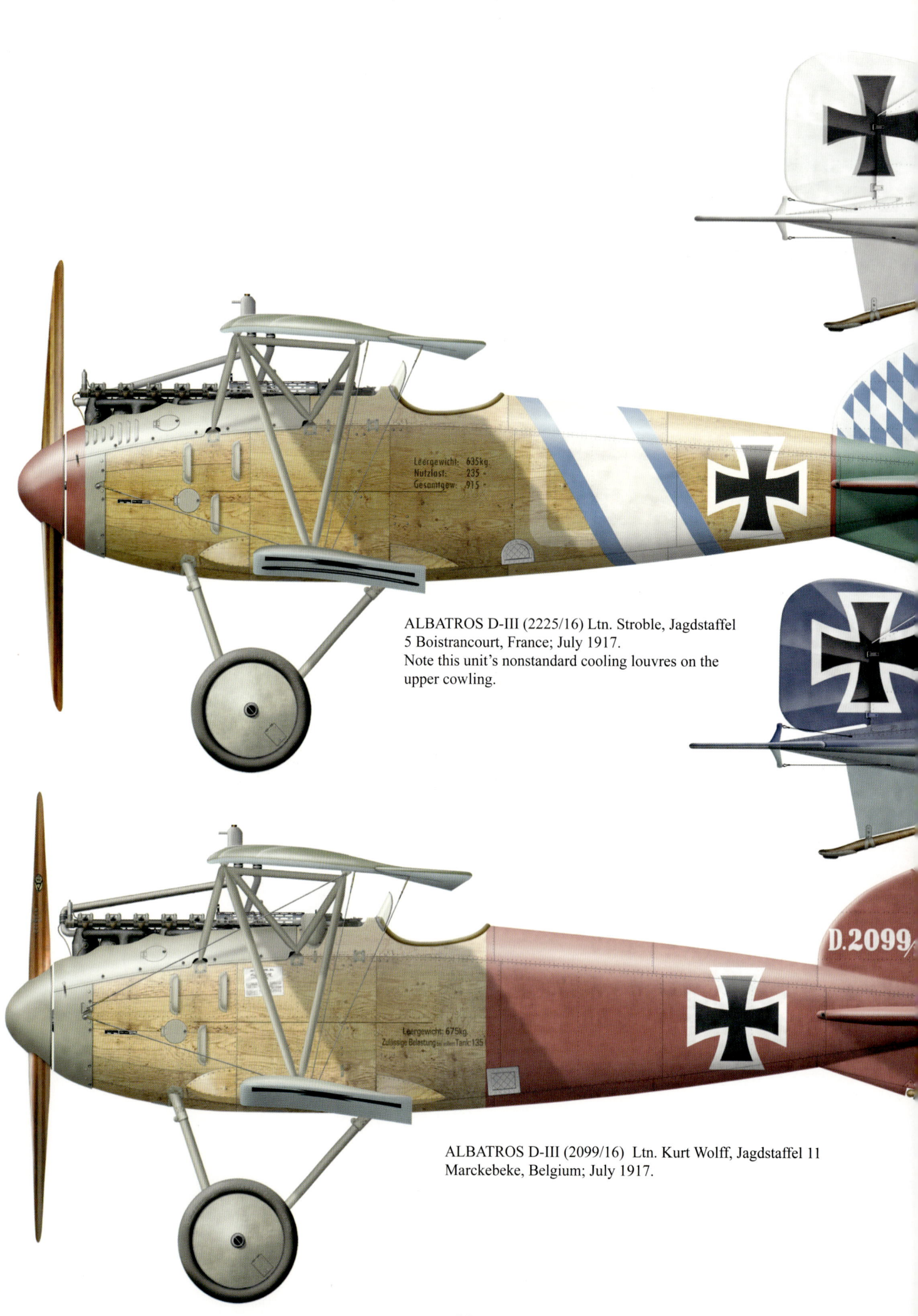

ALBATROS D-III (2225/16) Ltn. Stroble, Jagdstaffel 5 Boistrancourt, France; July 1917.
Note this unit's nonstandard cooling louvres on the upper cowling.

ALBATROS D-III (2099/16) Ltn. Kurt Wolff, Jagdstaffel 11 Marckebeke, Belgium; July 1917.

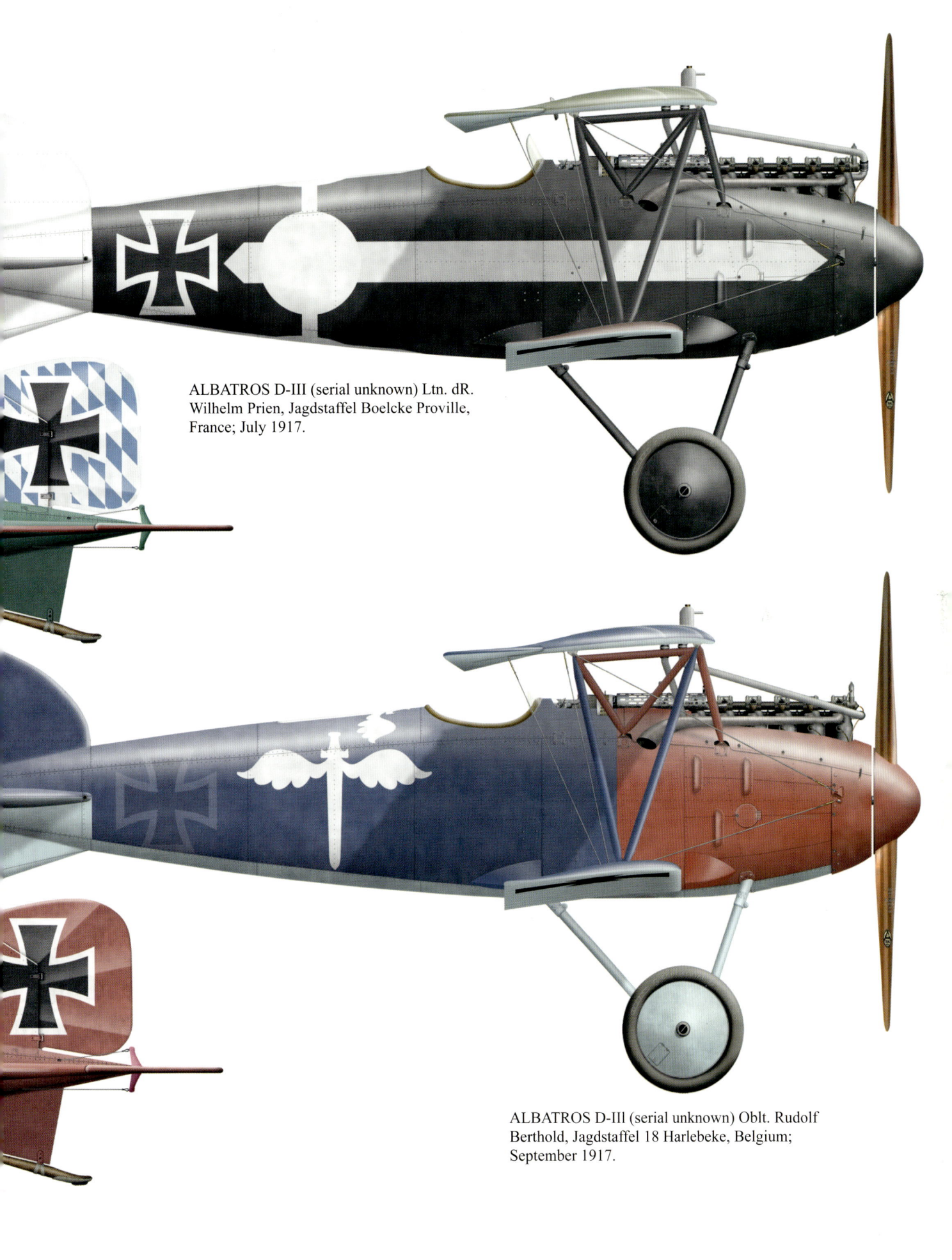

ALBATROS D-III (serial unknown) Ltn. dR. Wilhelm Prien, Jagdstaffel Boelcke Proville, France; July 1917.

ALBATROS D-Ill (serial unknown) Oblt. Rudolf Berthold, Jagdstaffel 18 Harlebeke, Belgium; September 1917.

ALBATROS D-III (O.A.W.)

ALBATROS D-III (O.A.W.) (serial unknown) Ltn d R. Wilhelm Papenmeyer, Jagdstaffel Boelcke Bavichove, France; November 1917.

ALBATROS D-III (O.A.W.) (5127-17) Off Stv. Hermann Habich, Jagdstaffel 49 Villers Campeau, France; Early 1918.

ALBATROS D-III (O.A.W.) (serial unknown) Oblt. Josef Loeser, Jagdstaffel 39 San Fior, Italy; December 1917.
The stripes could also have been Black and White.

ALBATROS D-III (O.A.W.) (2385/17) Ltn d R. Paul Strähle, Jagdstaffel 57 Halluin, France; April 1918.

49

ROLAND D-II

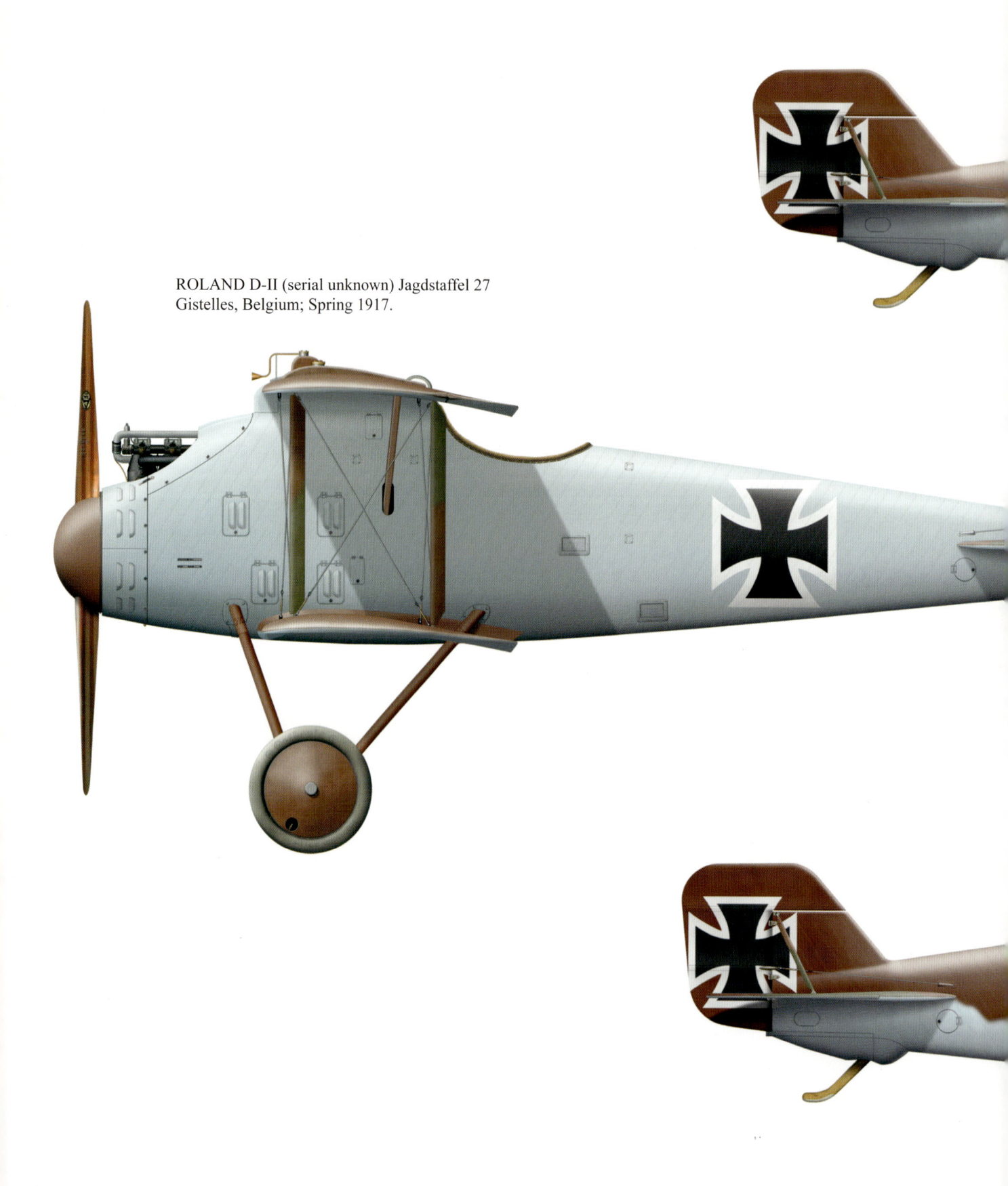

ROLAND D-II (serial unknown) Jagdstaffel 27
Gistelles, Belgium; Spring 1917.

ROLAND D-II (serial unknown) Jagdstaffel 32
Chery-les-Poilly, France; Spring 1917.

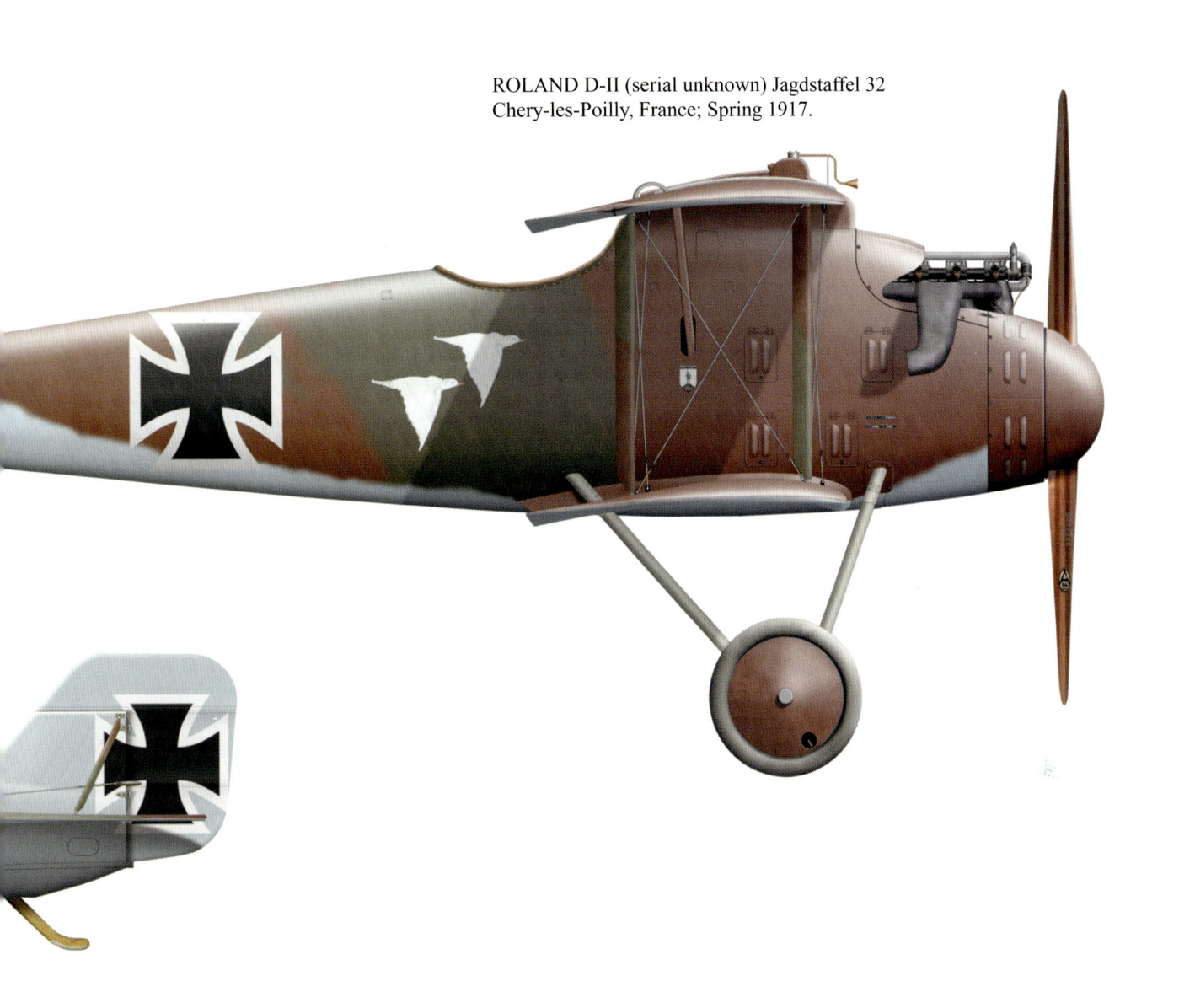

ROLAND D-II (serial unknown) (unit and location unknown)
Mid-1917.

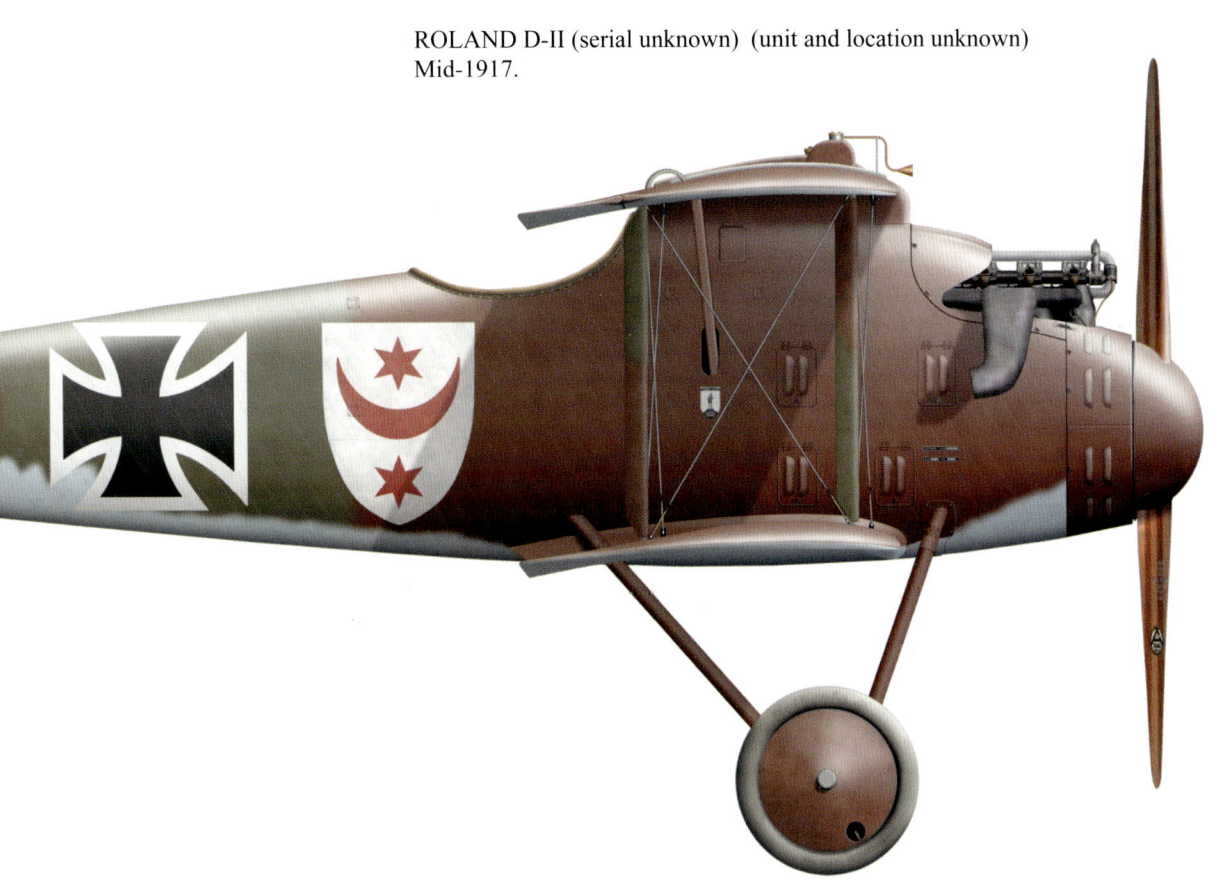

51

ROLAND D-IIA

ROLAND D-IIa (serial unknown) Vzfw. Paul Raetsch, Jagdstaffel 32
Chery-les-Poilly, France; March 1917.

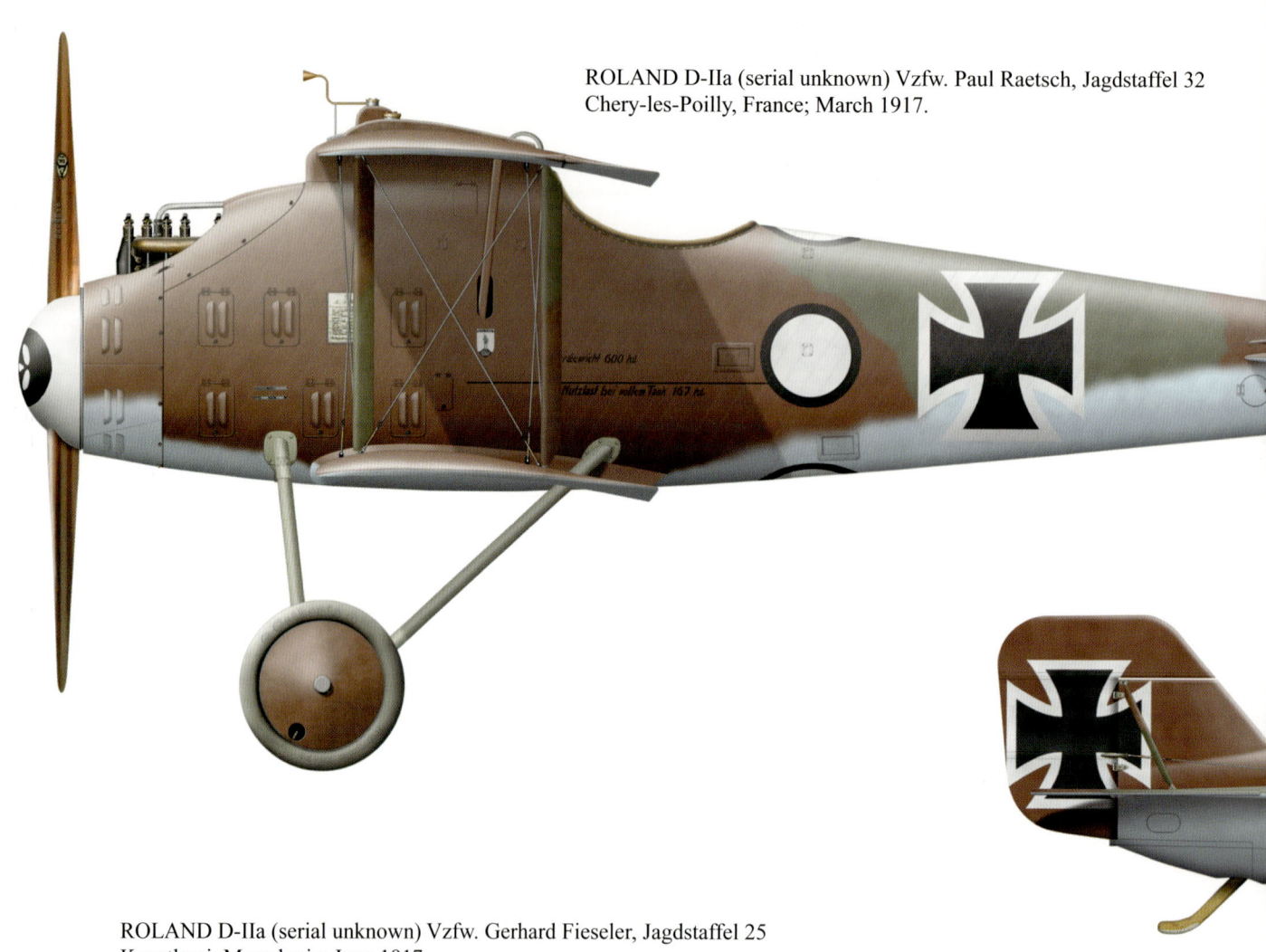

ROLAND D-IIa (serial unknown) Vzfw. Gerhard Fieseler, Jagdstaffel 25
Kanatlarci, Macedonia; June 1917.

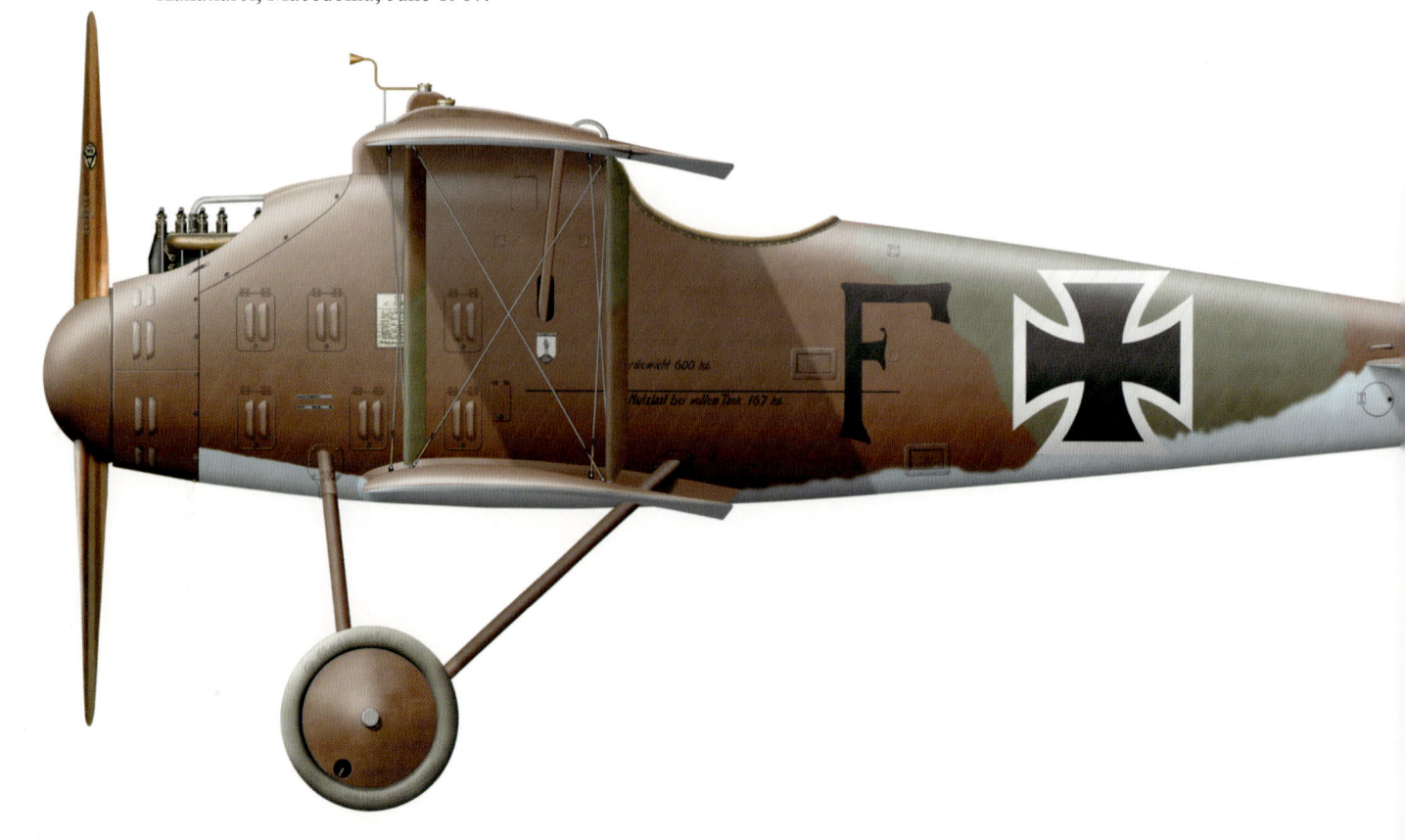

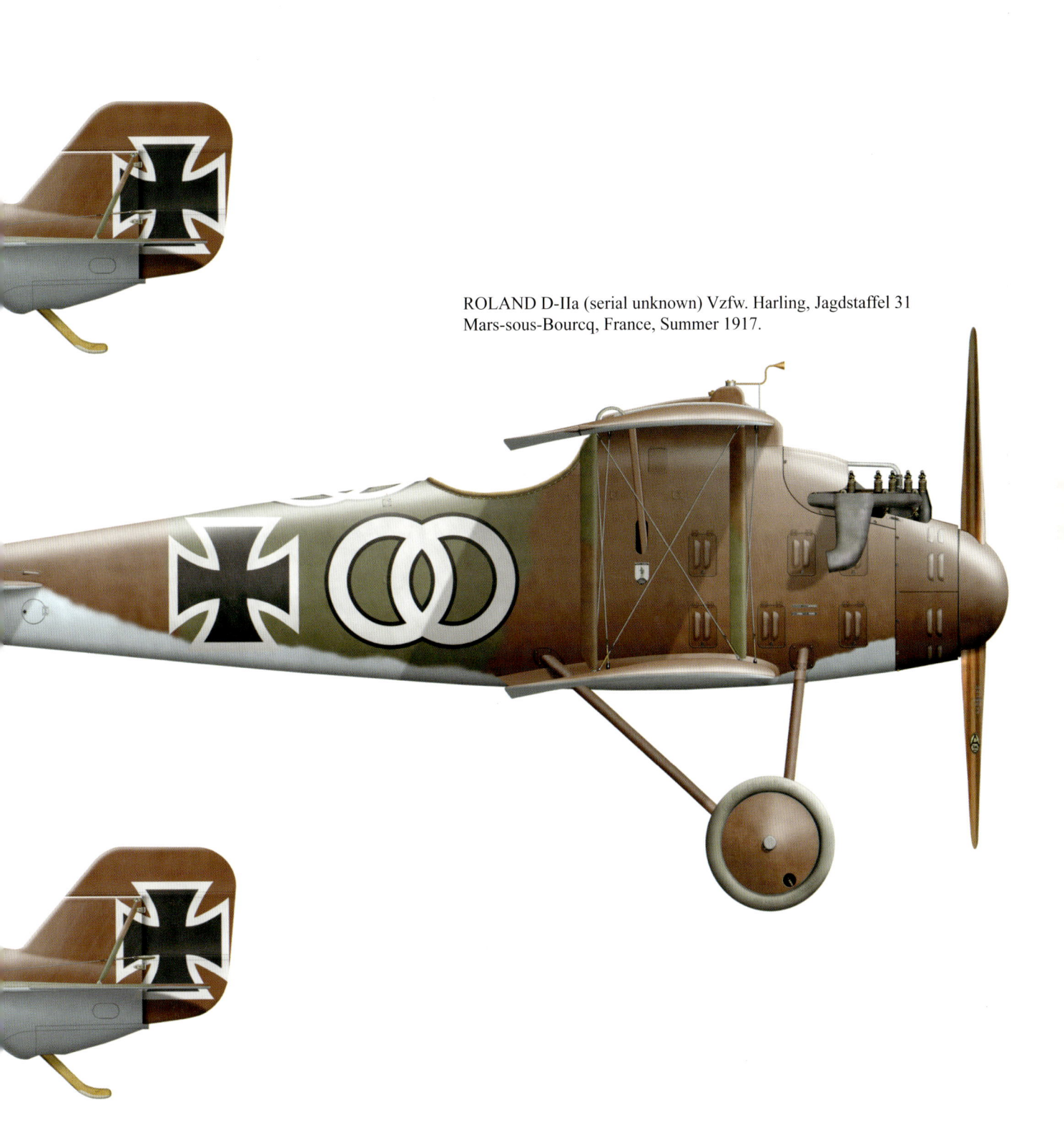

ROLAND D-IIa (serial unknown) Vzfw. Harling, Jagdstaffel 31
Mars-sous-Bourcq, France, Summer 1917.

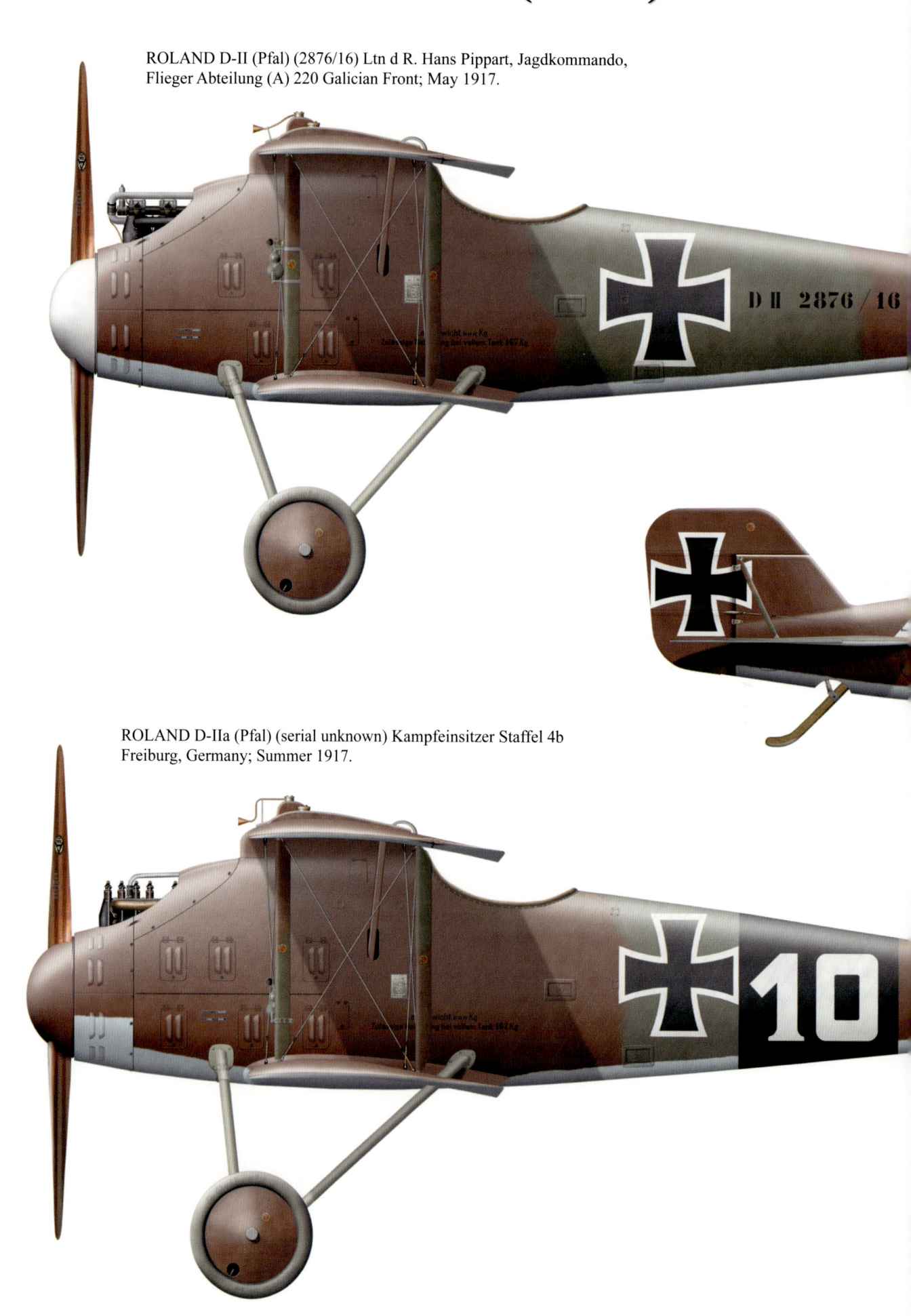

ROLAND D-IIA (PFAL)

ROLAND D-II (Pfal) (2876/16) Ltn d R. Hans Pippart, Jagdkommando, Flieger Abteilung (A) 220 Galician Front; May 1917.

ROLAND D-IIa (Pfal) (serial unknown) Kampfeinsitzer Staffel 4b Freiburg, Germany; Summer 1917.

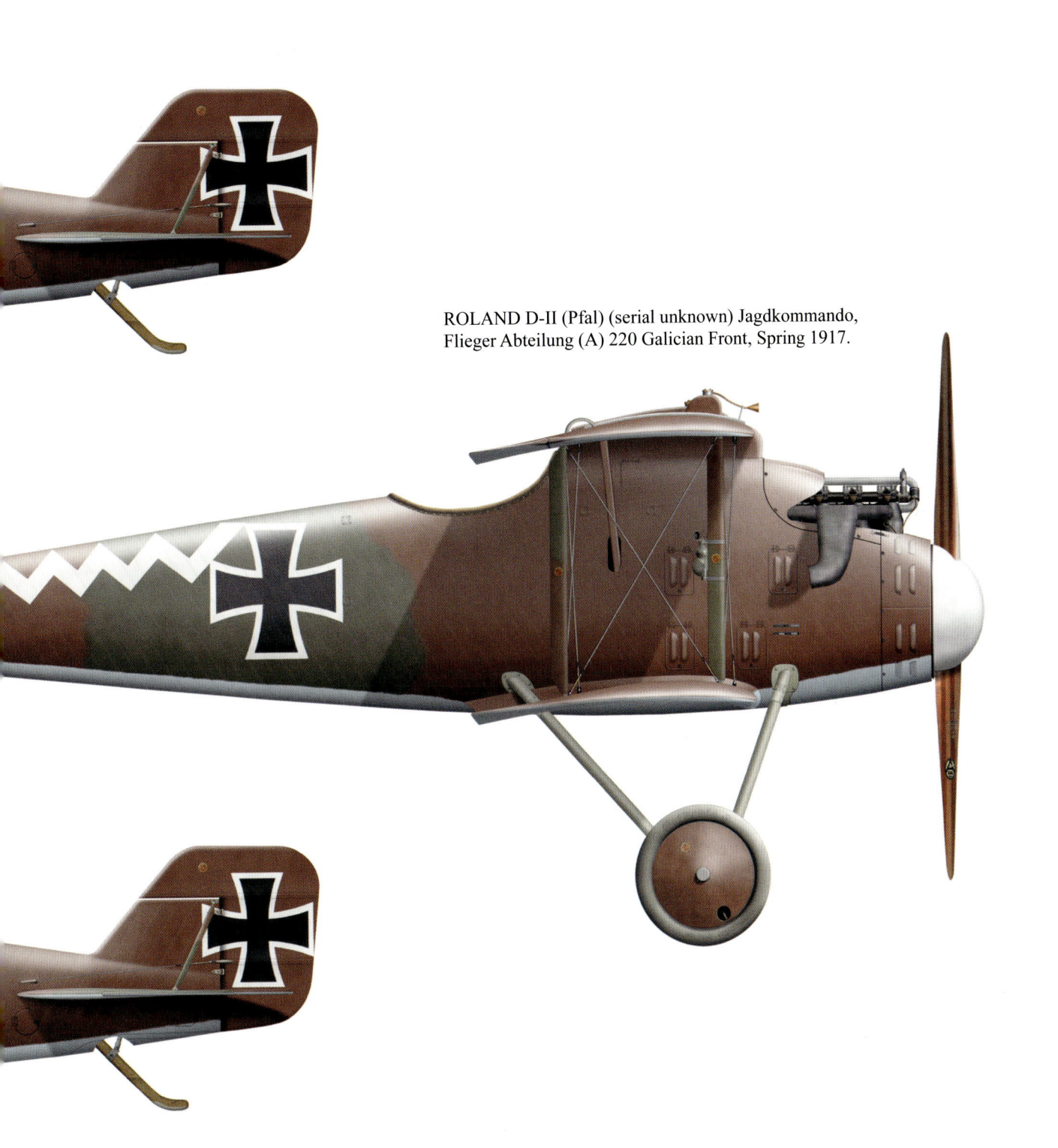

ROLAND D-II (Pfal) (serial unknown) Jagdkommando, Flieger Abteilung (A) 220 Galician Front, Spring 1917.

SIEMENS-SCHUCKERT D-I

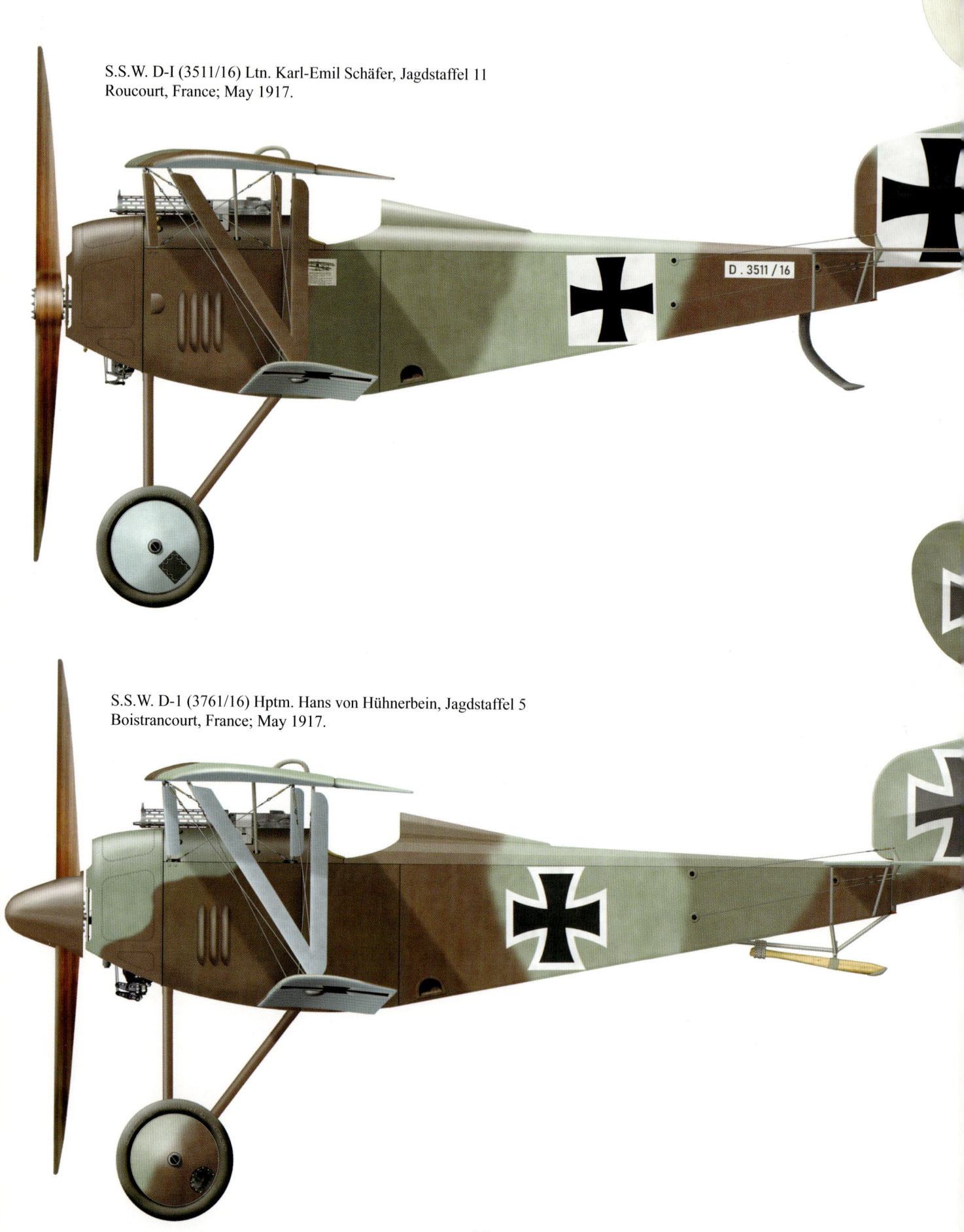

S.S.W. D-I (3511/16) Ltn. Karl-Emil Schäfer, Jagdstaffel 11
Roucourt, France; May 1917.

S.S.W. D-1 (3761/16) Hptm. Hans von Hühnerbein, Jagdstaffel 5
Boistrancourt, France; May 1917.

S.S.W. D-I (3503/16) First prototype
Döberitz, Germany; October 1916.

S.S.W. D-1 (3505/16) Jagdstaffel 7
Procher, France; Spring 1917.

ALBATROS D-V

ALBATROS D-V (2065/17) Oblt. Richard Flashar, Jagdstaffel 5
Boistrancourt, France; July 1917.
Note the flare tube sticking out of the side of the fuselage.

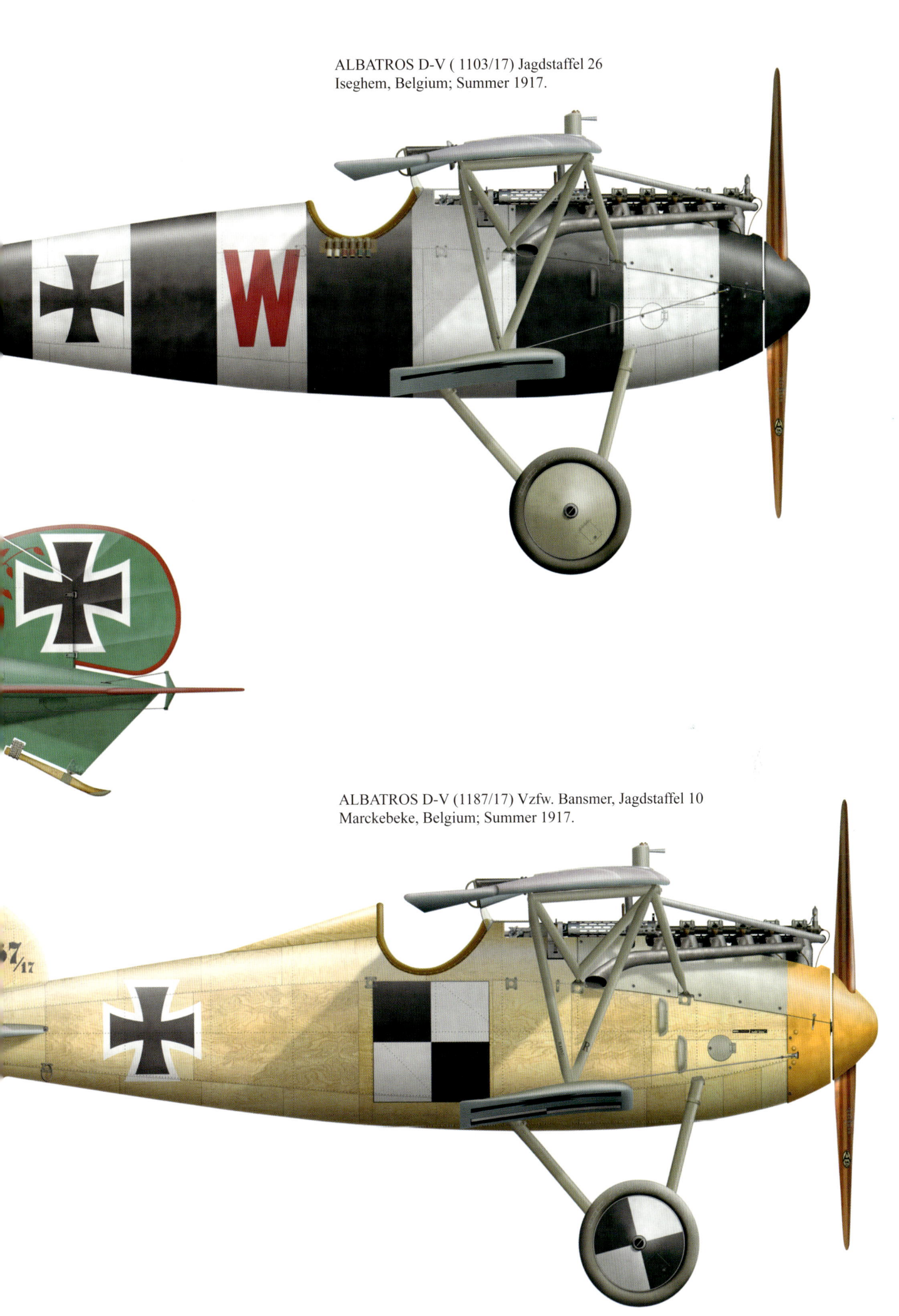

ALBATROS D-V (1103/17) Jagdstaffel 26
Iseghem, Belgium; Summer 1917.

ALBATROS D-V (1187/17) Vzfw. Bansmer, Jagdstaffel 10
Marckebeke, Belgium; Summer 1917.

59

ALBATROS D-V (serial unknown) Ltn.
Kurt Monnington, Jagdstaffel 15
Leffincourt, France; July 1917.

ALBATROS D-V (2030/17) Ltn. Alfred Lenz,
Jagstaffel 22 Vivaise, France; Summer 1917.

ALBATROS D-V (serial unknown)
Ltn d R. Theodor Rumpel, Jagdstaffel
16b Spincourt, France; Summer 1917.

ALBATROS D-V (2263/17) Ltn. Otto Kissenberth,
Jagdstaffel 23b Jametz, France; Summer 1917.

ALBATROS D-V (serial unknown) Oblt. Hubertus Rudno-Rudzinski, Jagdstaffel 17 Wasquehal, France; October 1917.

62

ALBTROS D-V (1055/17) Ltn d R. Rudolf Windisch,
Jagdstaffel 32b Landreville, France; September 1917.

ALBATROS D-V (serial unknown) Ltn. Kurt Monnington,
Jagdstaffel 15 Le Clos Ferme-Boncourt, France; October 1917.

ALBATROS D-VA

ALBATROS D-Va (serial unknown) Oblt.
Rudolf von Esebeck, Jagdstaffel 17
Douilly, France; Autumn 1917.

ALBATROS D-Va (5784/17) Uffz. Kretschmar, Jagdstaffel 44
Leffincourt, France; Early 1918.

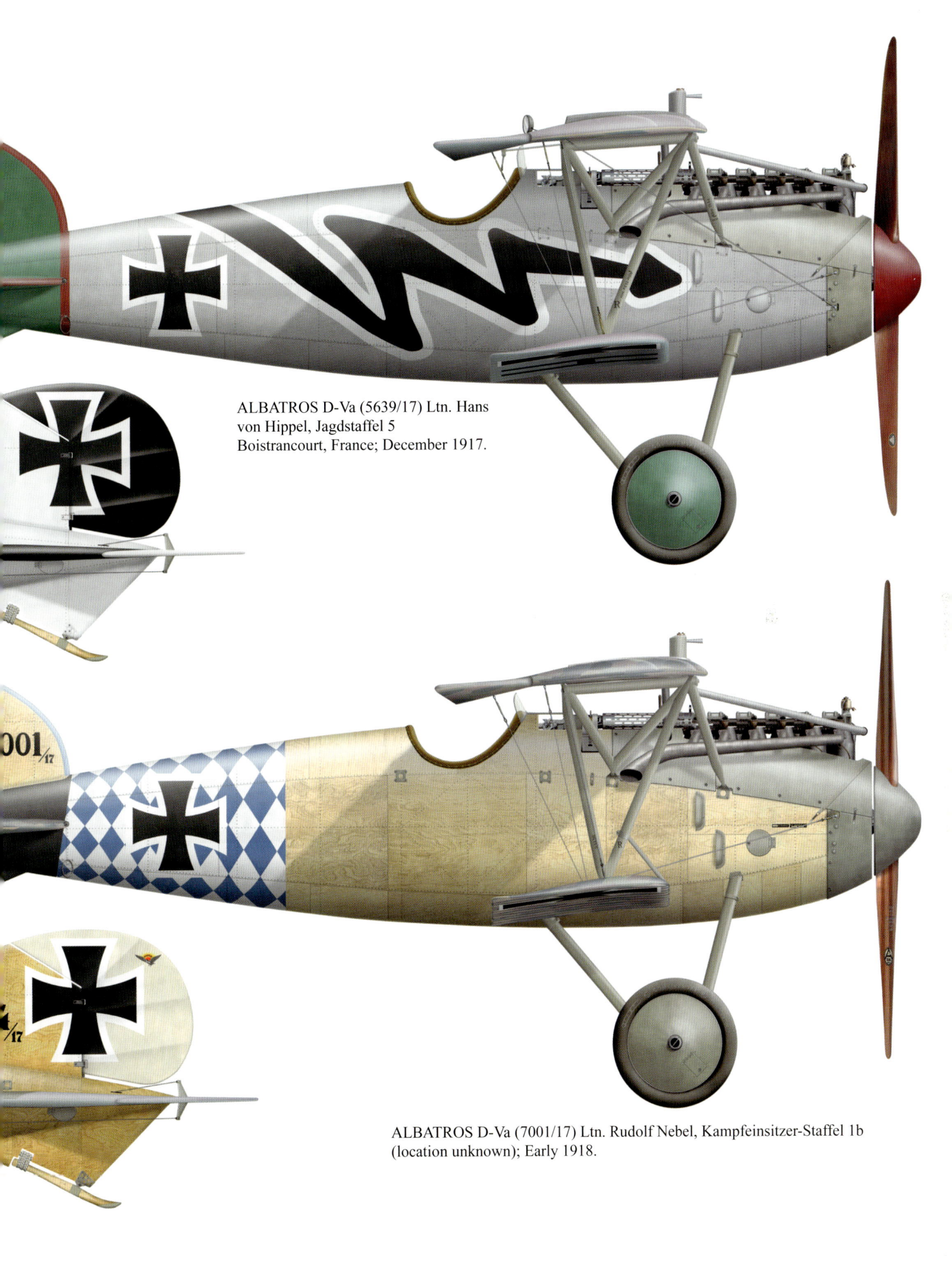

ALBATROS D-Va (5639/17) Ltn. Hans von Hippel, Jagdstaffel 5
Boistrancourt, France; December 1917.

ALBATROS D-Va (7001/17) Ltn. Rudolf Nebel, Kampfeinsitzer-Staffel 1b (location unknown); Early 1918.

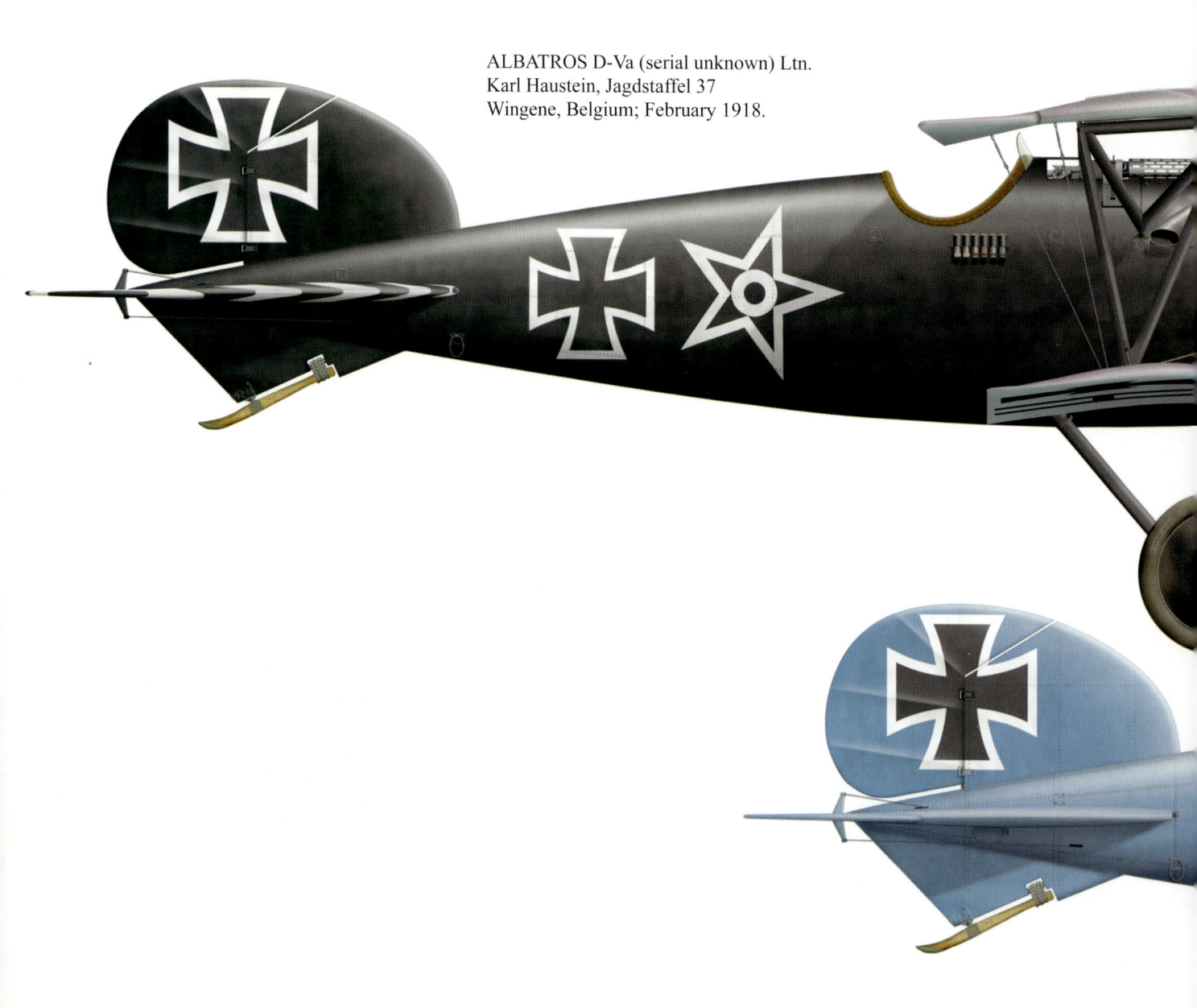

ALBATROS D-Va (serial unknown) Ltn. Karl Haustein, Jagdstaffel 37
Wingene, Belgium; February 1918.

ALBATROS D-Va (5358/17)
Marine Feld Jagdstaffel I
Koolkerke, Belgium; March 1918.

ALBATROS D-Va (serial unknown)
Ltn. Otto Fuchs, Jagdstaffel 77b
Le Cateau, France; March 1918.

67

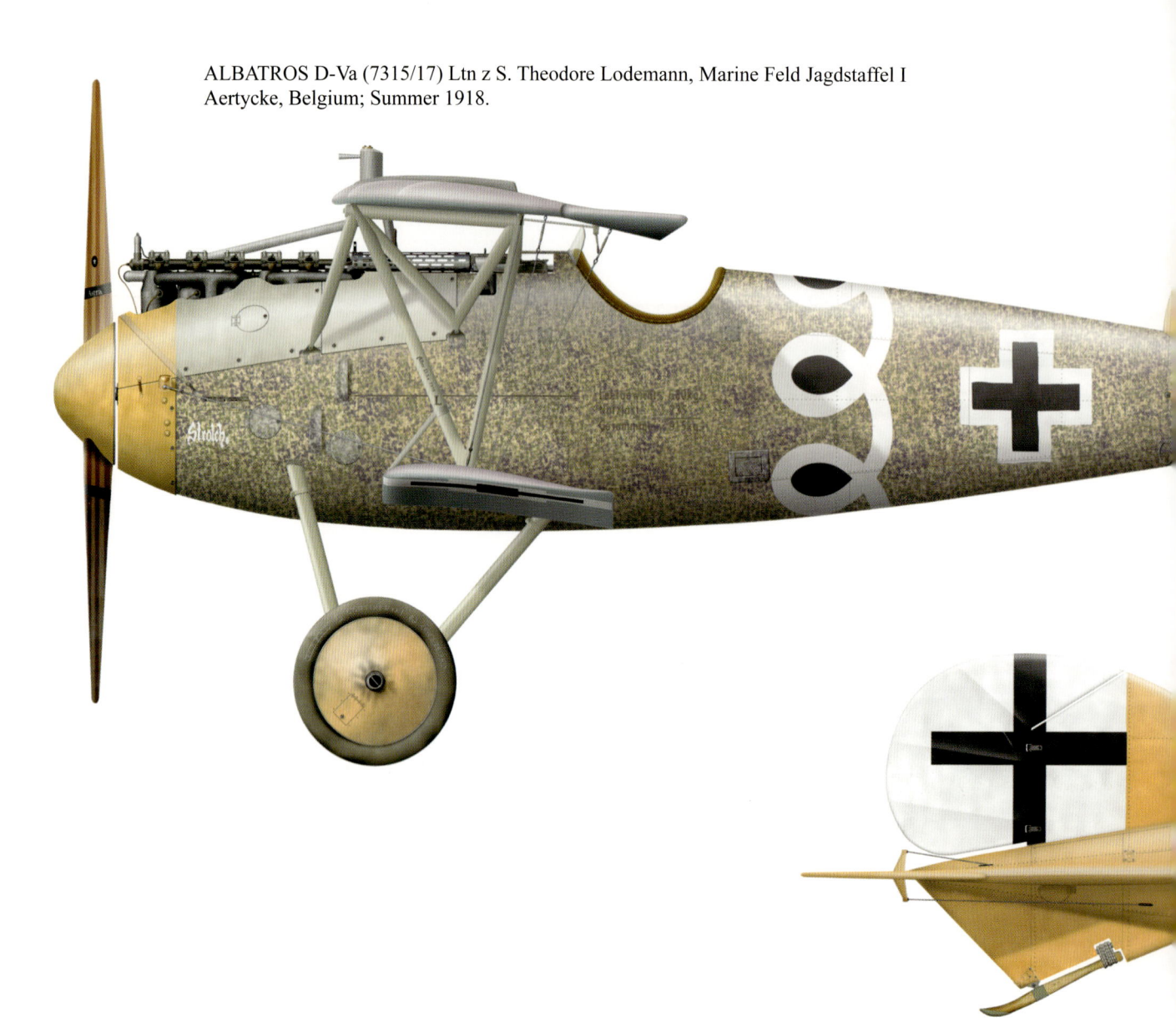

ALBATROS D-Va (7315/17) Ltn z S. Theodore Lodemann, Marine Feld Jagdstaffel I
Aertycke, Belgium; Summer 1918.

ALBATROS D-Va (serial unknown) Ltn. Max Näther, Jagdstaffel 62
Balatre, France; June 1918.

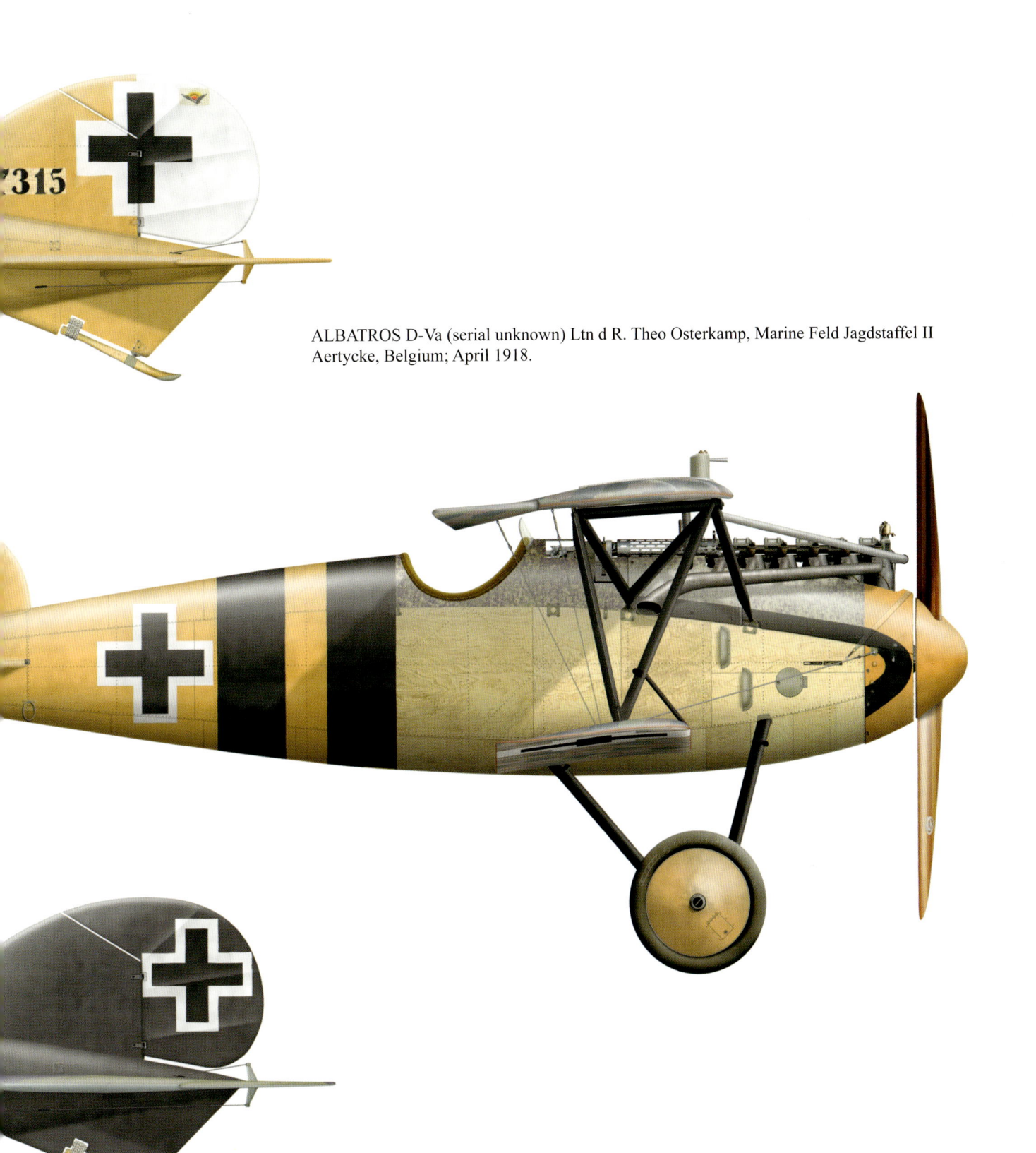

ALBATROS D-Va (serial unknown) Ltn d R. Theo Osterkamp, Marine Feld Jagdstaffel II
Aertycke, Belgium; April 1918.

69

ALBATROS D-VA (O.A.W.)

ALBATROS D-Va (O.A.W.) (6553/17) Jagdstaffel 73
Mars-sous-Bourcq, France; April 1918.

ALBATROS D-Va (O.A.W.) (serial unknown)
Ltn. Fritz Röth, Jagdstaffel 23b
St Mard, France; January 1918.

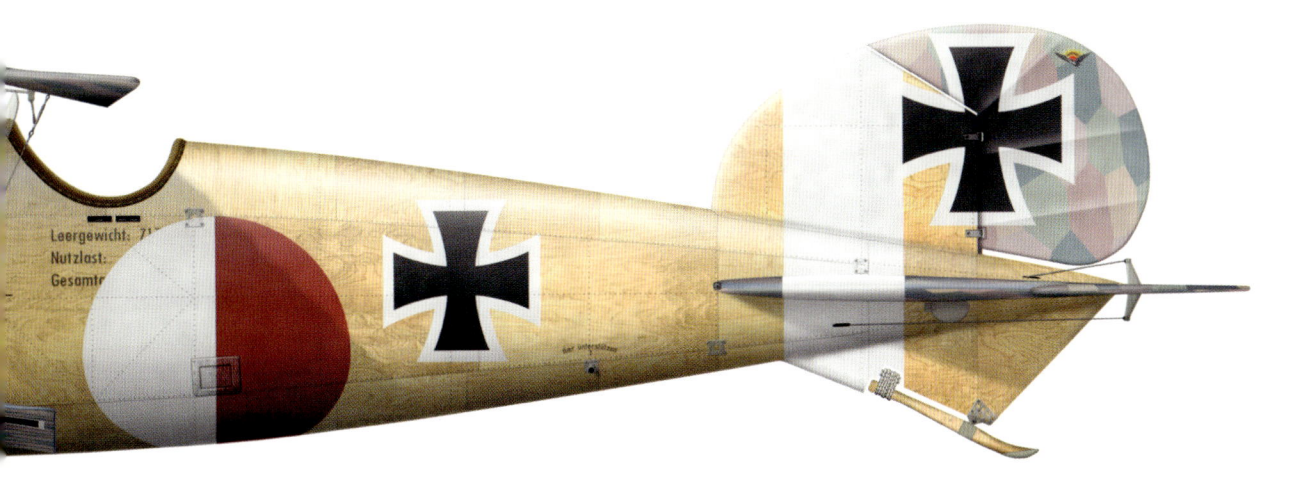

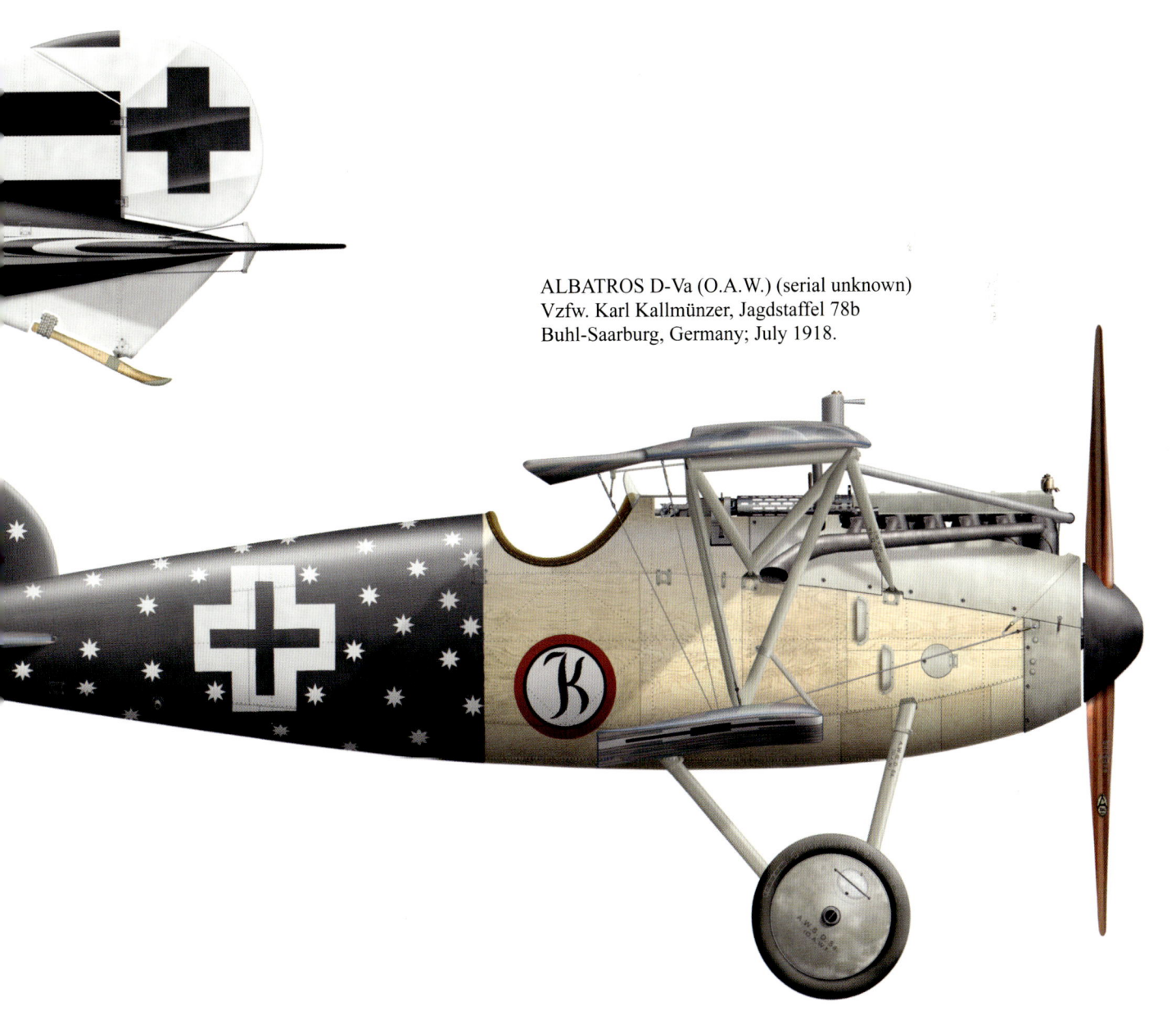

ALBATROS D-Va (O.A.W.) (serial unknown)
Vzfw. Karl Kallmünzer, Jagdstaffel 78b
Buhl-Saarburg, Germany; July 1918.

71

PFALZ D-III

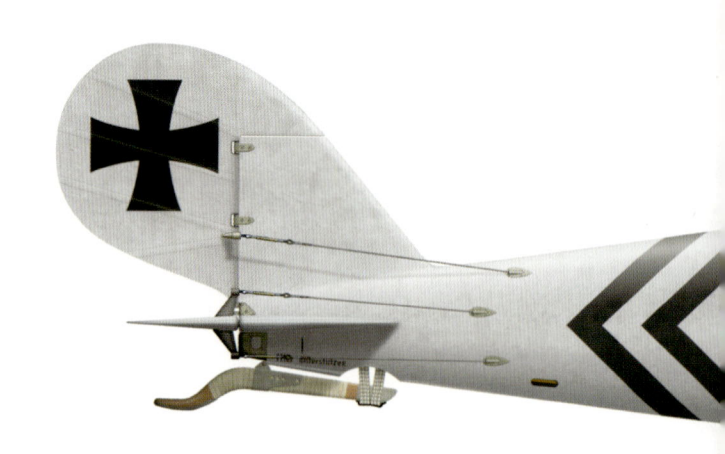

PFALZ D-III (1370/17) Ltn. Werner Voss, Jagdstaffel 10
Marcke, Belgium; September 1917.

PFALZ D-III (serial unknown) Ltn d R. Alfred Wunsch, Jagdstaffel 22
Soissons, France; September 1917.

PFALZ D-III (1369/17) Jagdstaffel 11
Marckebeke, Belgium; October 1917.

PFALZ D-III (serial unknown) Ltn. d R. Hans Klein, Jagdstaffel 10
Marcke, Belgium; November 1917.

PFALZ D-III (4011/17) Ltn d R. Fritz Höhn, Jagdstaffel 21s
Villers la Chévre, France; December 1917.

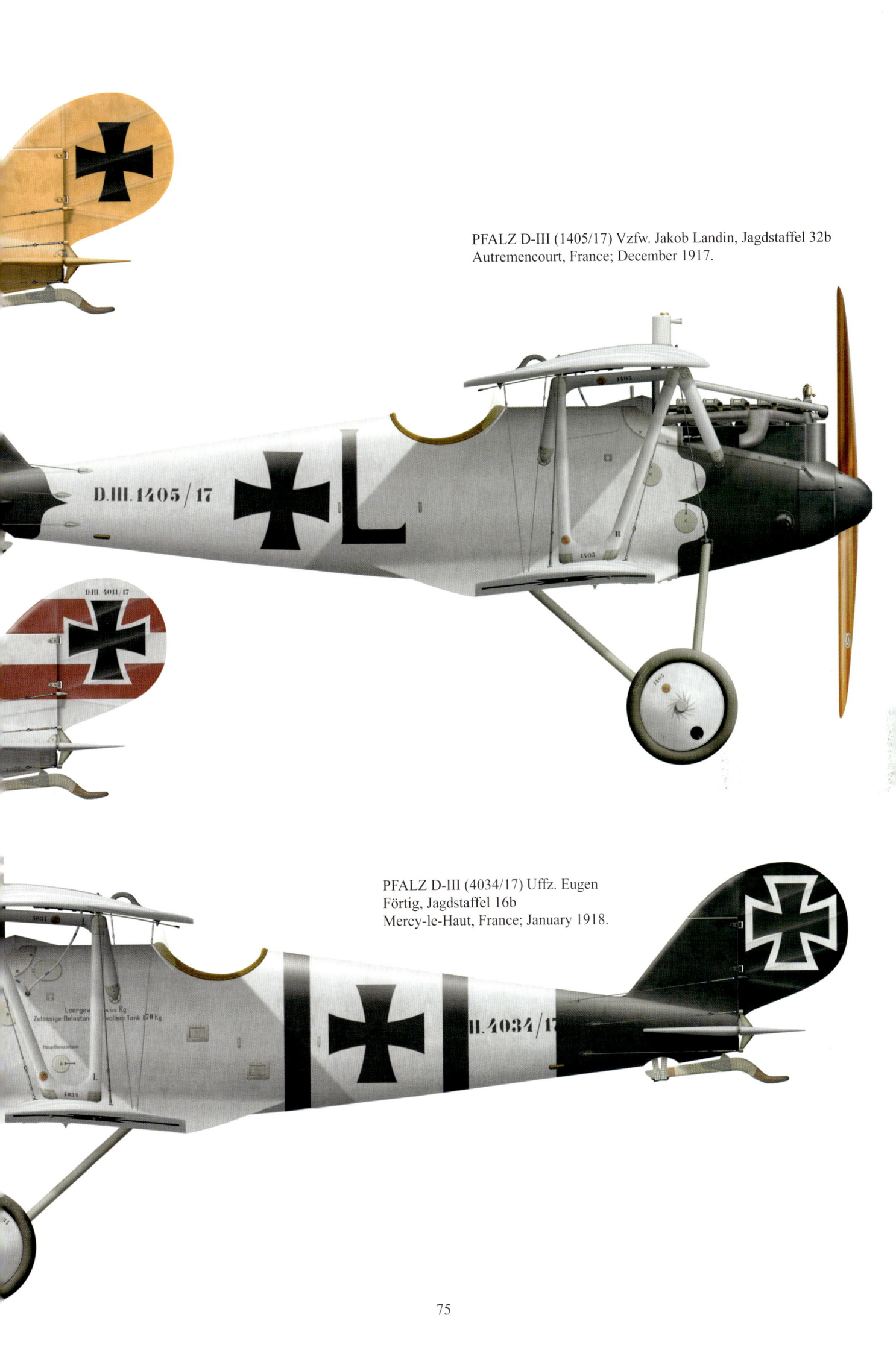

PFALZ D-III (1405/17) Vzfw. Jakob Landin, Jagdstaffel 32b
Autremencourt, France; December 1917.

PFALZ D-III (4034/17) Uffz. Eugen
Förtig, Jagdstaffel 16b
Mercy-le-Haut, France; January 1918.

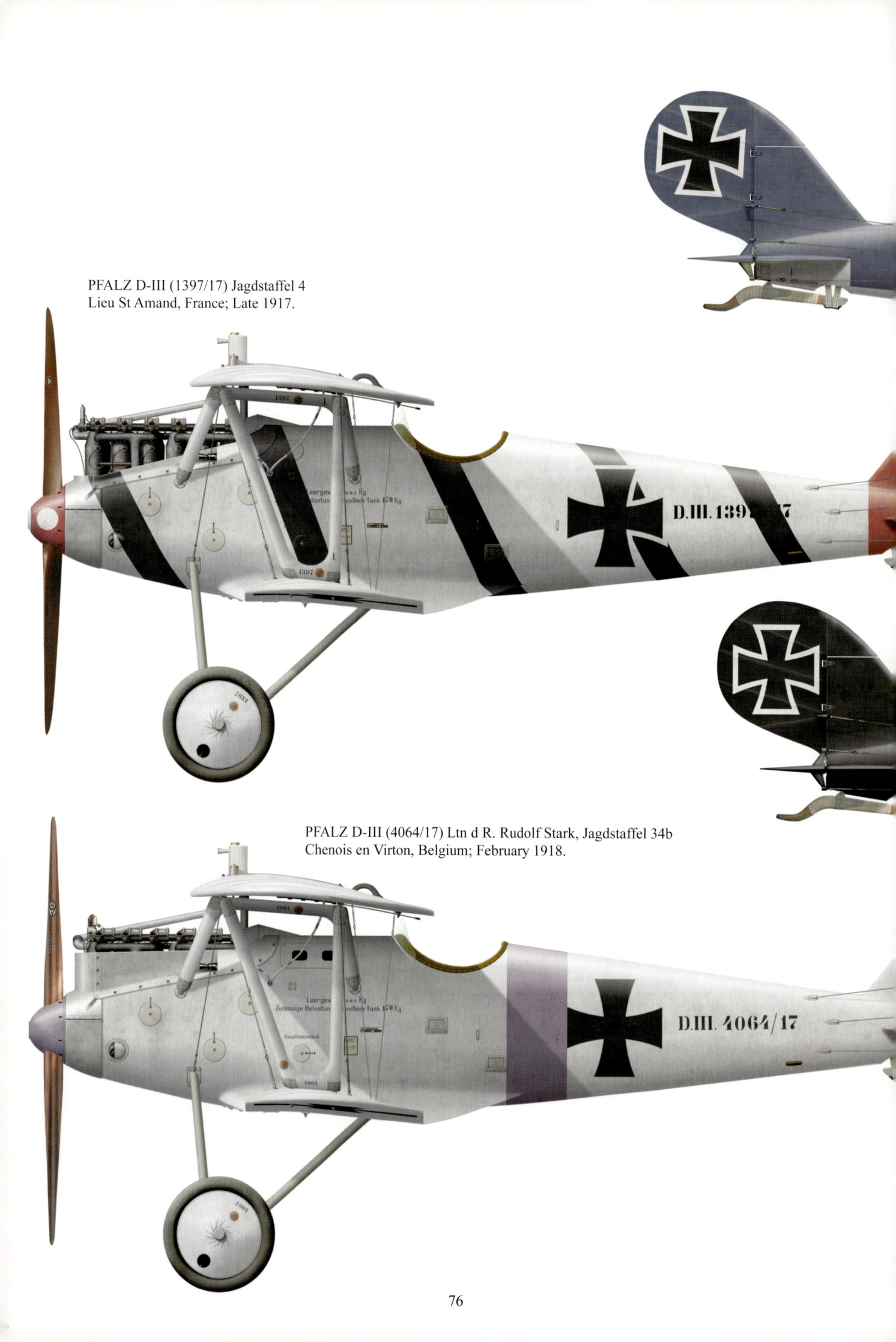

PFALZ D-III (1397/17) Jagdstaffel 4
Lieu St Amand, France; Late 1917.

PFALZ D-III (4064/17) Ltn d R. Rudolf Stark, Jagdstaffel 34b
Chenois en Virton, Belgium; February 1918.

PFALZ D-III (serial unknown) Ltn. Hans Burkhard von Buttlar, Jagdstaffel 18 Avelin, France; January 1918.

PFALZ D-III (4013/17) Ltn d R. August Handl, Jagdstaffel 16b Aertrycke, Belgium; February 1918.

PFALZ D-IIIA

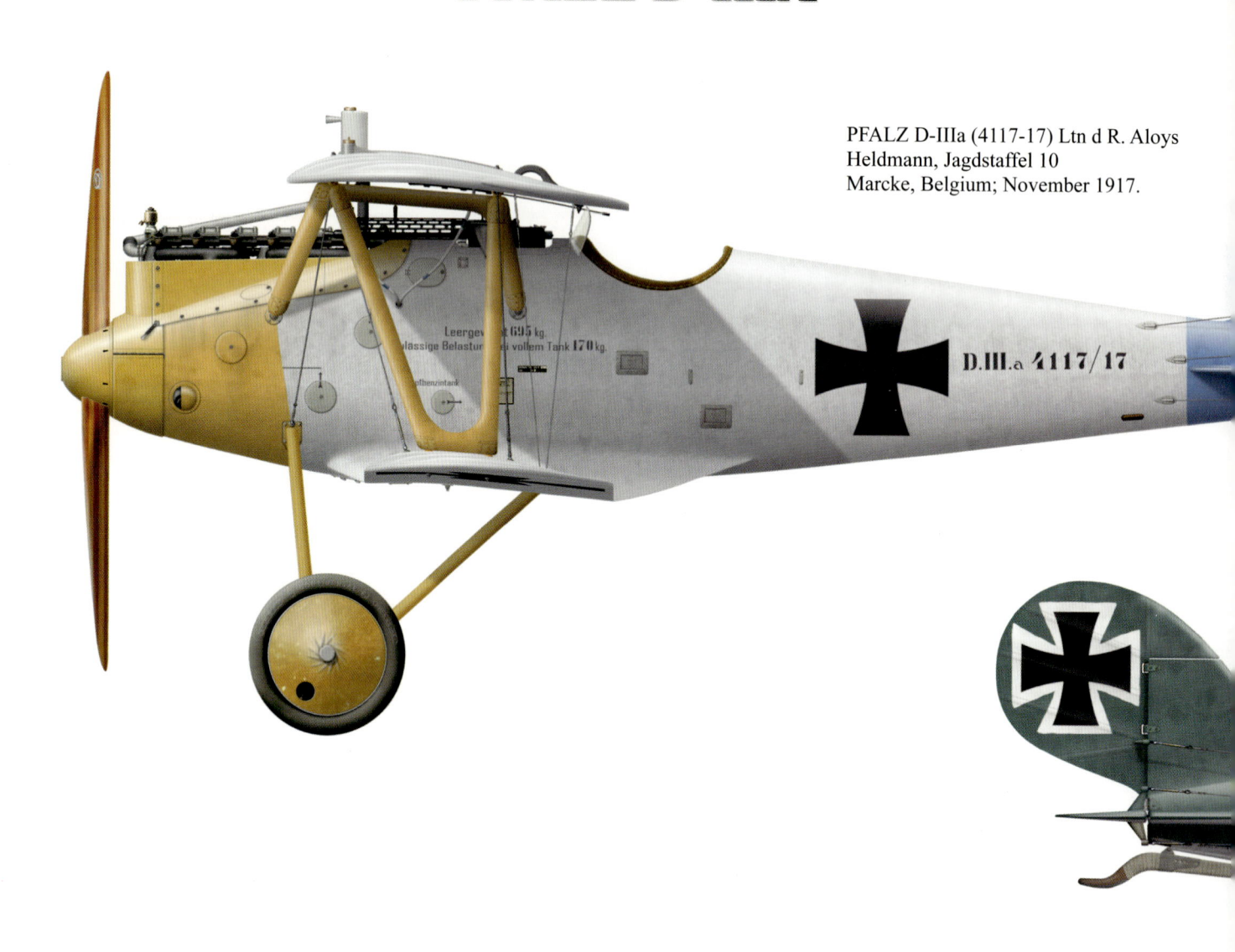

PFALZ D-IIIa (4117-17) Ltn d R. Aloys Heldmann, Jagdstaffel 10
Marcke, Belgium; November 1917.

PFALZ D-IIIa (8009/17) Ltn d R. Fritz Höhn, Jagdstaffel 21s
St Mard, France; March 1918.
Note Teddy Bear fixed behind the cockpit.

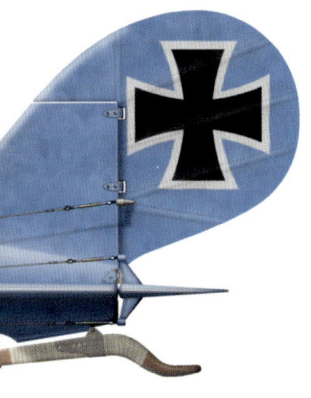

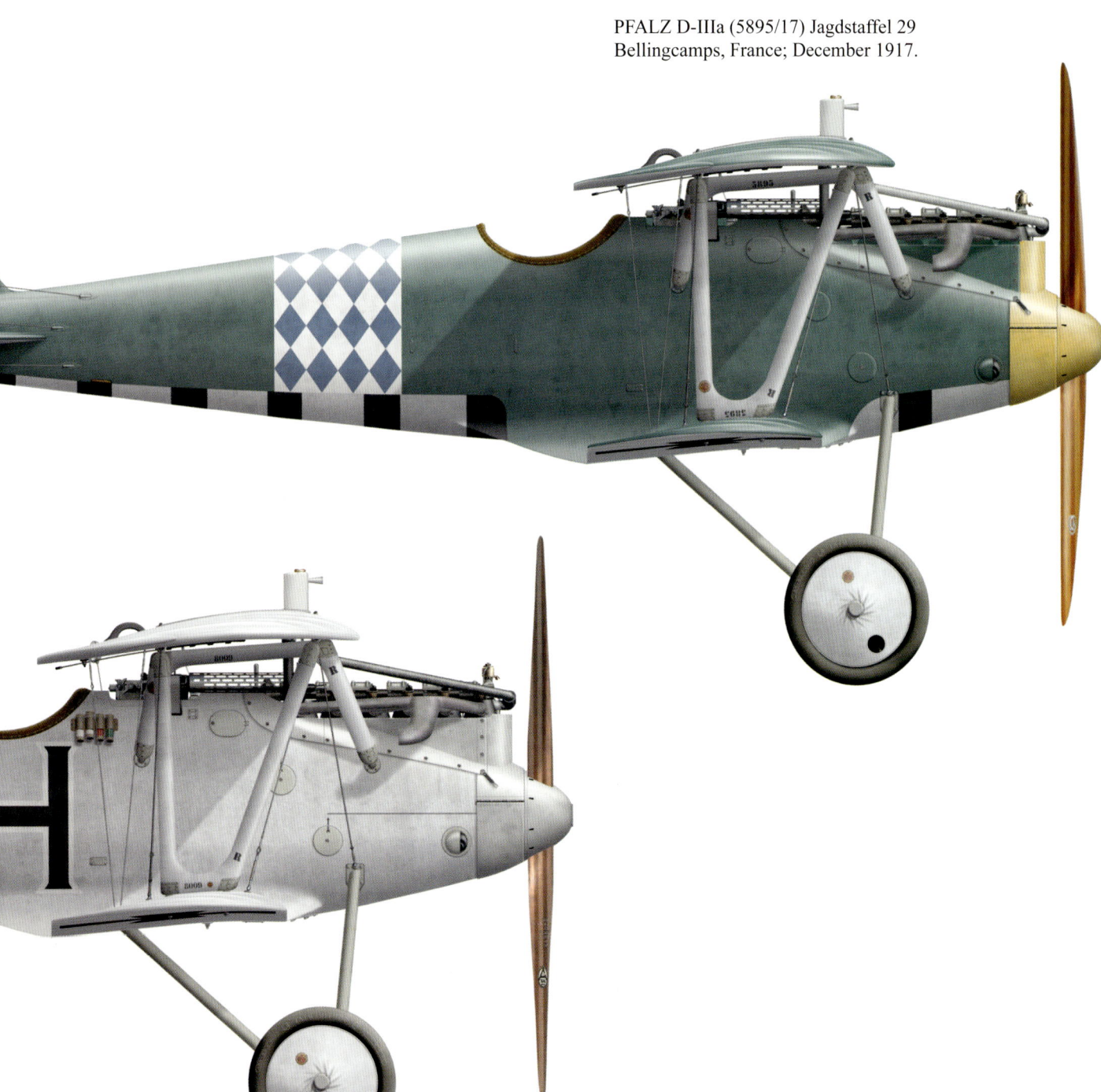

PFALZ D-IIIa (5895/17) Jagdstaffel 29
Bellingcamps, France; December 1917.

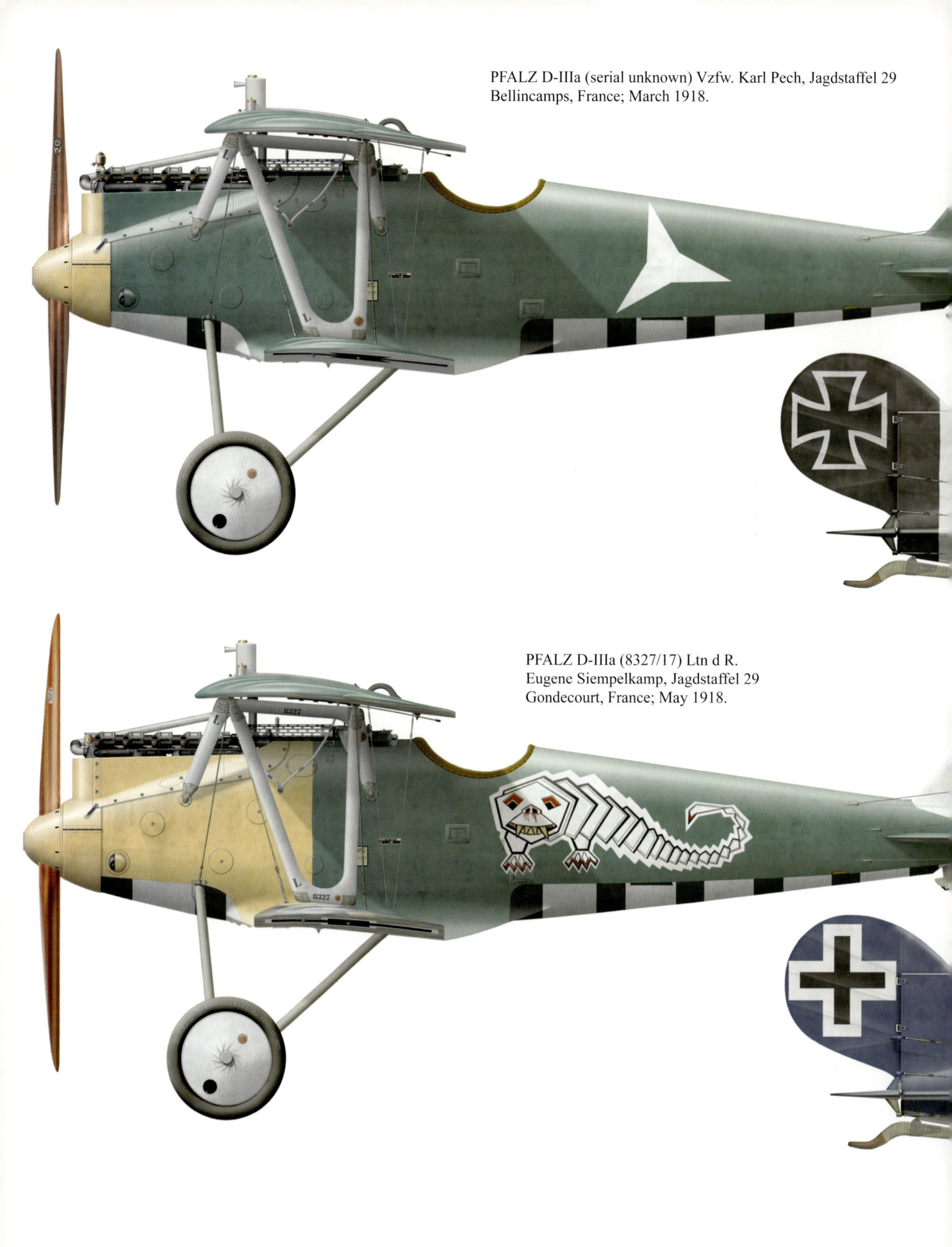

PFALZ D-IIIa (serial unknown) Vzfw. Karl Pech, Jagdstaffel 29
Bellincamps, France; March 1918.

PFALZ D-IIIa (8327/17) Ltn d R.
Eugene Siempelkamp, Jagdstaffel 29
Gondecourt, France; May 1918.

80

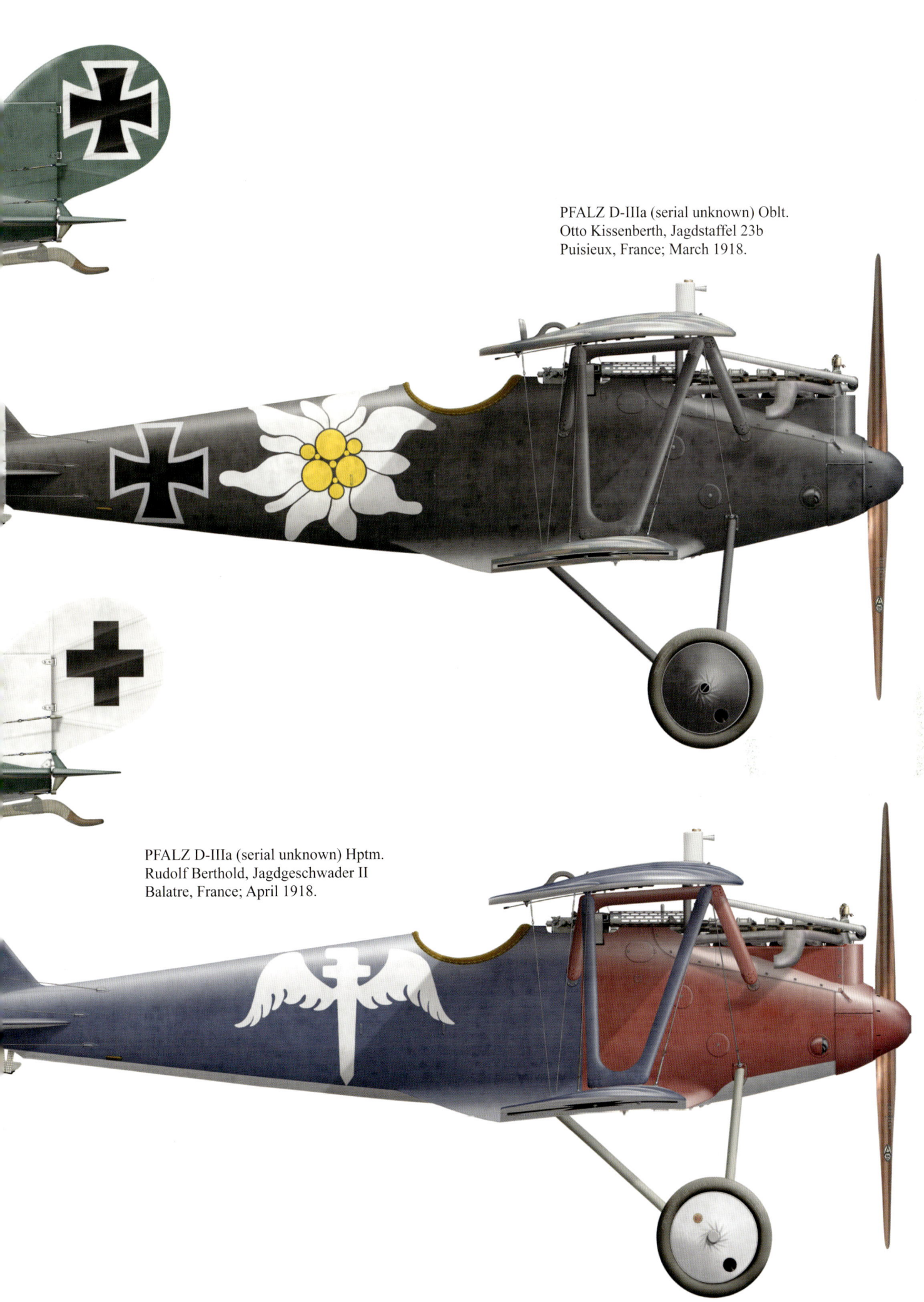

PFALZ D-IIIa (serial unknown) Oblt.
Otto Kissenberth, Jagdstaffel 23b
Puisieux, France; March 1918.

PFALZ D-IIIa (serial unknown) Hptm.
Rudolf Berthold, Jagdgeschwader II
Balatre, France; April 1918.

81

PFALZ D-IIIa (serial unknown) Ltn. Hans-Georg von der Marwitz, Jagdstaffel 30
Phalempin, France; May 1918.

PFALZ D-IIIa (serial unknown) Ltn. Busso von Alvensleben, Jagdstaffel 21s
Boncourt, France; June 1918.

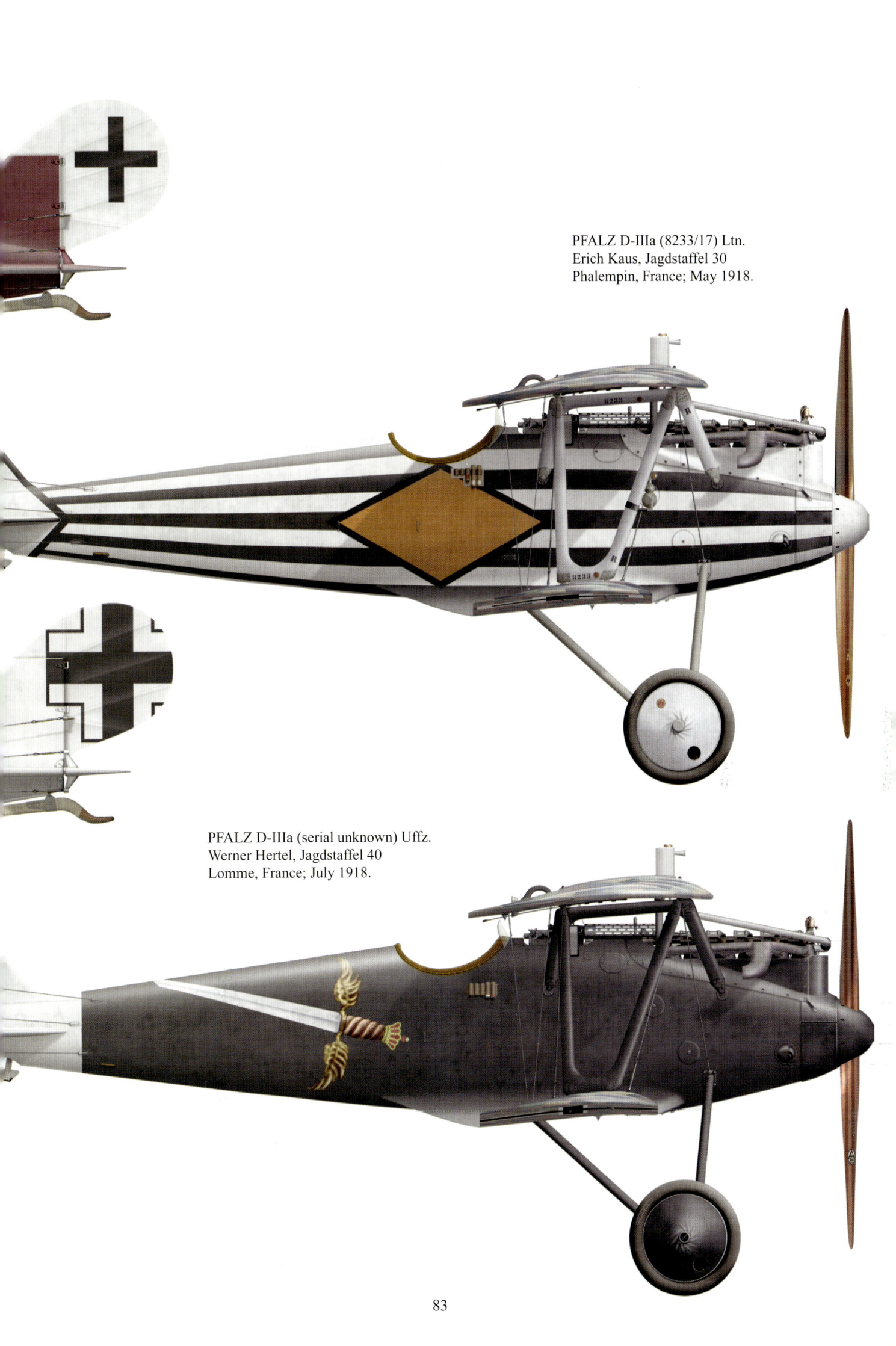

PFALZ D-IIIa (8233/17) Ltn.
Erich Kaus, Jagdstaffel 30
Phalempin, France; May 1918.

PFALZ D-IIIa (serial unknown) Uffz.
Werner Hertel, Jagdstaffel 40
Lomme, France; July 1918.

FOKKER F-I

FOKKER F-I (101/17) Triplane prototype (V-5, Werk Nr. 1697)
Schwerin, Germany; July 1917.

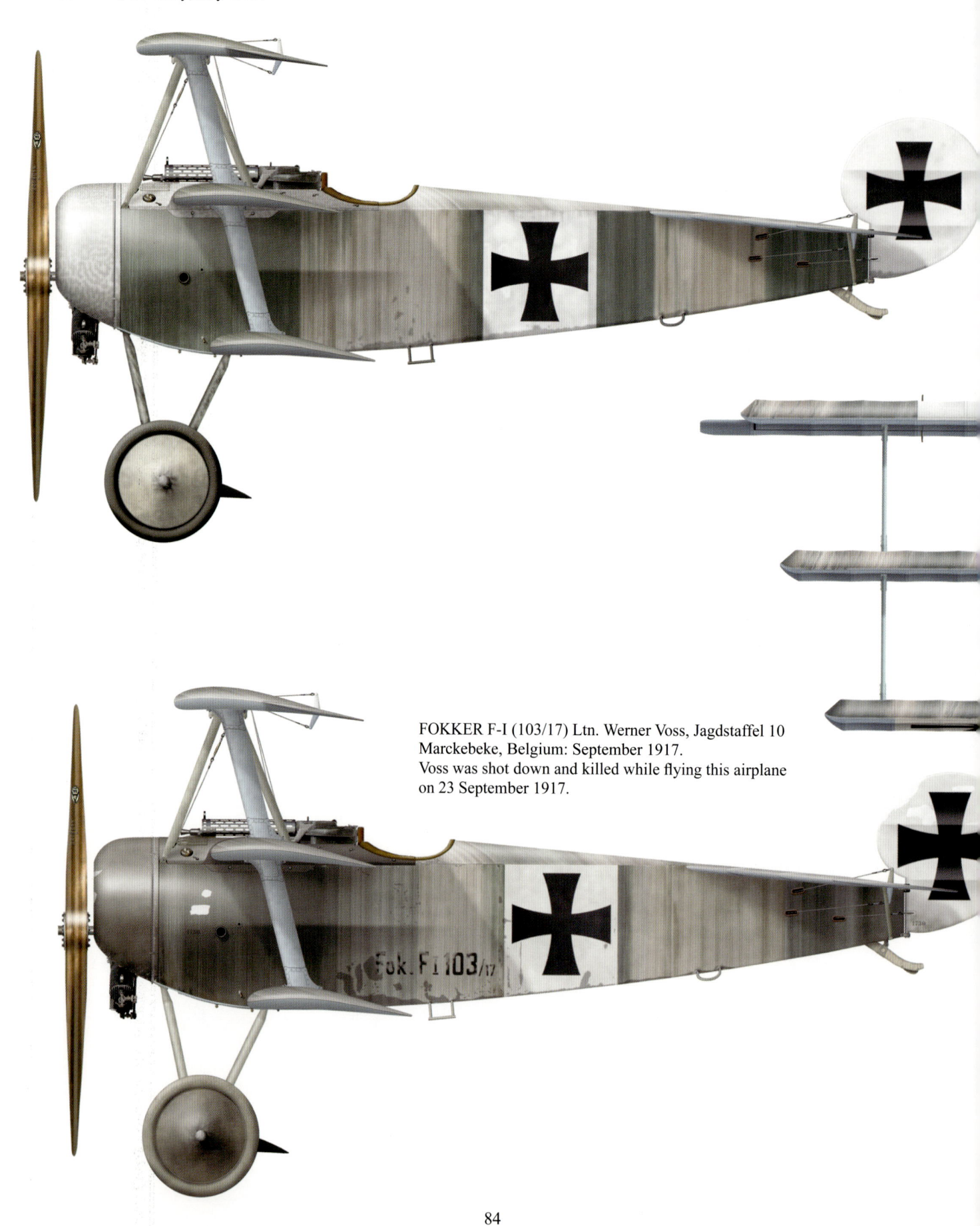

FOKKER F-I (103/17) Ltn. Werner Voss, Jagdstaffel 10
Marckebeke, Belgium: September 1917.
Voss was shot down and killed while flying this airplane on 23 September 1917.

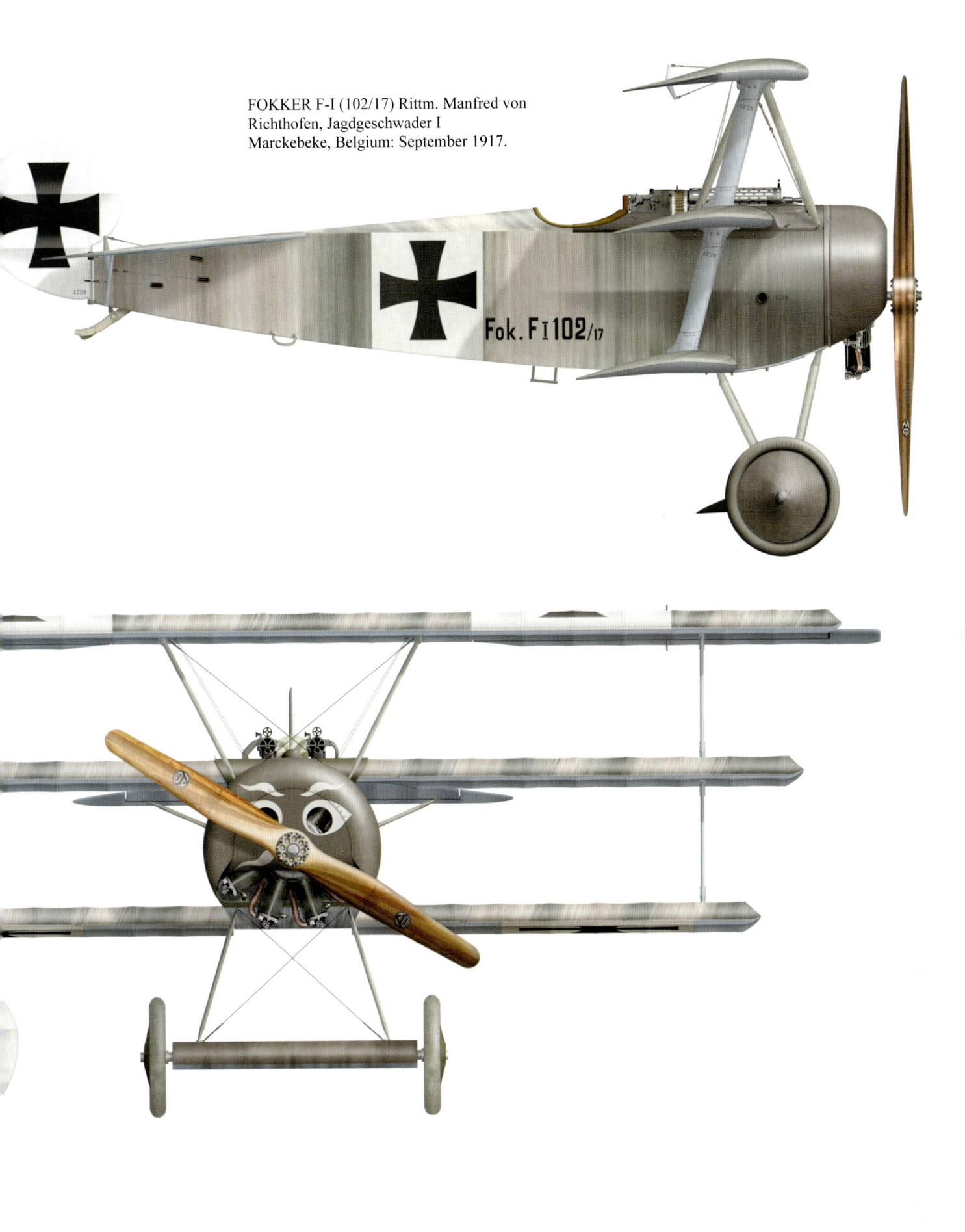

FOKKER F-I (102/17) Rittm. Manfred von Richthofen, Jagdgeschwader I
Marckebeke, Belgium: September 1917.

FOKKER DR-I

FOKKER Dr-I (425/17) Rittm. Manfred von Richthofen, Jagdgeschwader I
Cappy, France; April 1918.
Manfred von Richthofen was killed in this airplane on 21 April 1918.

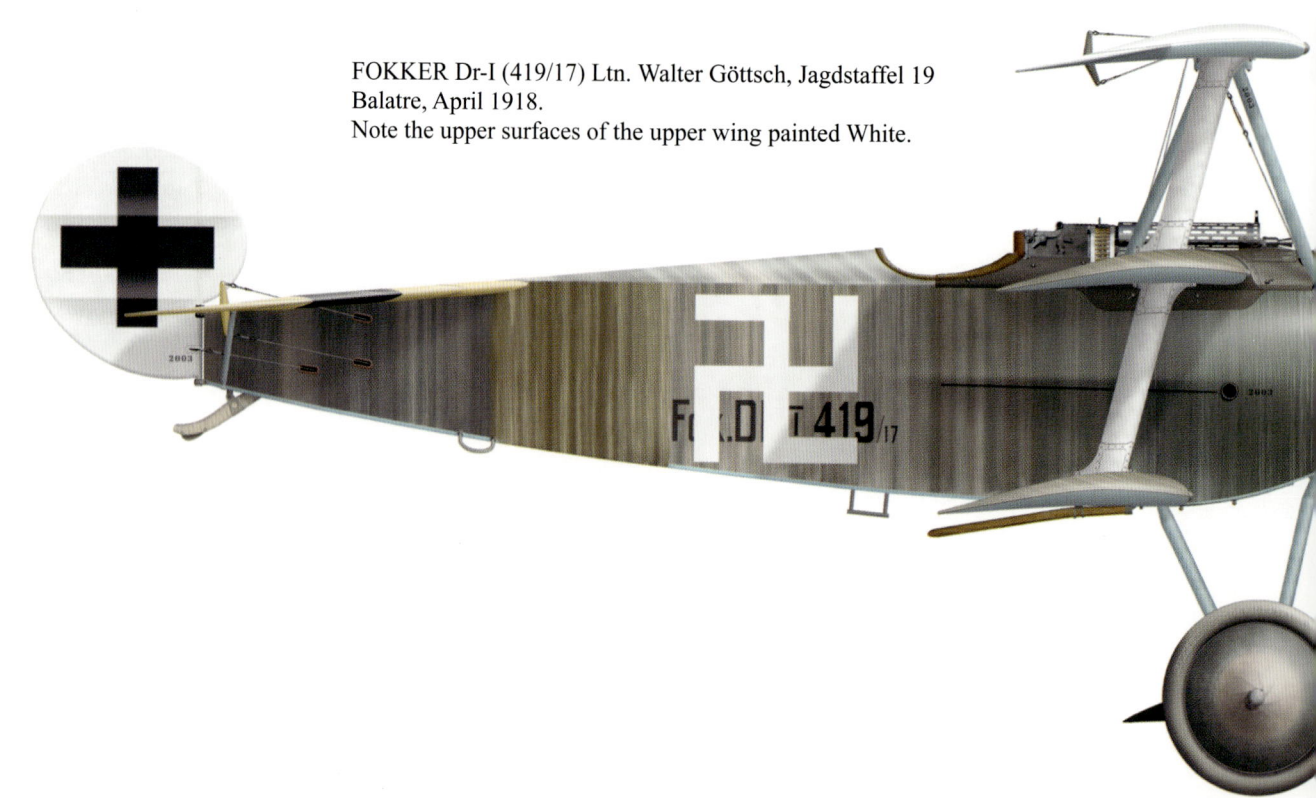

FOKKER Dr-I (419/17) Ltn. Walter Göttsch, Jagdstaffel 19
Balatre, April 1918.
Note the upper surfaces of the upper wing painted White.

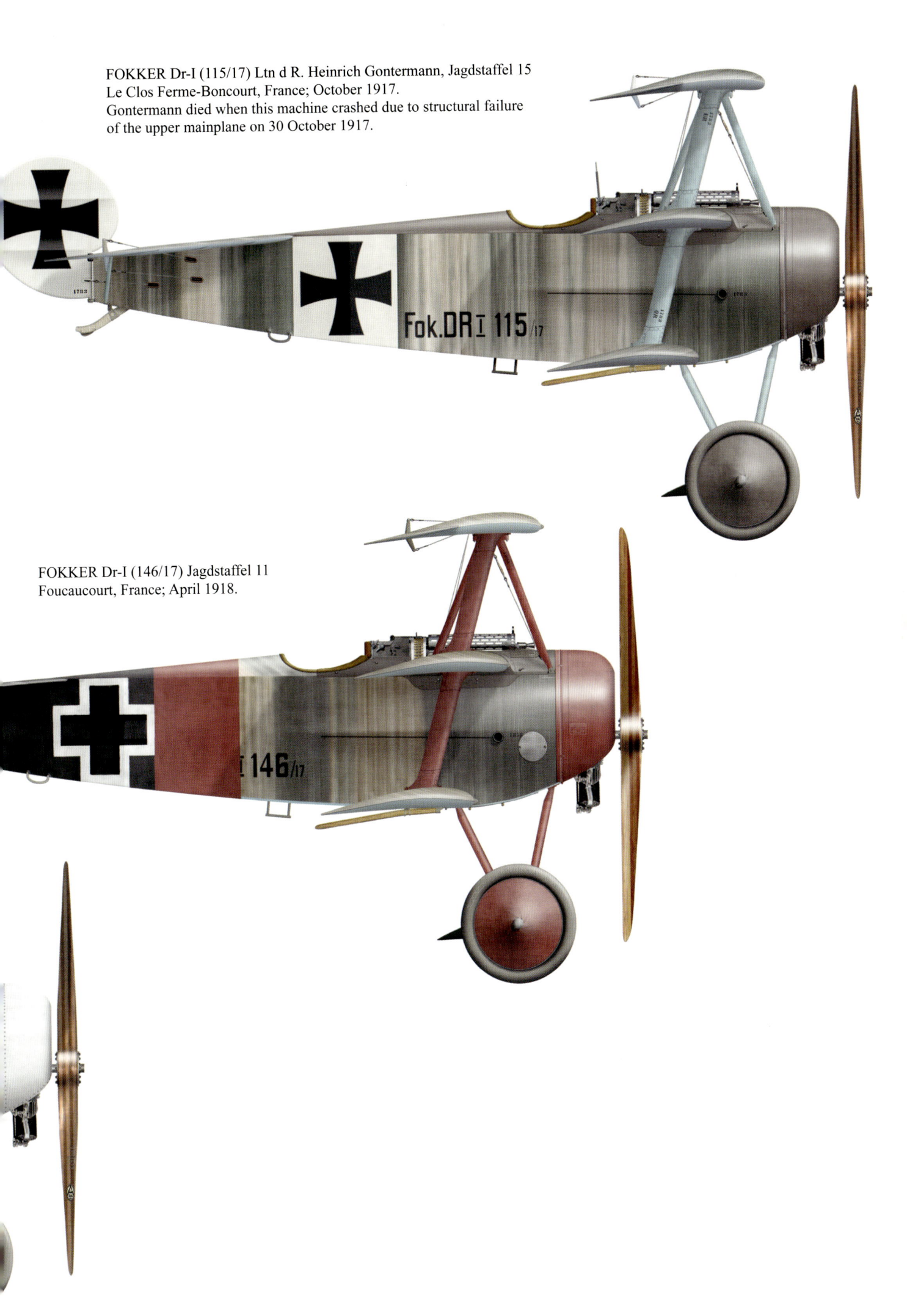

FOKKER Dr-I (115/17) Ltn d R. Heinrich Gontermann, Jagdstaffel 15
Le Clos Ferme-Boncourt, France; October 1917.
Gontermann died when this machine crashed due to structural failure
of the upper mainplane on 30 October 1917.

FOKKER Dr-I (146/17) Jagdstaffel 11
Foucaucourt, France; April 1918.

FOKKER Dr-I (503/17) Ltn. Hans Körner, Jagdstaffel 19
Balatre, France; May 1918.

FOKKER Dr-I (serial unknown) Ltn. Hermann Frommherz, Jagdstaffel Boelcke
Halluin-Ost, France; May 1918.

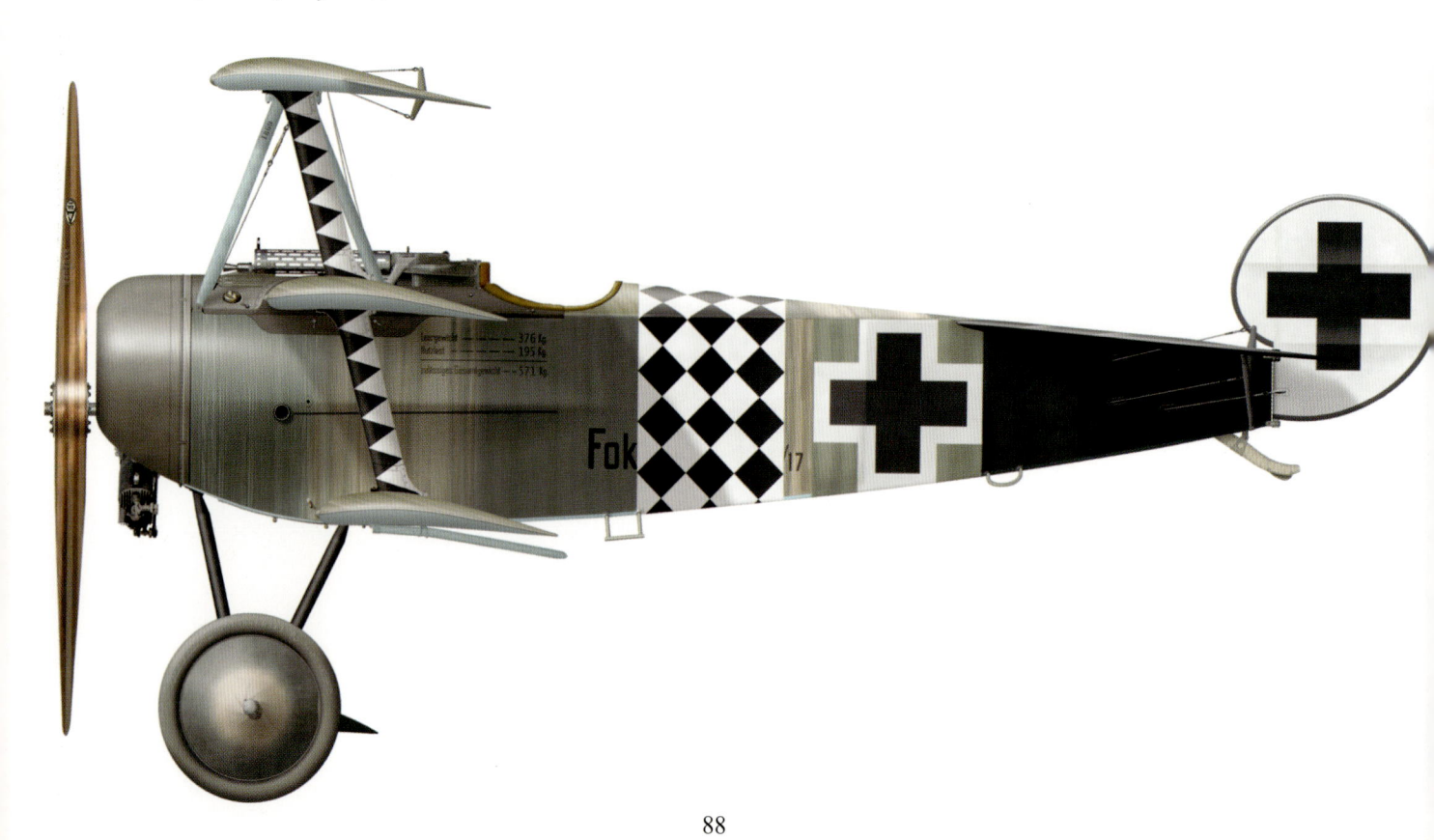

FOKKER Dr-I (206/17) Oblt. Hermann Göring, Jagdstaffel 27
Halluin, France; May 1918.

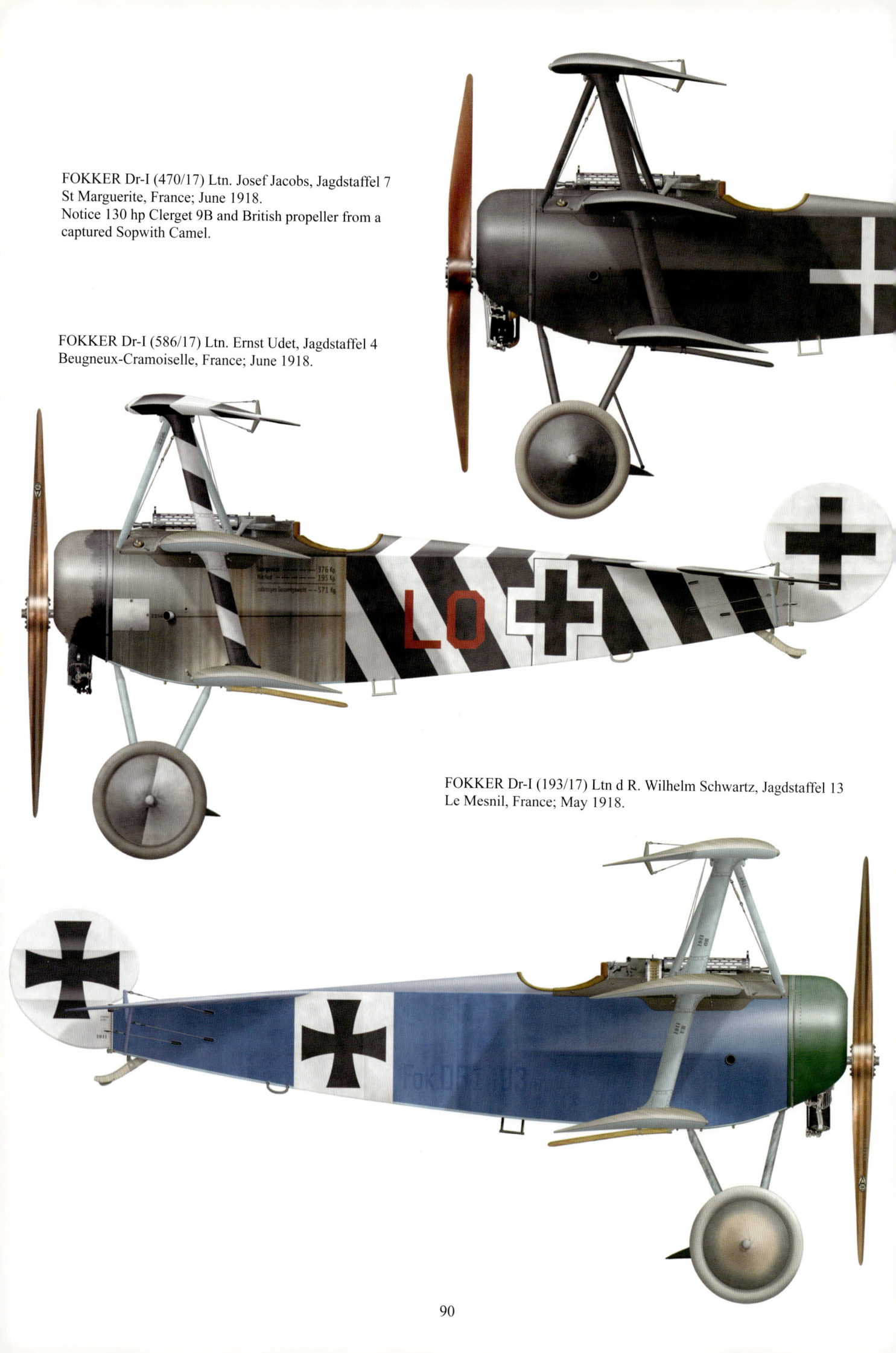

FOKKER Dr-I (470/17) Ltn. Josef Jacobs, Jagdstaffel 7
St Marguerite, France; June 1918.
Notice 130 hp Clerget 9B and British propeller from a
captured Sopwith Camel.

FOKKER Dr-I (586/17) Ltn. Ernst Udet, Jagdstaffel 4
Beugneux-Cramoiselle, France; June 1918.

FOKKER Dr-I (193/17) Ltn d R. Wilhelm Schwartz, Jagdstaffel 13
Le Mesnil, France; May 1918.

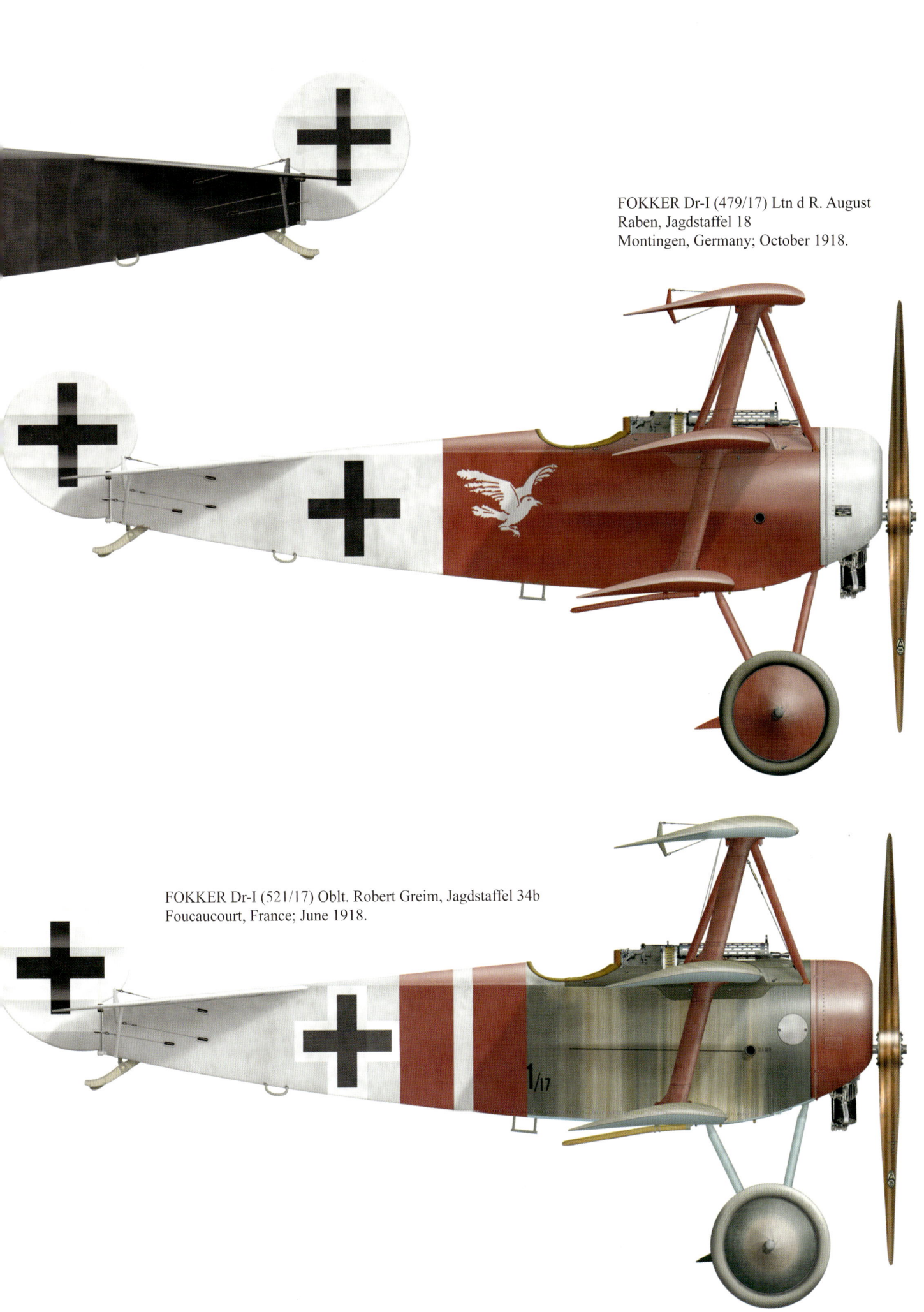

FOKKER Dr-I (479/17) Ltn d R. August Raben, Jagdstaffel 18
Montingen, Germany; October 1918.

FOKKER Dr-I (521/17) Oblt. Robert Greim, Jagdstaffel 34b
Foucaucourt, France; June 1918.

PFALZ D-VIII

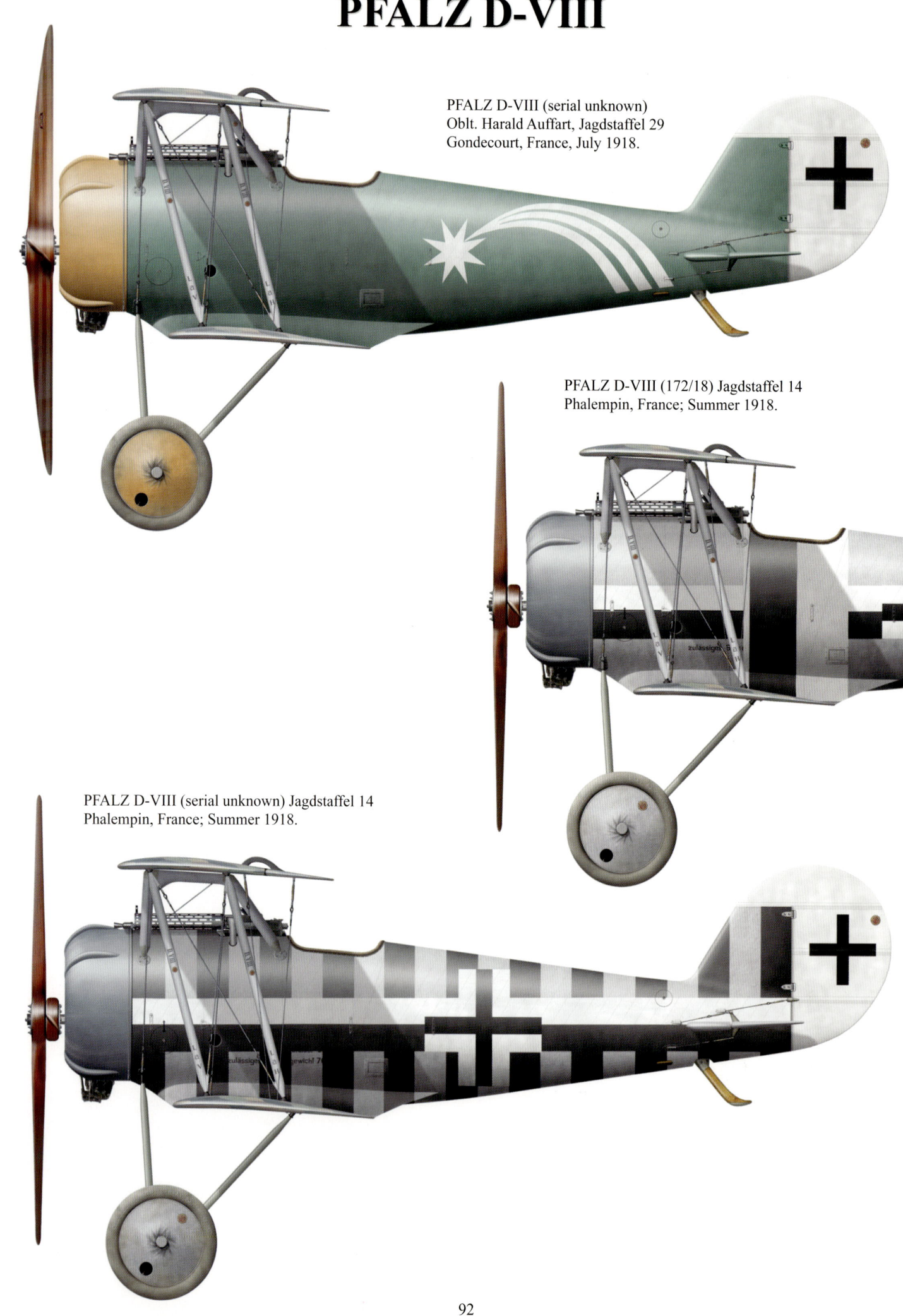

PFALZ D-VIII (serial unknown)
Oblt. Harald Auffart, Jagdstaffel 29
Gondecourt, France, July 1918.

PFALZ D-VIII (172/18) Jagdstaffel 14
Phalempin, France; Summer 1918.

PFALZ D-VIII (serial unknown) Jagdstaffel 14
Phalempin, France; Summer 1918.

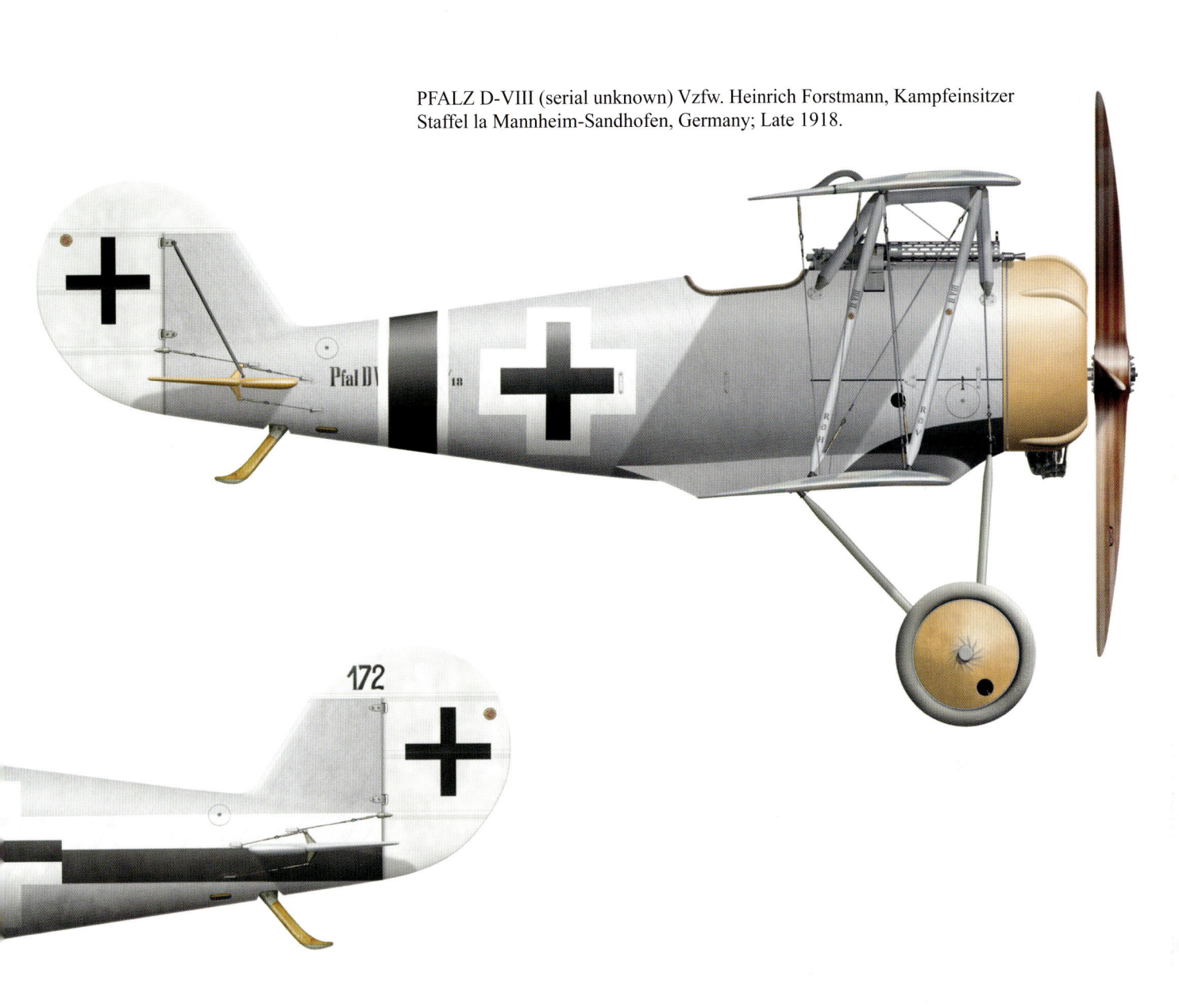

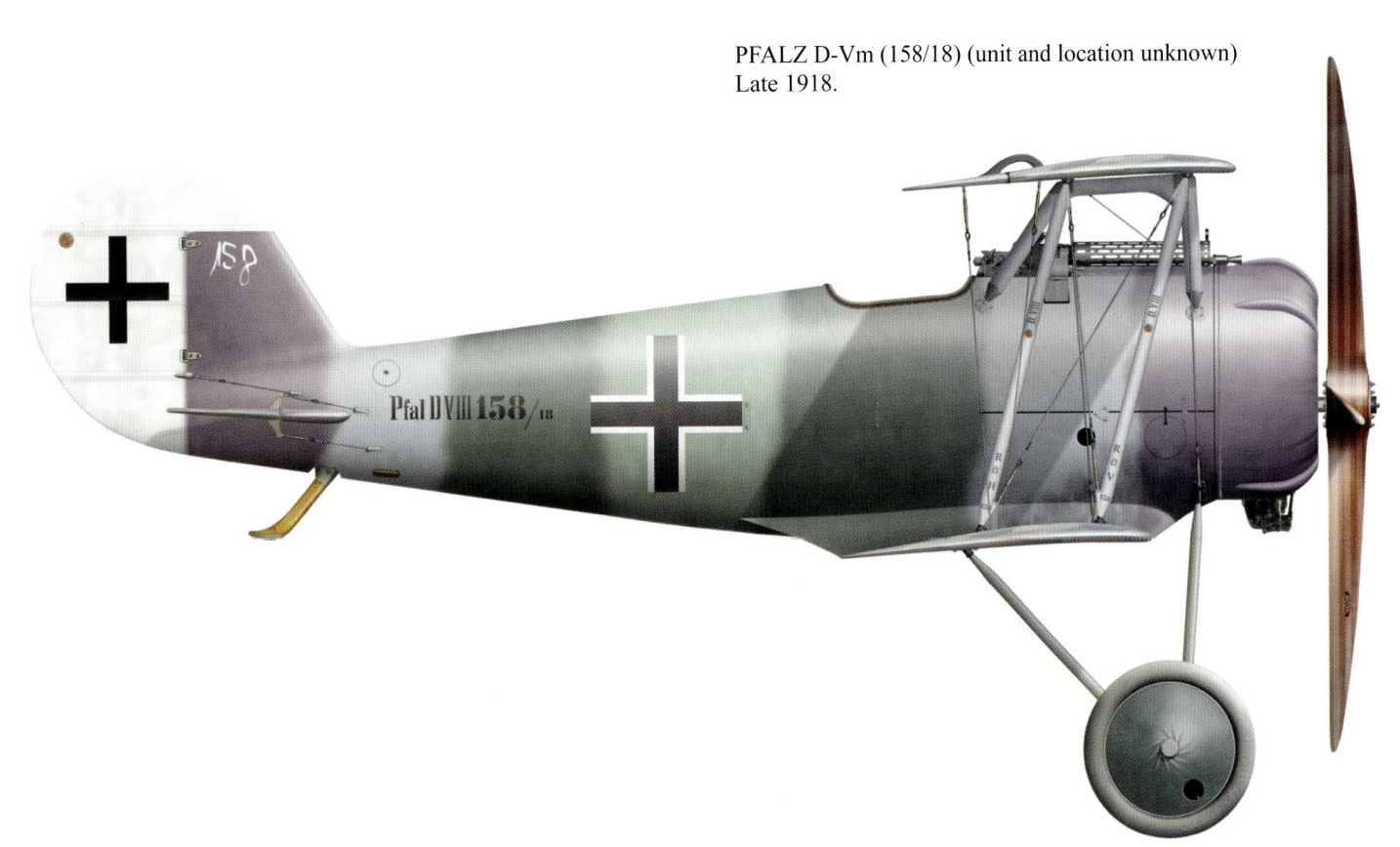

PFALZ D-VIII (serial unknown) Vzfw. Heinrich Forstmann, Kampfeinsitzer
Staffel 1a Mannheim-Sandhofen, Germany; Late 1918.

PFALZ D-Vm (158/18) (unit and location unknown)
Late 1918.

ROLAND D-VIA

ROLAND D-VIa (serial unknown) Jagdstaffel 23b
Epinoy, France; June 1918.

ROLAND D-VIa (1222/18) Ltn d R. Emil Koch, Jagdstaffel 32b
Epinoy, France; June 1918.

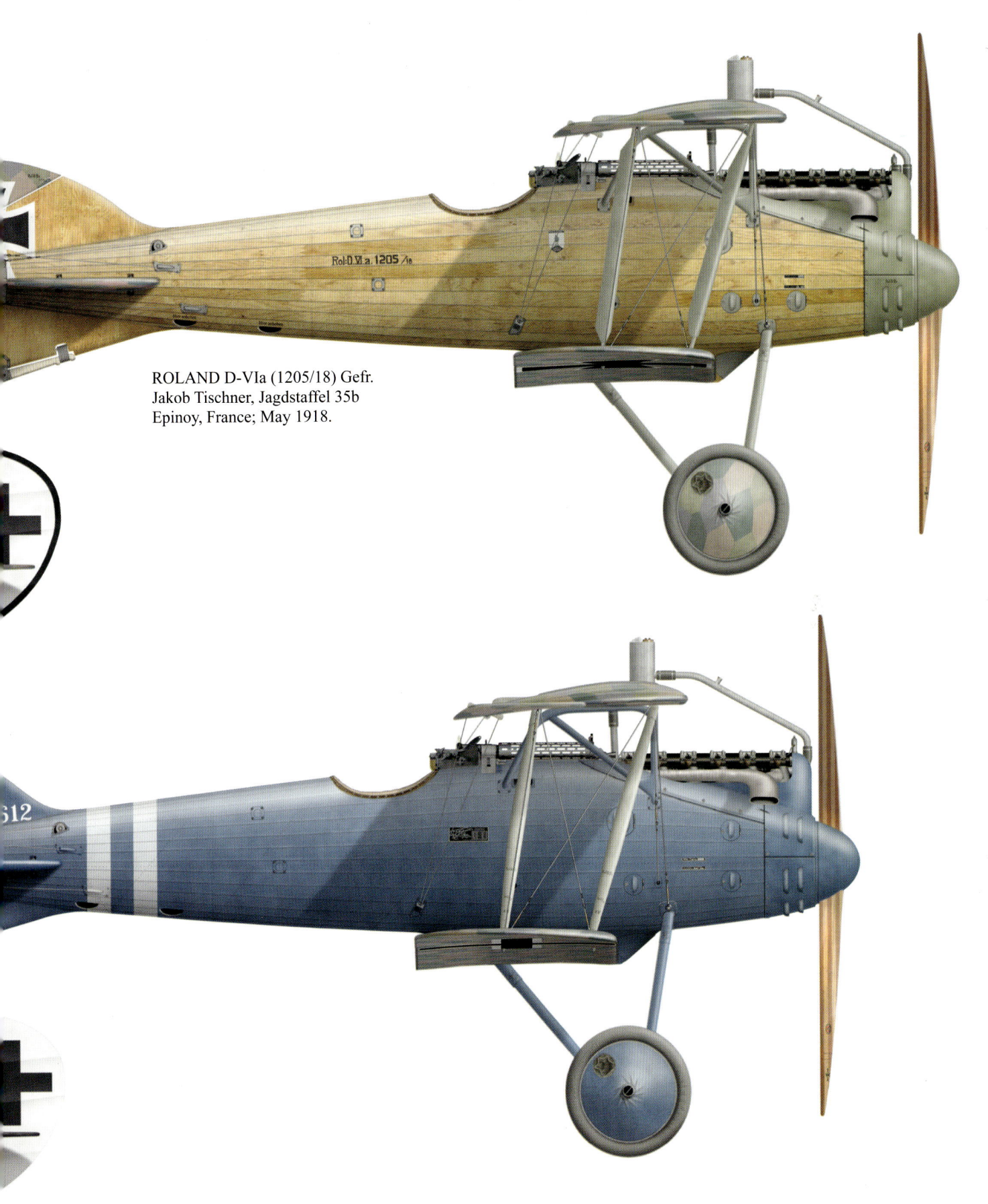

ROLAND D-VIa (1205/18) Gefr.
Jakob Tischner, Jagdstaffel 35b
Epinoy, France; May 1918.

ROLAND D-VIa (3612/18) (unit and location unknown)
Summer 1918.

ROLAND D-VIB

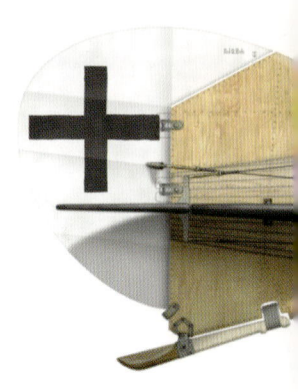

ROLAND D-VIb (serial unknown) Jagdstaffel 59
Roucourt, France; Summer 1918.

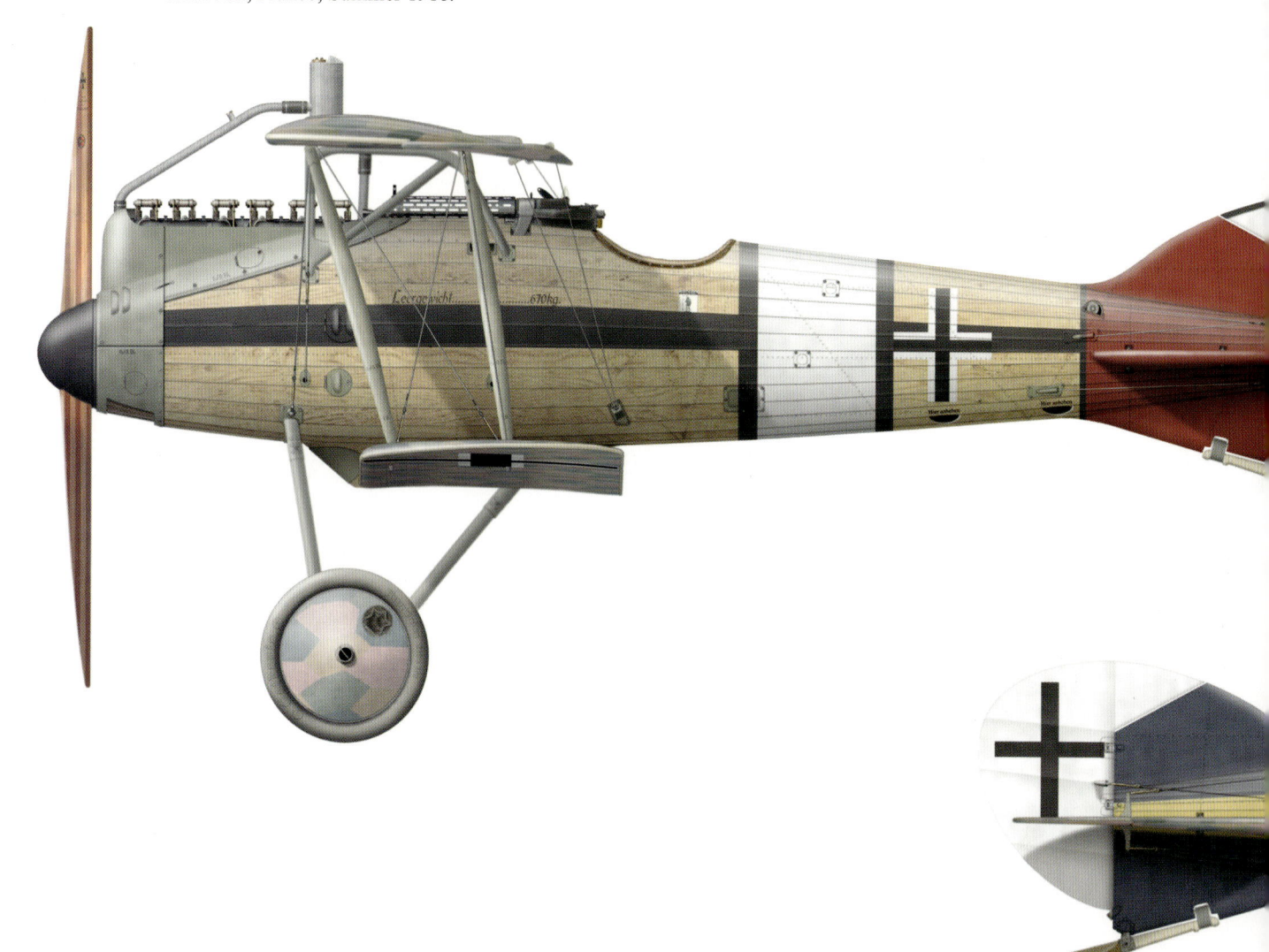

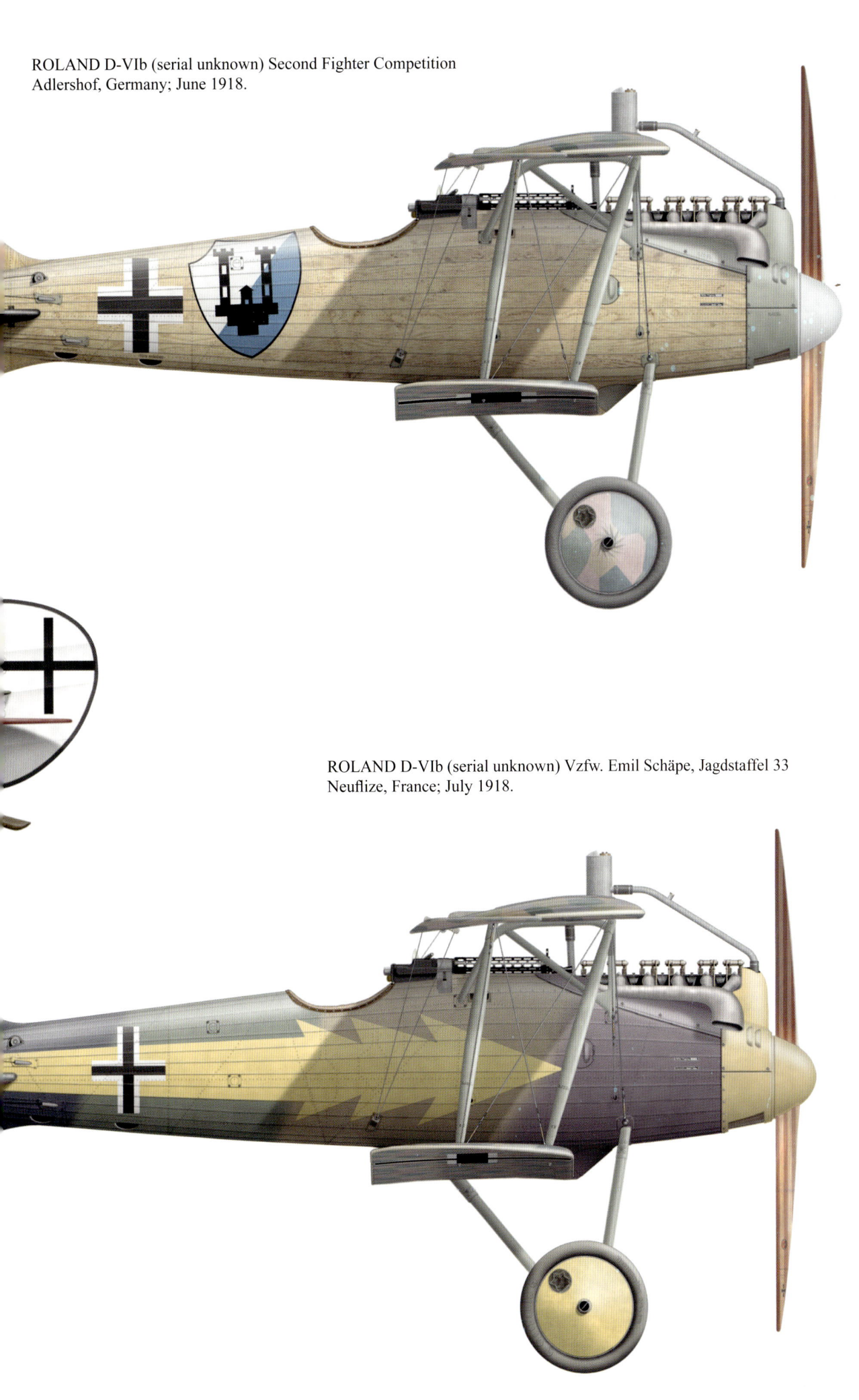

ROLAND D-VIb (serial unknown) Second Fighter Competition
Adlershof, Germany; June 1918.

ROLAND D-VIb (serial unknown) Vzfw. Emil Schäpe, Jagdstaffel 33
Neuflize, France; July 1918.

FOKKER D-VI

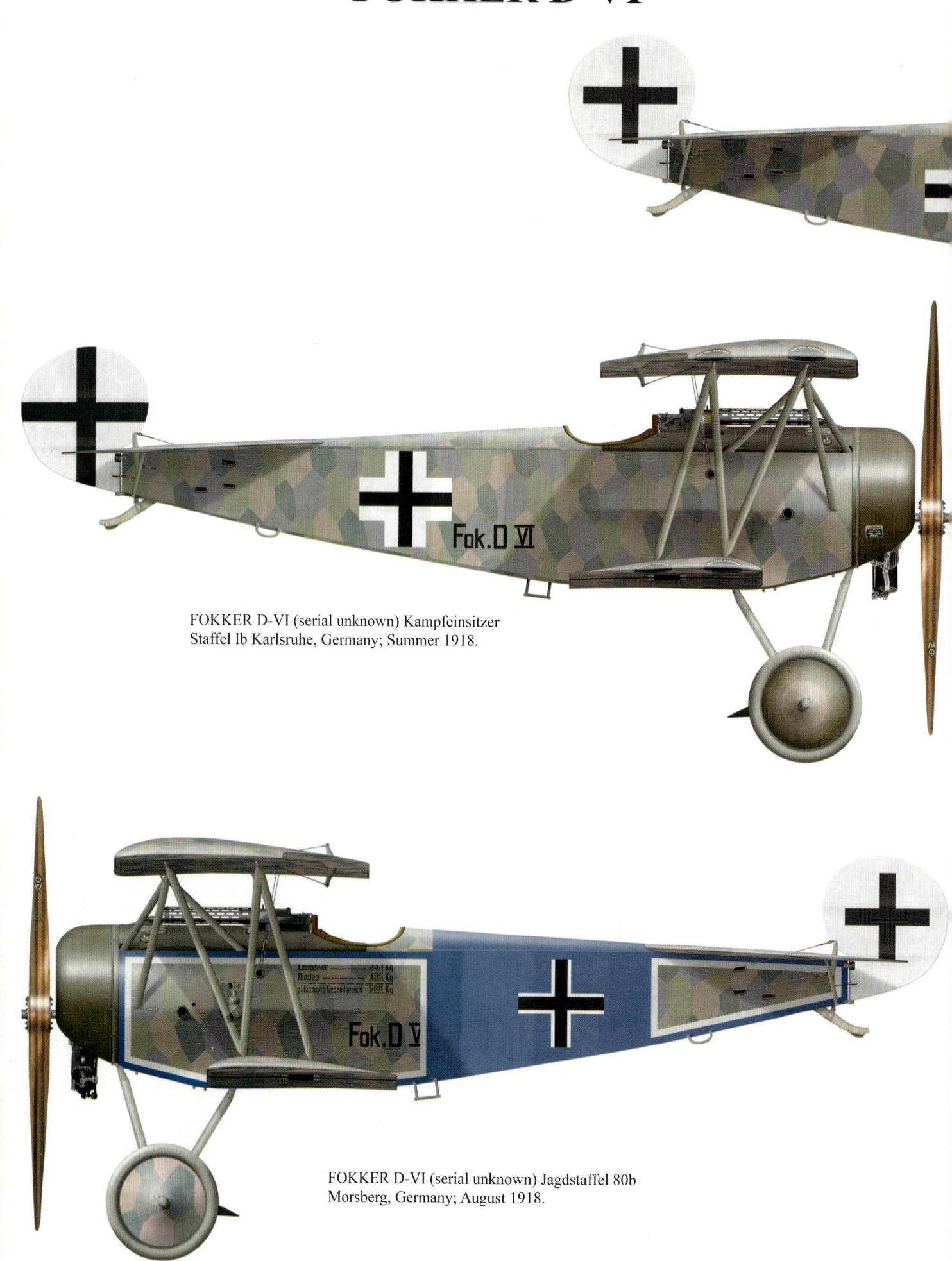

FOKKER D-VI (serial unknown) Kampfeinsitzer
Staffel lb Karlsruhe, Germany; Summer 1918.

FOKKER D-VI (serial unknown) Jagdstaffel 80b
Morsberg, Germany; August 1918.

FOKKER D-VI (serial unknown) Kampfeinsitzer
Staffel 1a Mannheim, Germany; Summer 1918.

FOKKER D-VI (serial unknown) Jagdstaffel 80b
Morsberg, Germany; August 1918.

FOKKER D-VI (serial unknown) Ltn. Kurt Seit, Jagdstaffel 80b
Morsberg, Germany; August 1918.

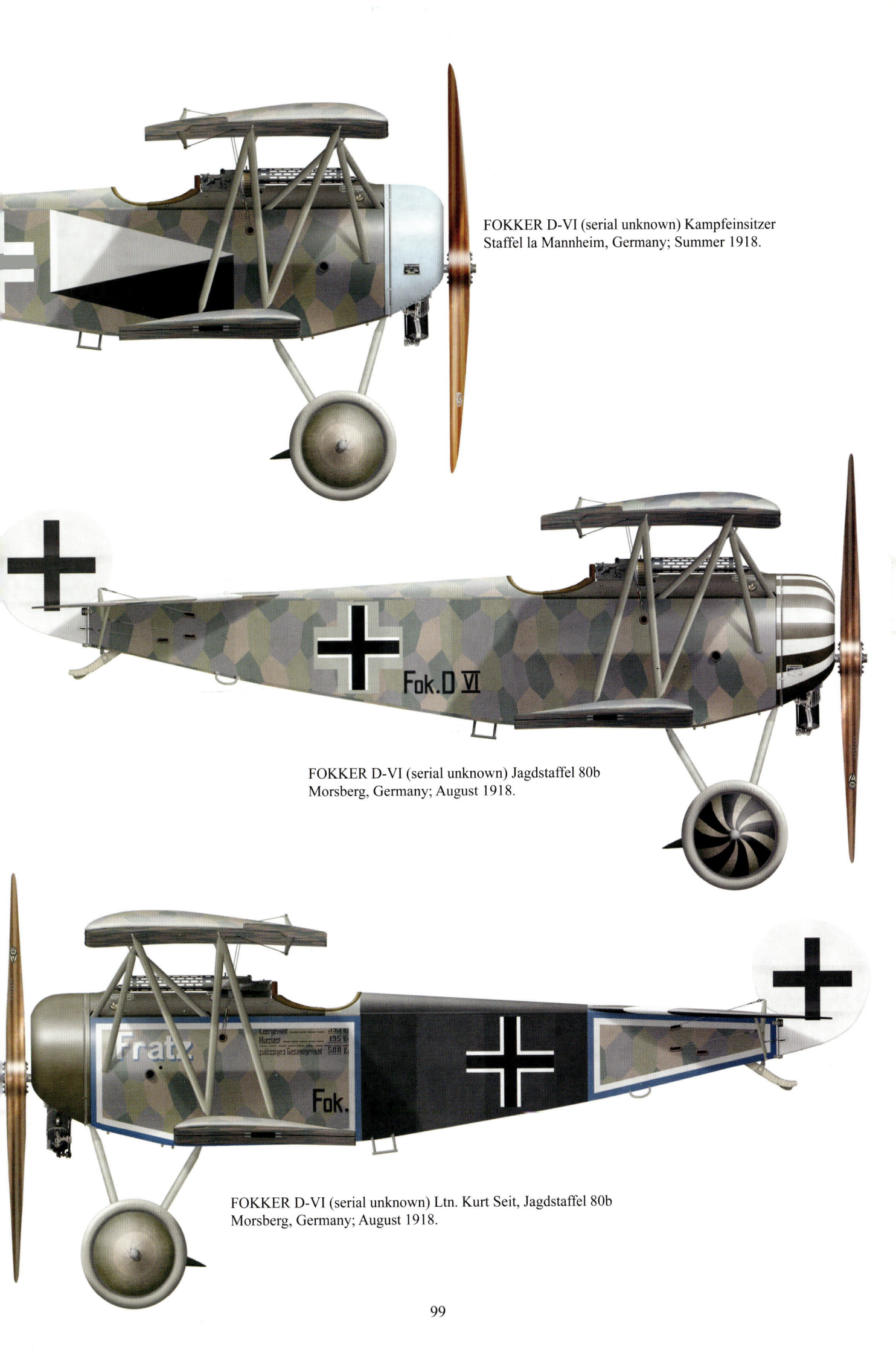

FOKKER D-VII

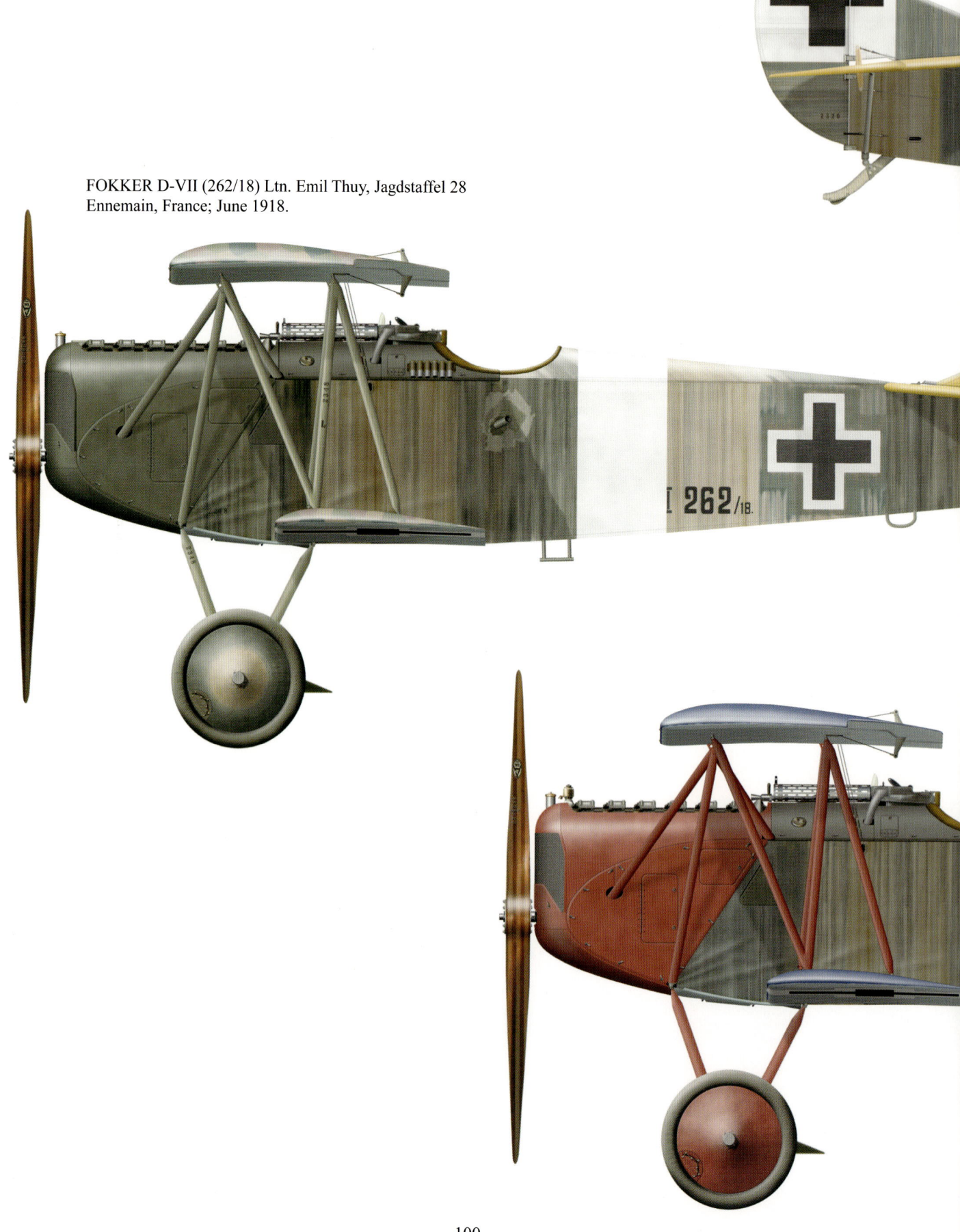

FOKKER D-VII (262/18) Ltn. Emil Thuy, Jagdstaffel 28
Ennemain, France; June 1918.

FOKKER D-VII (234/18) Ltn. Fritz Friedrichs, Jagdstaffel 10
Cappy, France; May 1918.

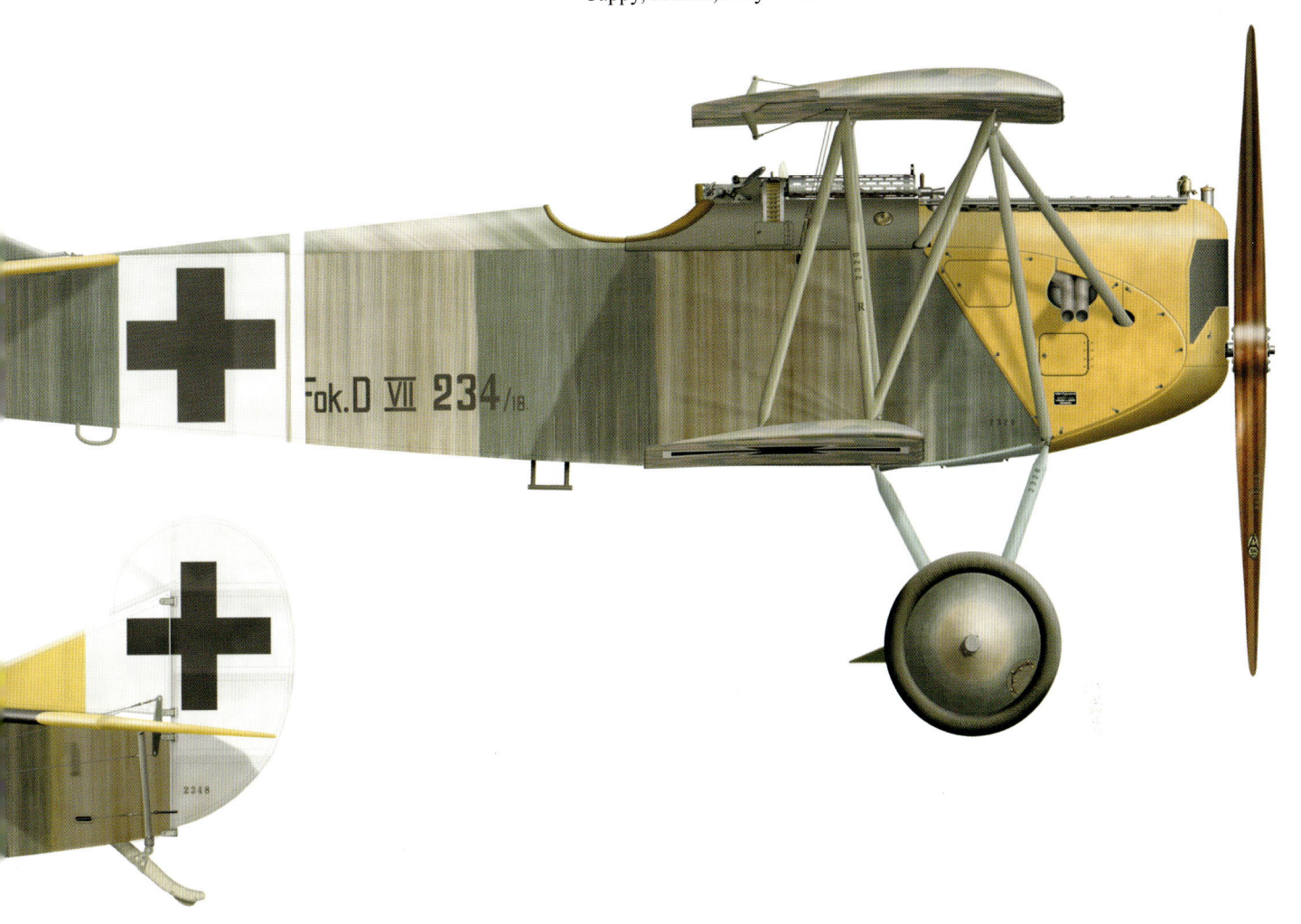

FOKKER D-VII (serial unknown) Haupt. Rudolf
Berthold, Jagdgeschwader II
Le Mesnil, France; June 1918.

FOKKER D-VII (332/18) Ltn d R. Otto Löffler, Jagdstaffel Boelcke
Mont Soissons Ferme, France; July 1918.

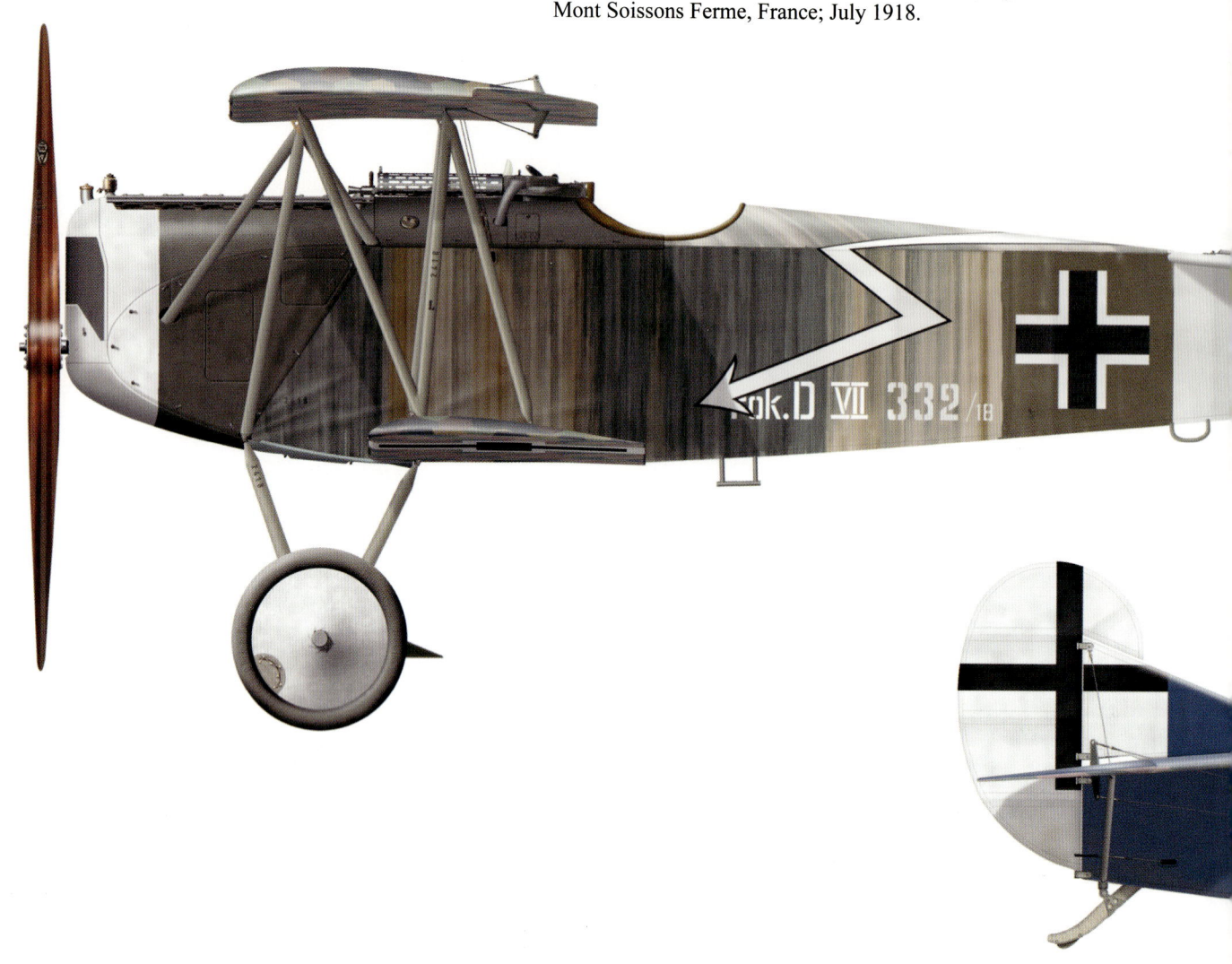

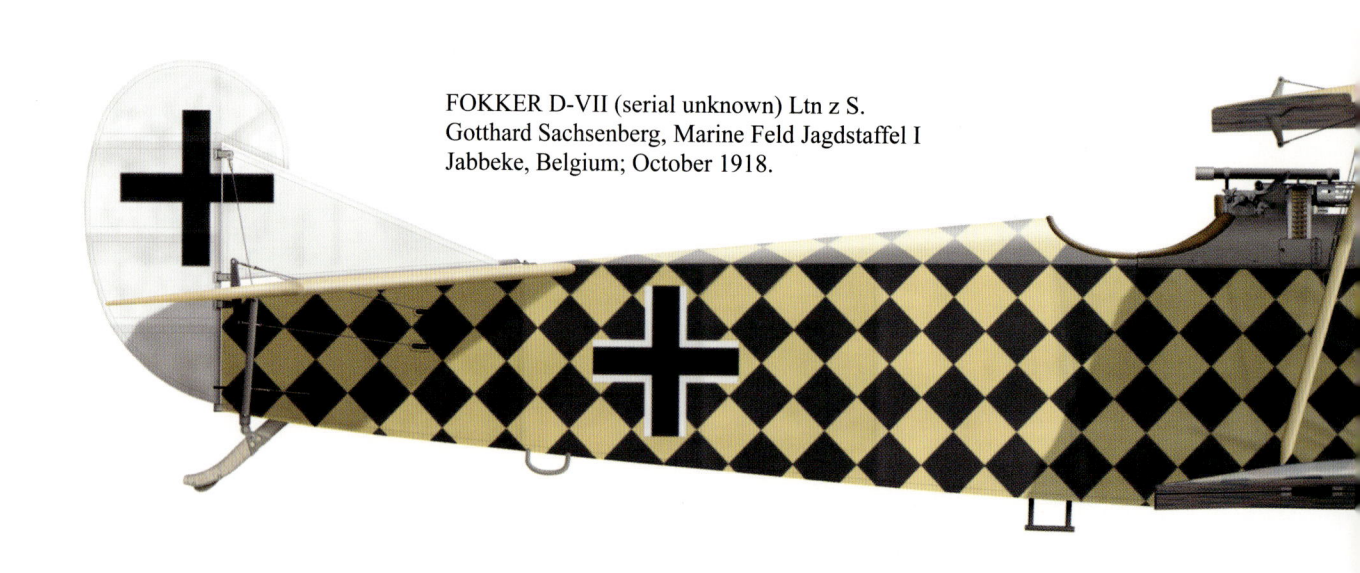

FOKKER D-VII (serial unknown) Ltn z S.
Gotthard Sachsenberg, Marine Feld Jagdstaffel I
Jabbeke, Belgium; October 1918.

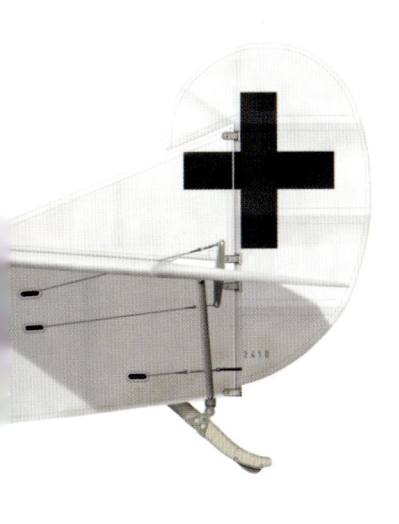

FOKKER D-VII (serial unknown) Ltn d R. Grimm, Jagdstaffel 13
Tichemont, France; September 1918.

FOKKER D-VII F

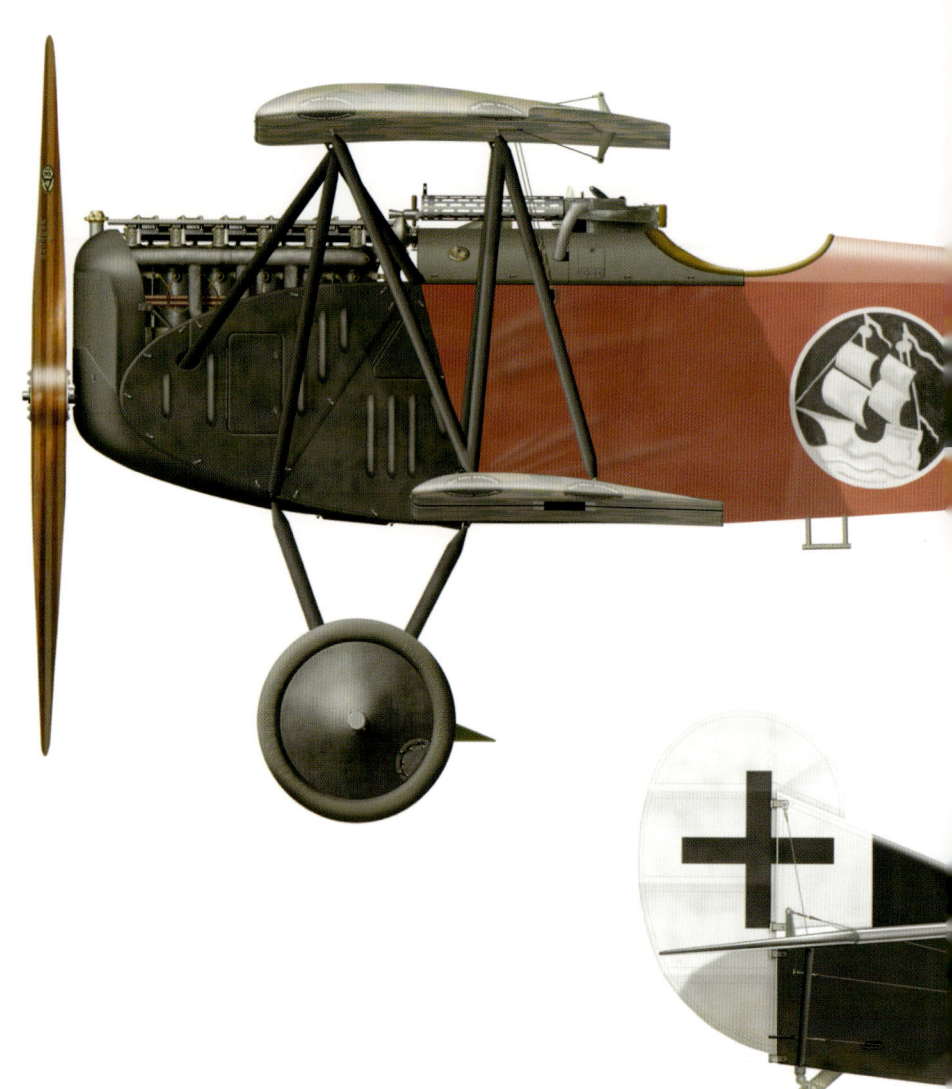

FOKKER D-VII F (serial unknown) Ltn d R. Josef Veltjens, Jagdstaffel 15
Chéry-les-Pouilly, France; August 1918.

104

FOKKER D-VII F (serial unknown) Ltn d R. Heinrich Drekmann, Jagdstaffel 4
Monthussart, France; June 1918.

FOKKER D-VII F (460/18) Ltn d R. Erich Just, Jagdstaffel 11
Bernes, France; Summer 1918.

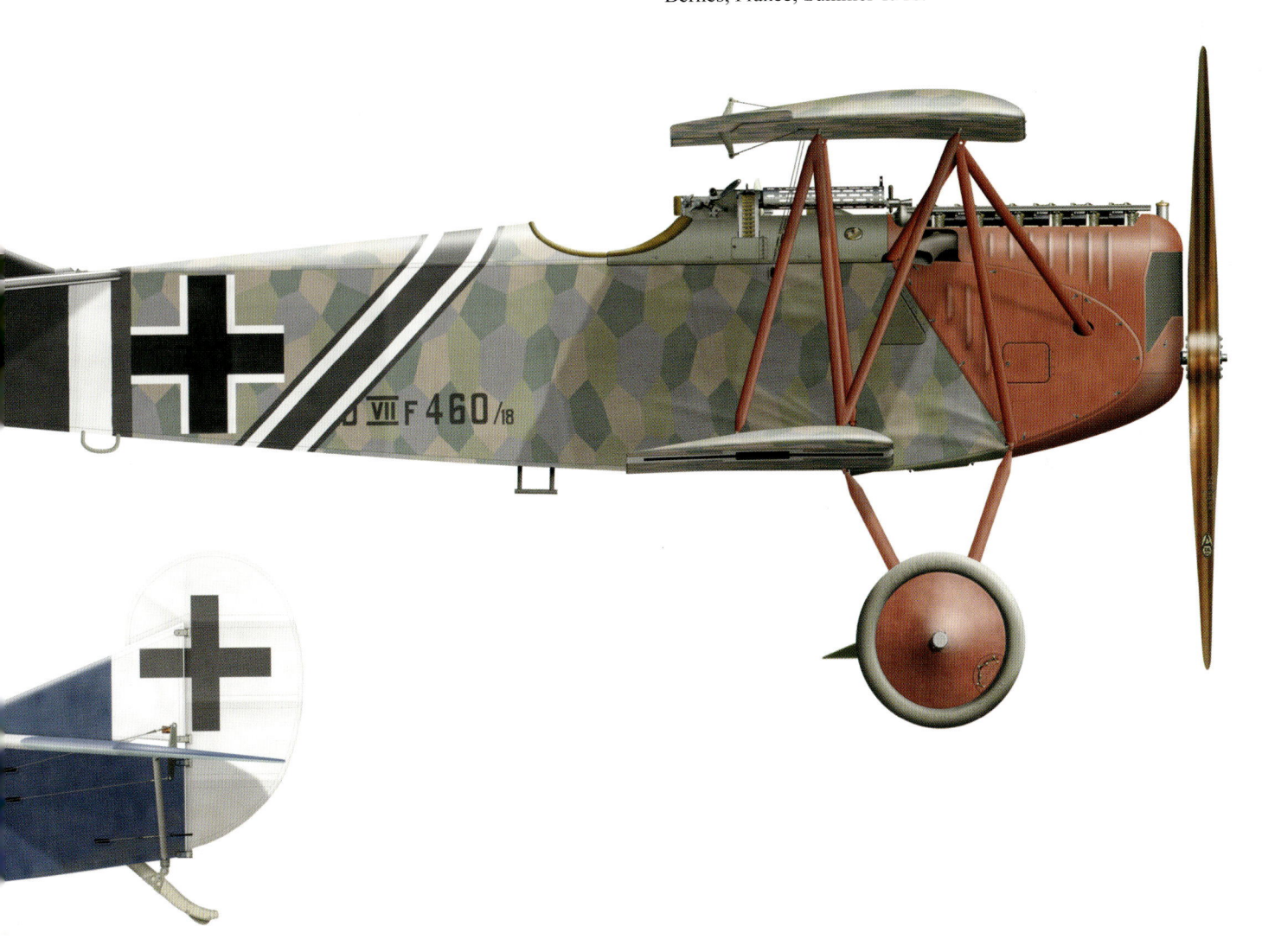

FOKKER D-VII F (serial unknown) Ltn.
Lothar von Richthofen, Jagdstaffel 11
Puisieux Ferme, France; August 1918.

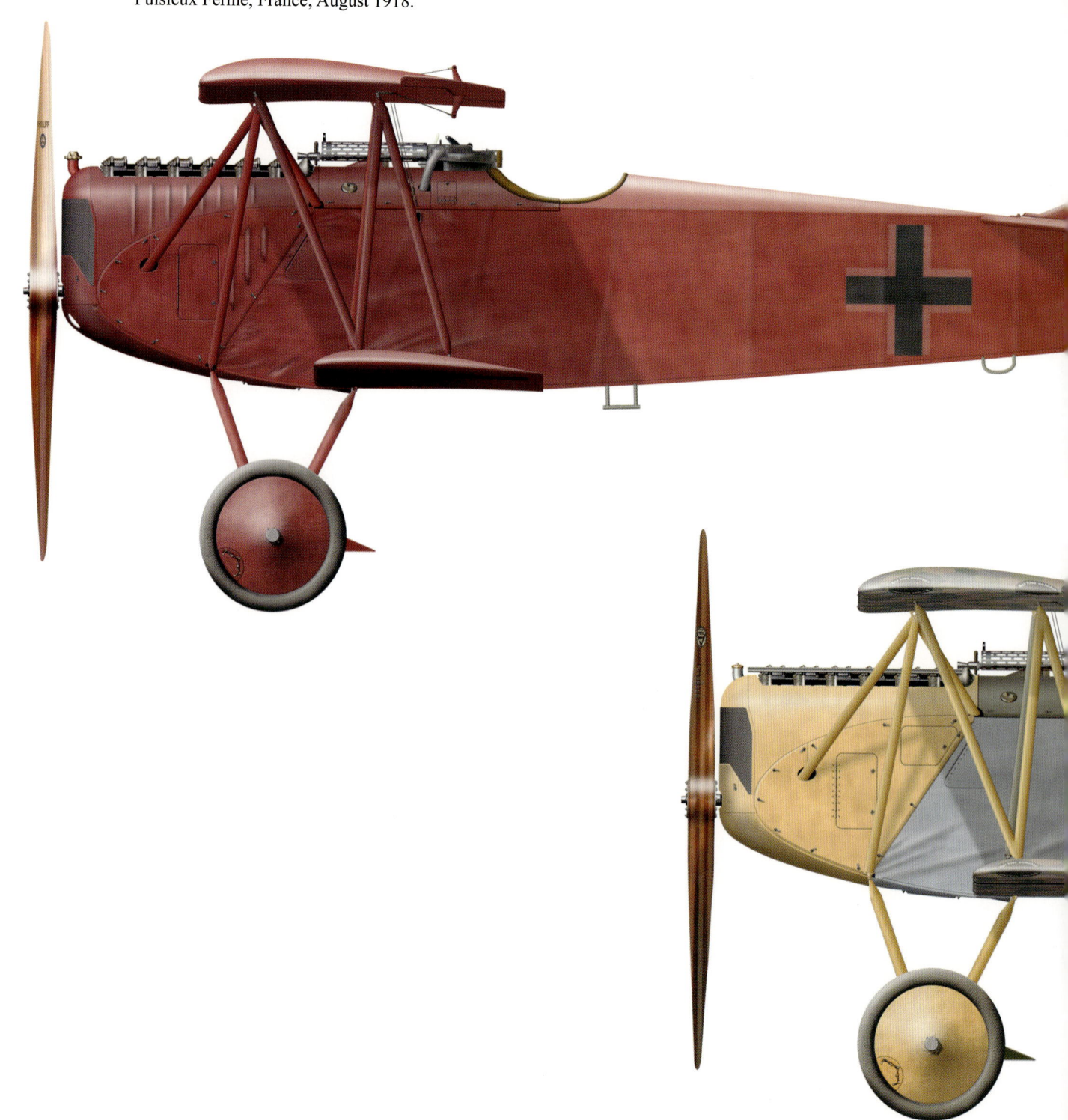

FOKKER D-VII F (465/18) Ltn.
Georg von Hantelmann, Jagdstaffel 15
Tichemont, France; September 1918.

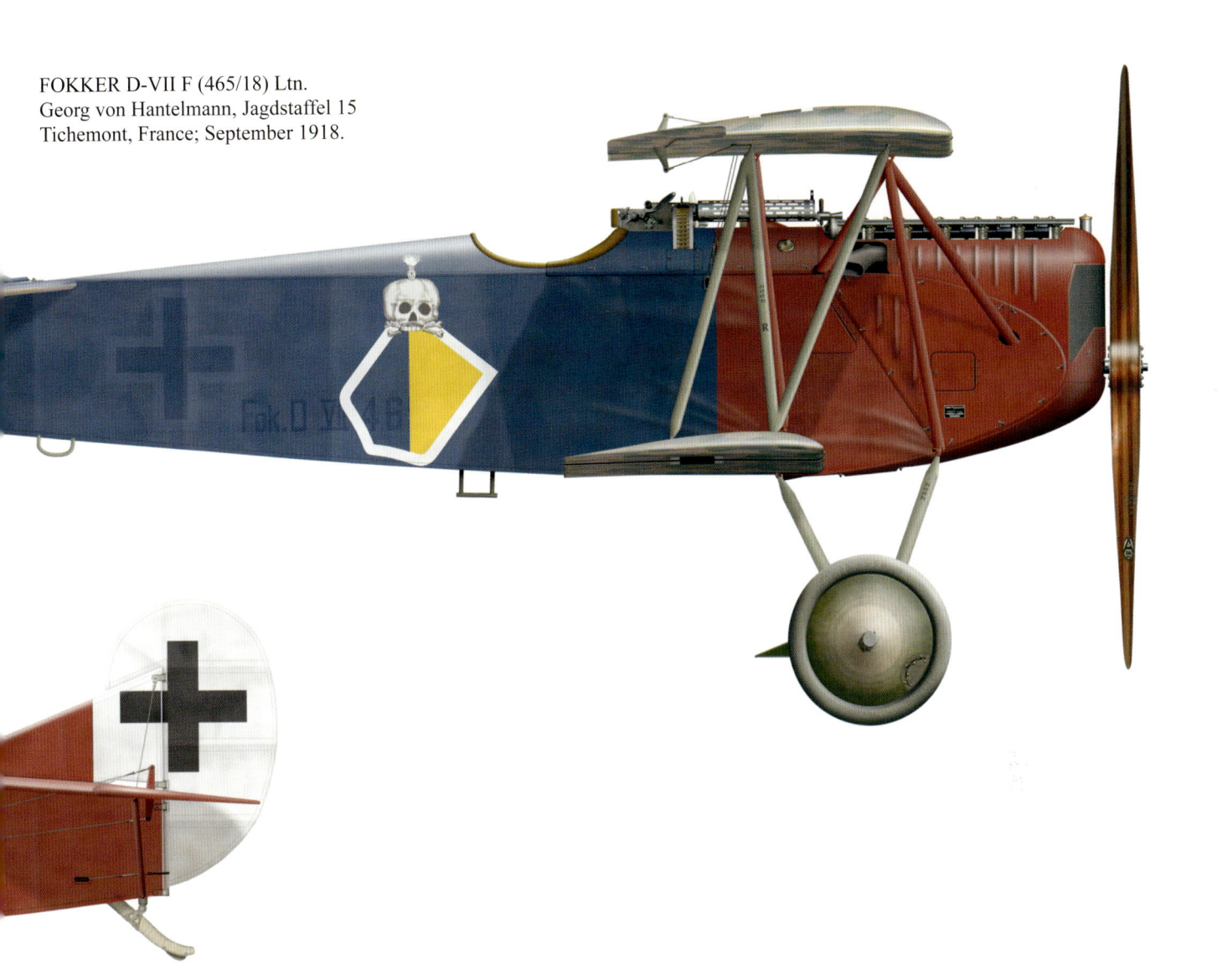

FOKKER D-VIIF (serial unknown) Jagdstaffel 56
Rumbeke, Belgium; September 1918.

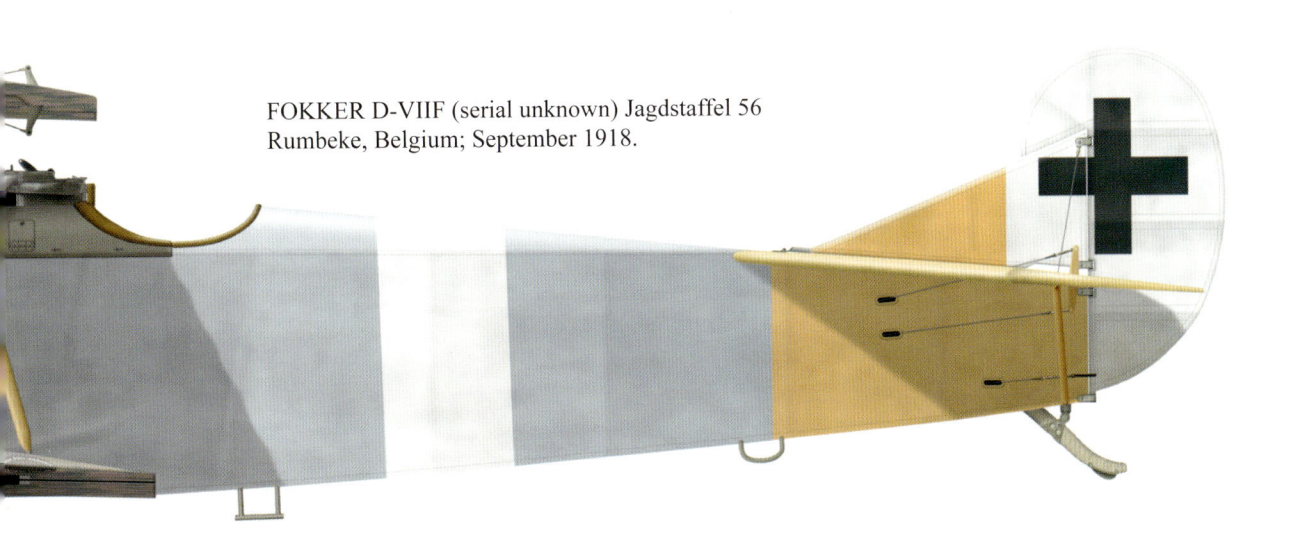

107

FOKKER D-VII F (5125/18) Oblt. Hermann Göring, Jagdgeschwader I
Marville, France; October 1918.

FOKKER D-VII F (serial unknown)
Oblt. Carl Bolle, Jagdstaffel Boelcke
Aniche, France; November 1918.

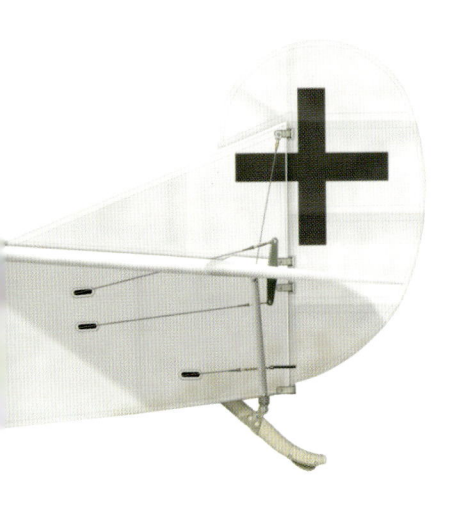

FOKKER D-VII F (4361/18) Jagdstaffel Boelcke
Lens, Belgium; November 1918.

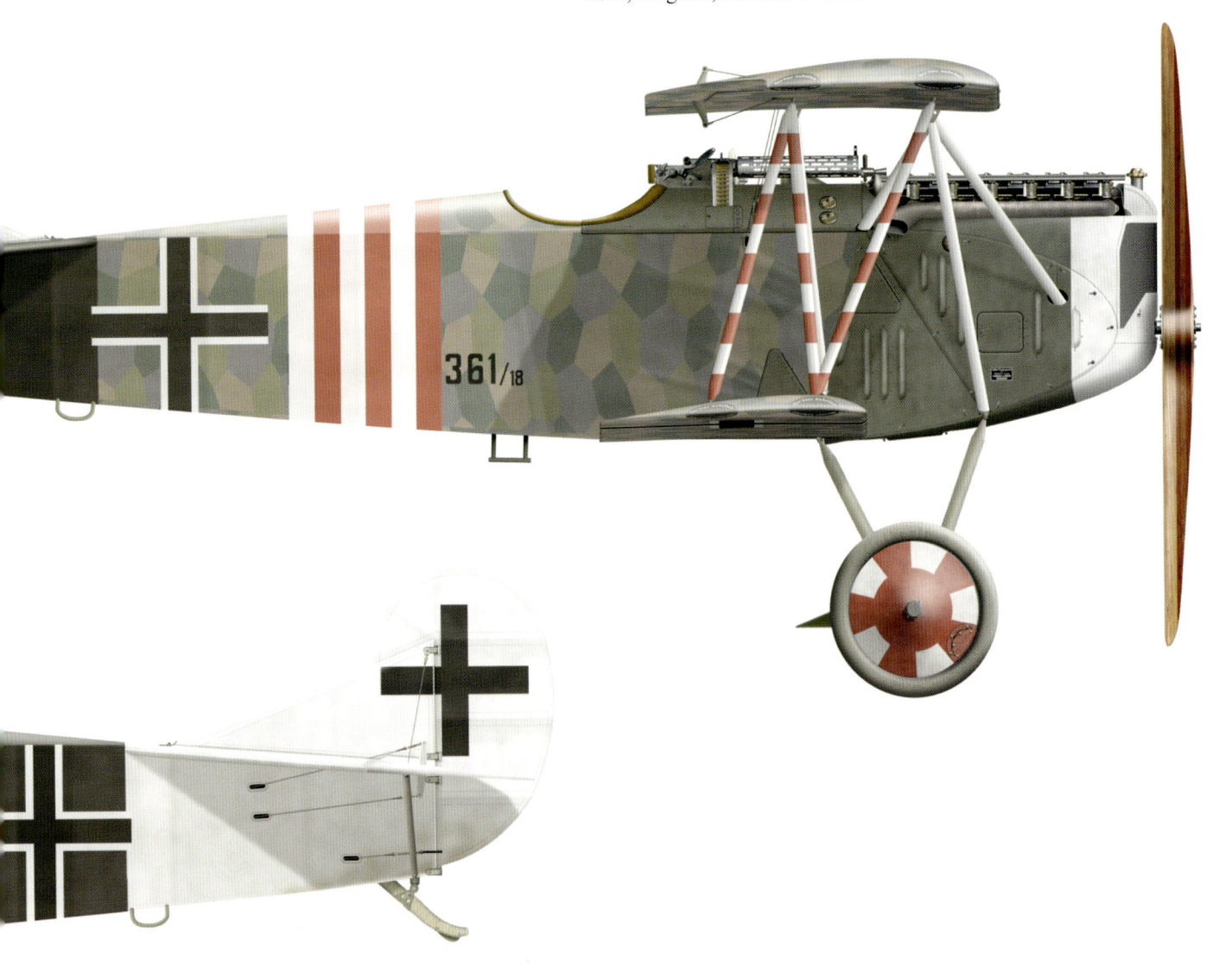

FOKKER D-VII (ALB)

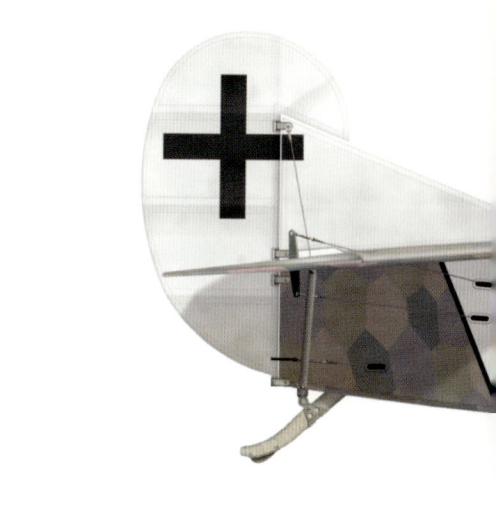

FOKKER D-VII (Alb) (serial unknown)
Ltn. Günther Schuster, Jagdstaffel 17
Mars-sous-Bourcq, France; July 1918.

110

FOKKER D-VII (Alb) (serial unknown) Ltn. Schultz von Dratzig, Jagdstaffel 73
St Remy-le-Petit, France; July 1918.
Note replacement O.A.W. starboard wheel.

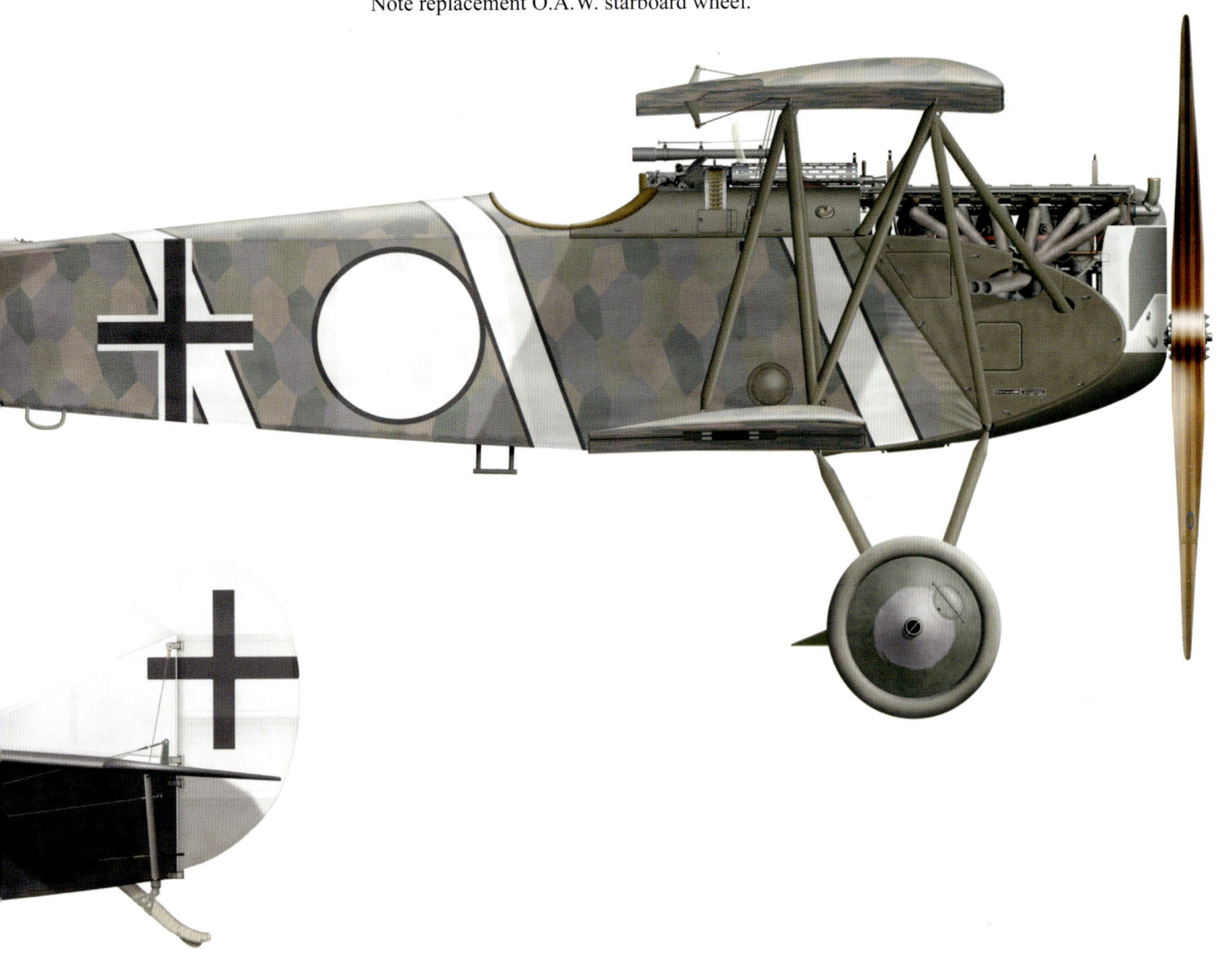

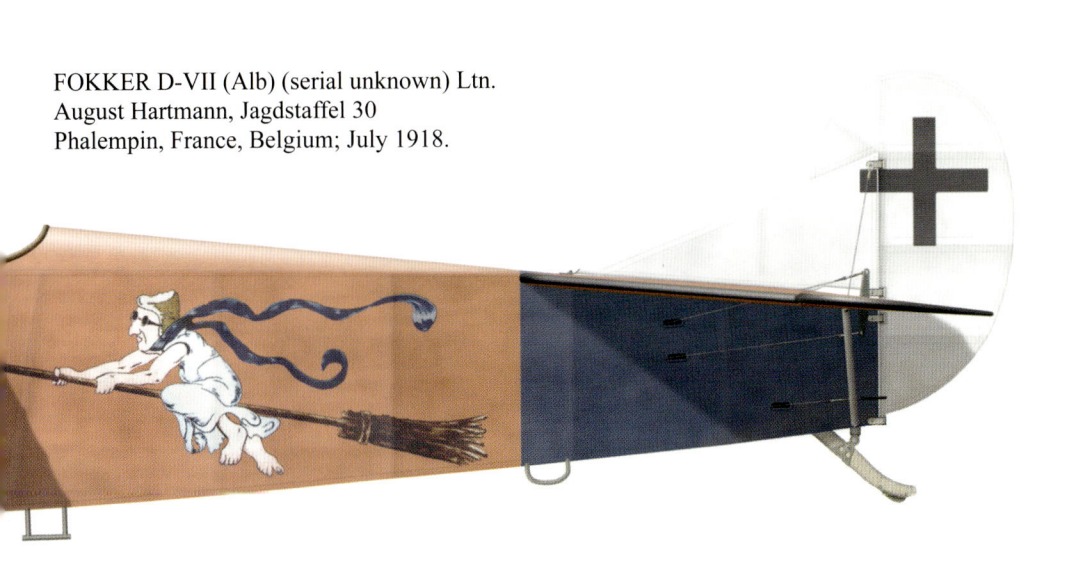

FOKKER D-VII (Alb) (serial unknown) Ltn.
August Hartmann, Jagdstaffel 30
Phalempin, France, Belgium; July 1918.

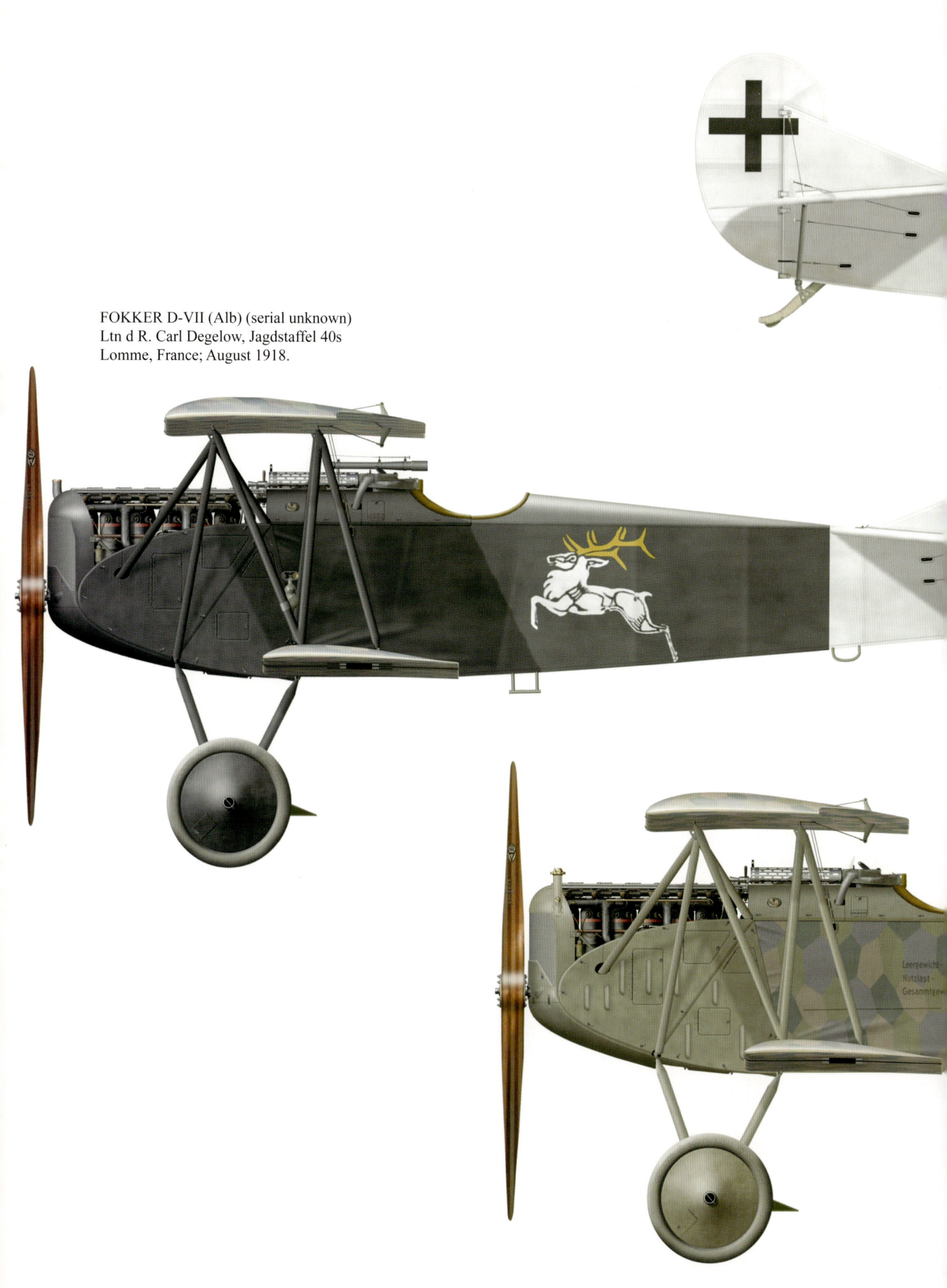

FOKKER D-VII (Alb) (serial unknown)
Ltn d R. Carl Degelow, Jagdstaffel 40s
Lomme, France; August 1918.

FOKKER D-VII (Alb) (serial unknown) Ltn d R. Friedrich Jakobs, Jagdstaffel 43
Haubourdin-Lille, France; August 1918.

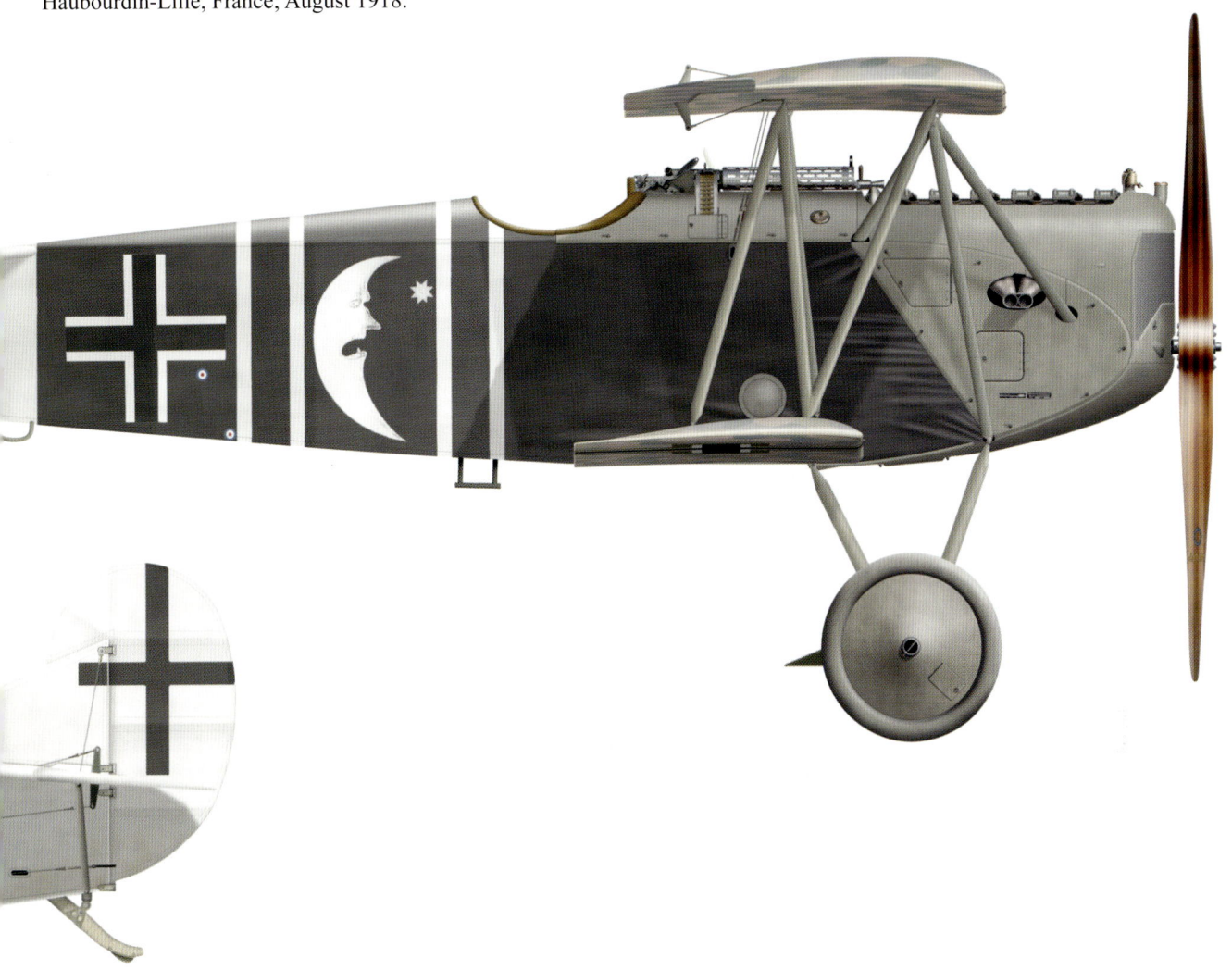

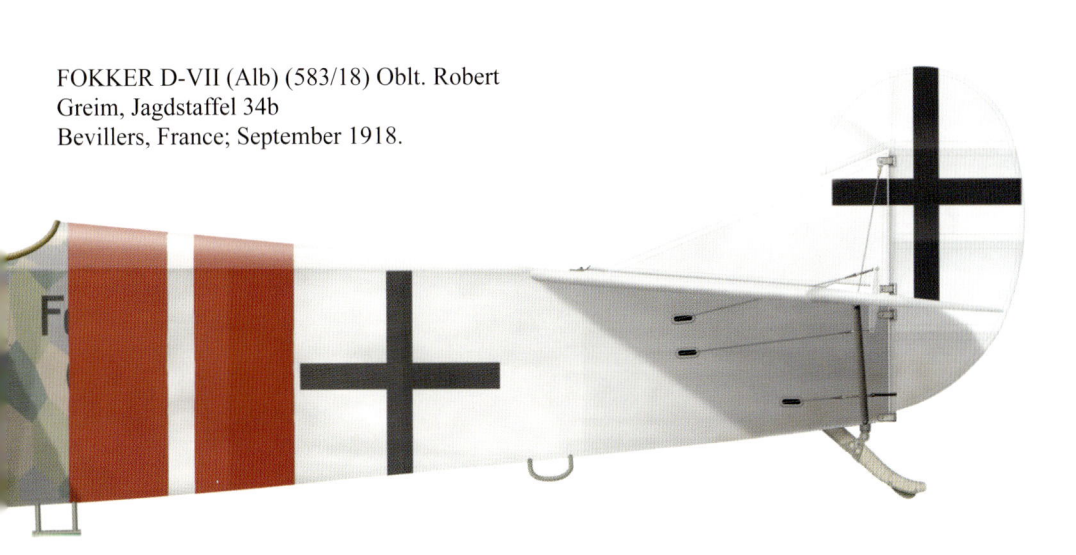

FOKKER D-VII (Alb) (583/18) Oblt. Robert
Greim, Jagdstaffel 34b
Bevillers, France; September 1918.

FOKKER D-VII (O.A.W.)

FOKKER D-VII (O.A.W.) (2012/18) Ltn. Karl Meyer. Jagdstaffel 4
Monthussart, France; July 1918.

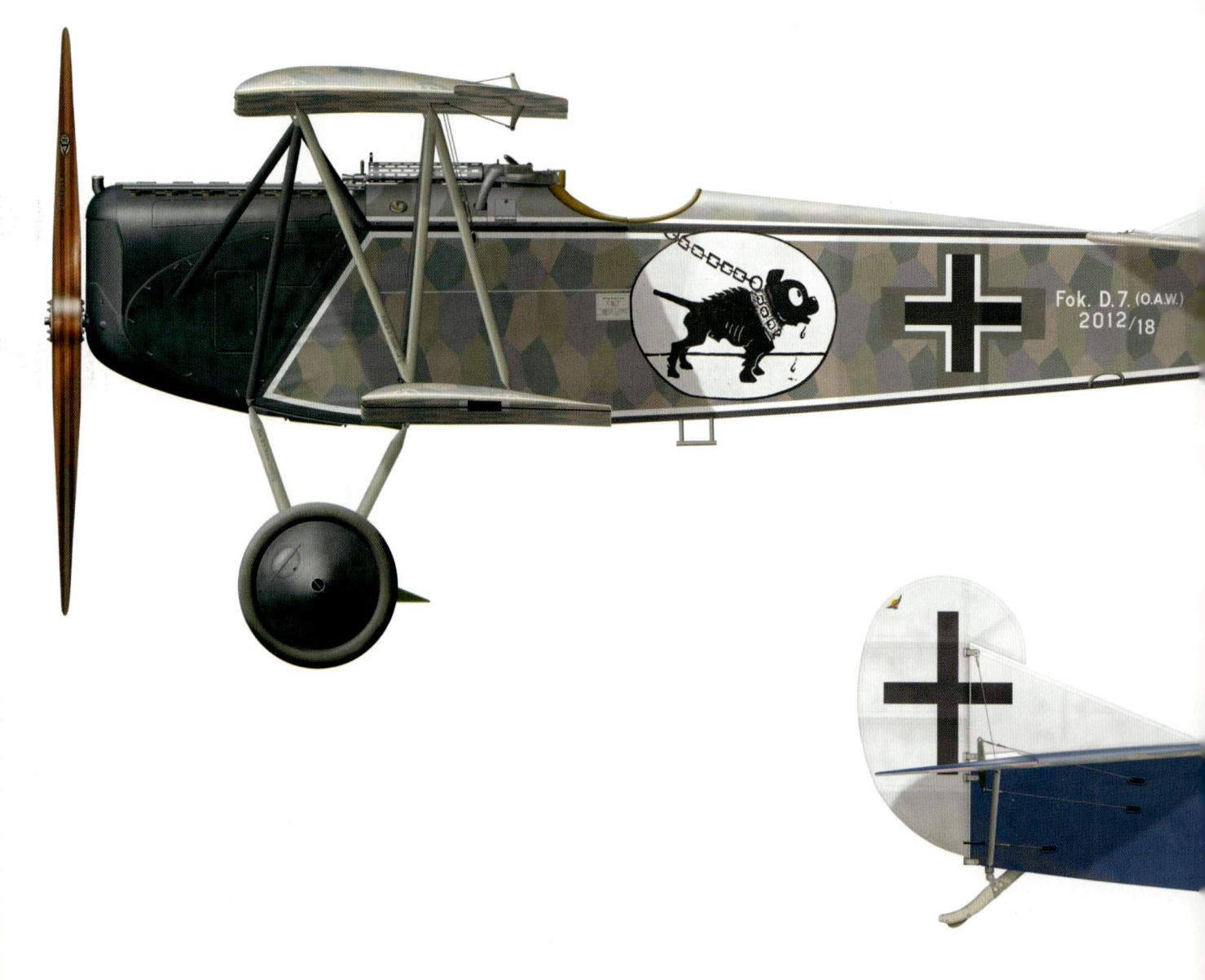

FOKKER D-VII (O.A.W.) (serial unknown) Ltn d R. Ernst Udet, Jagdstaffel 4
Beugneux, France; June 1918.

FOKKER D-VII (O.A.W.) (serial unknown)
Ltn d R. Hans Besser, Jagdstaffel 12
Chery-les-Pouilly, France; August 1918.

115

FOKKER D-VII (O.A.W.) (4649/18) Uffz.
Alfred Bäder, Jagdstaffel 65
Mars-la-Tour, France; Autumn 1918.

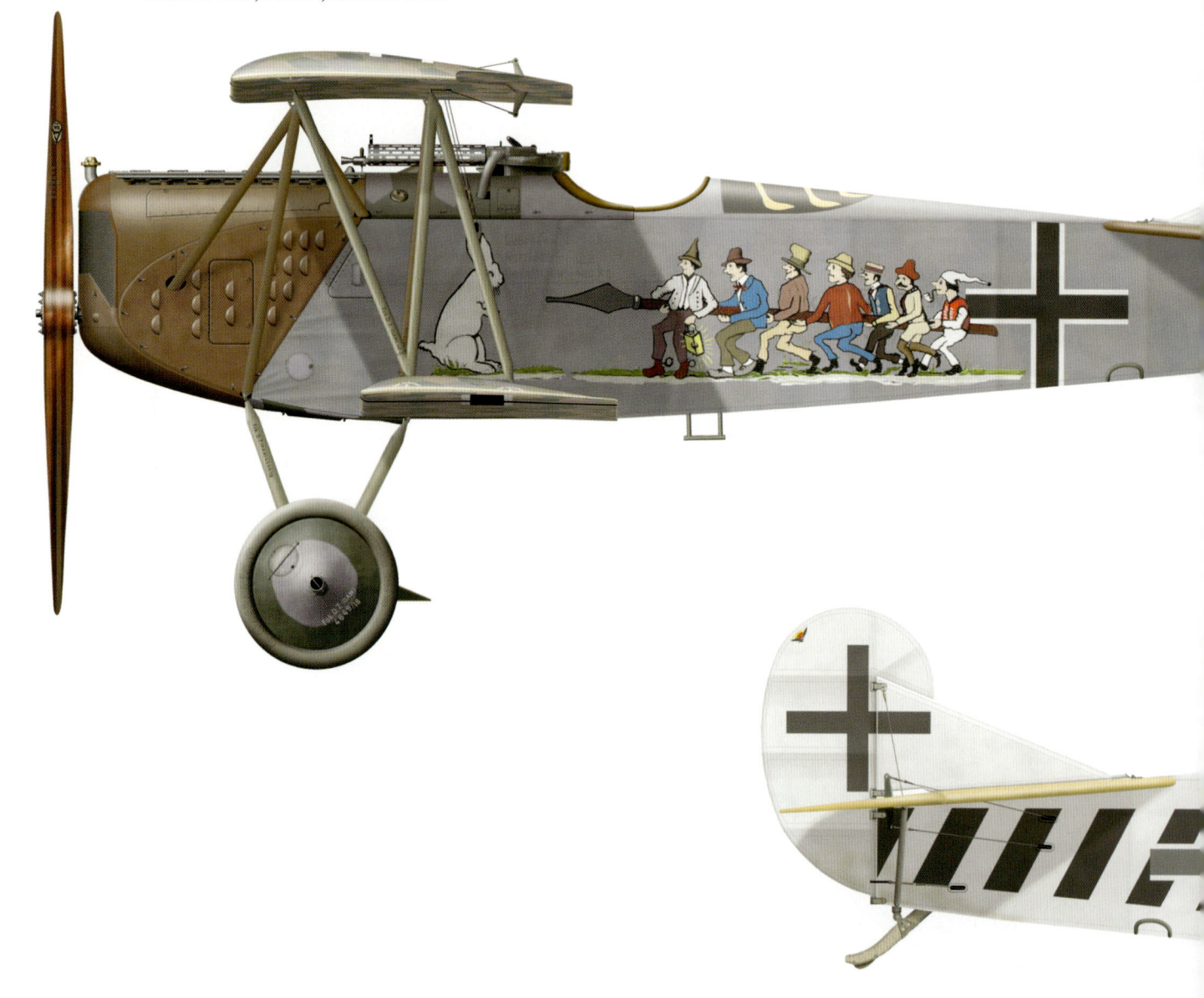

FOKKER D-VII (O.A.W.) (serial unknown)
Ltn d R. Kurt Monnington, Jagdstaffel 18
Montingen, France, August 1918.

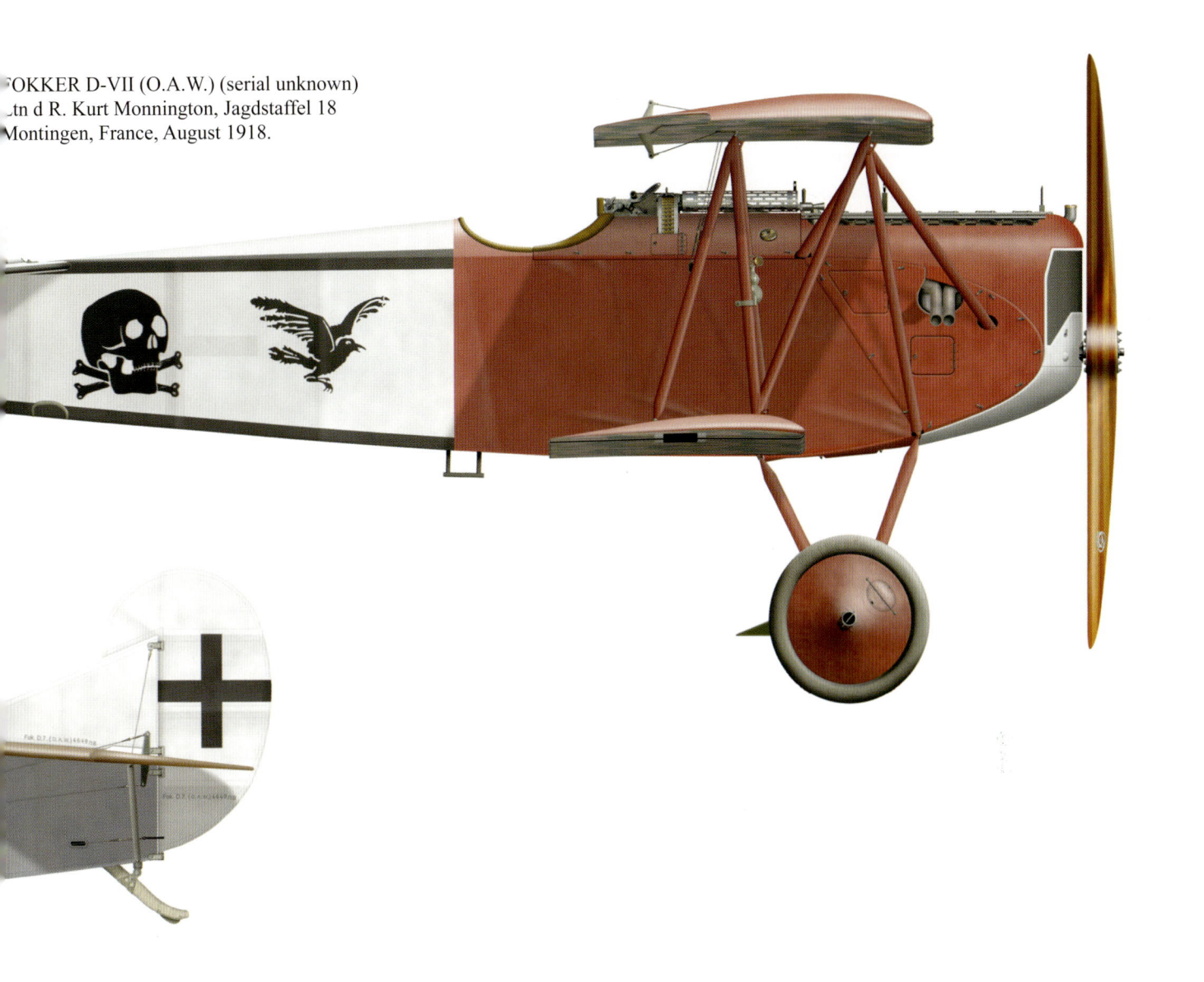

FOKKER D-VII (O.A.W.) (4499/18) Vzflgmstr.
Franz Mayer, Marine Feld Jagdstaffel III
Jabbeke, Belgium, September 1918.

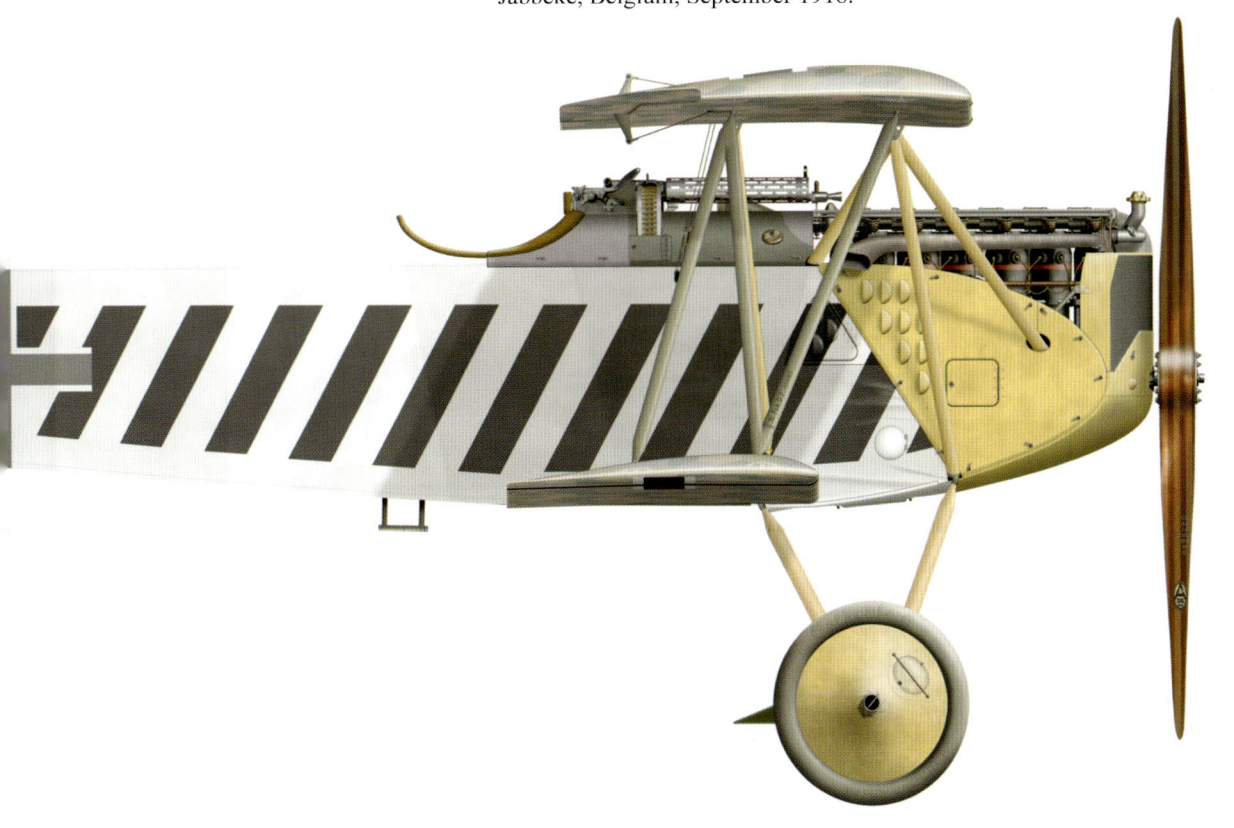

117

FOKKER D-VII (serial unknown) Hptm. Eduard Schleich, Jagdgeschwader IV
Bühl, Germany; October 1918.

FOKKER D-VII (O.A.W.) (serial unknown) Ltn. Franz Büchner, Jagdstaffel 13
Carignan, France; November 1918.

FOKKER D-VII (O.A.W.) (6468/18)
Oblt. Hasso von Wedel, Jagdstaffel 24
Guise, France, October 1918.

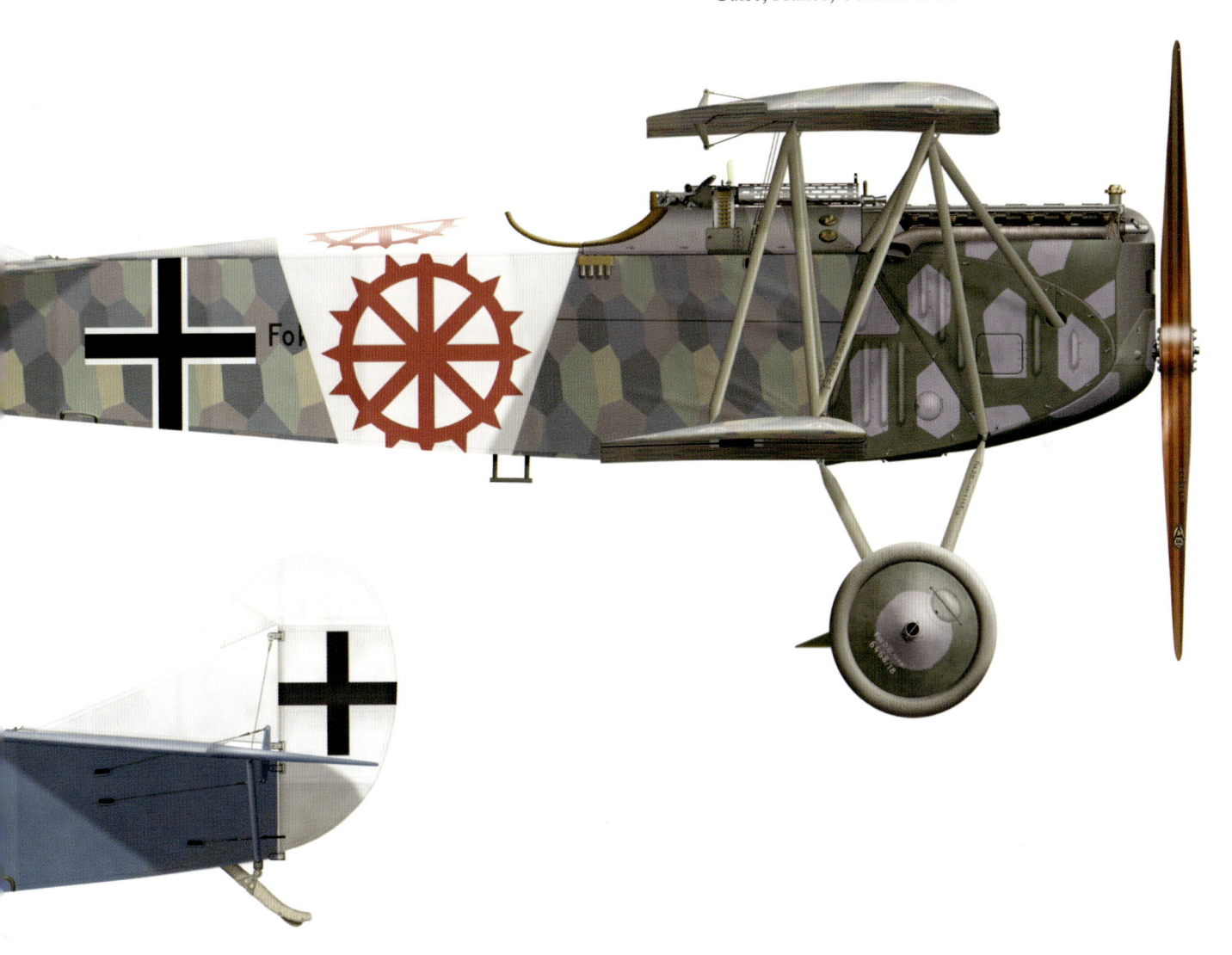

PFALZ D-XII

PFLAZ D-XII (1443/18) Jagdstaffel 77b
Foucaucourt, France; Summer 1918

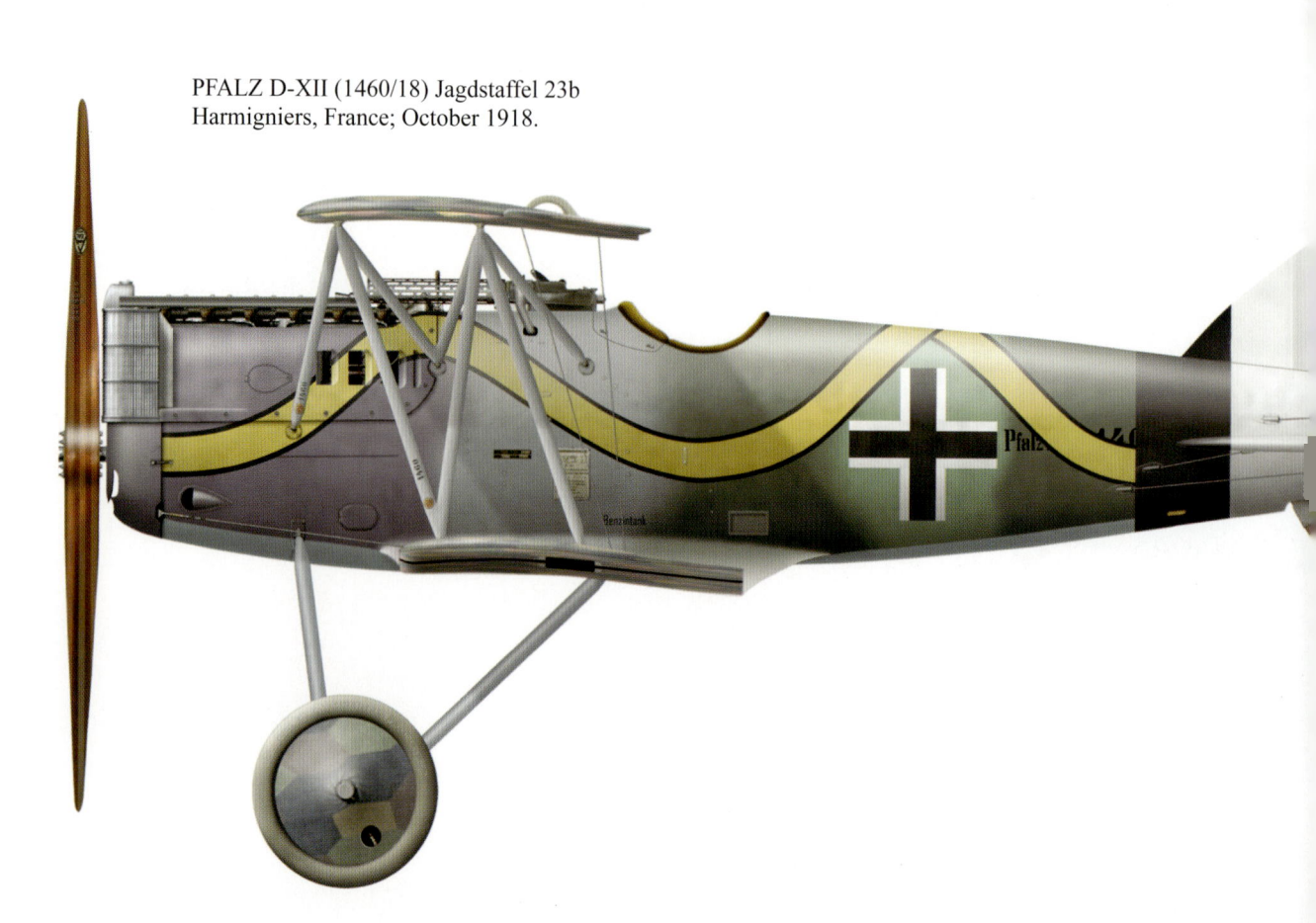

PFALZ D-XII (1460/18) Jagdstaffel 23b
Harmigniers, France; October 1918.

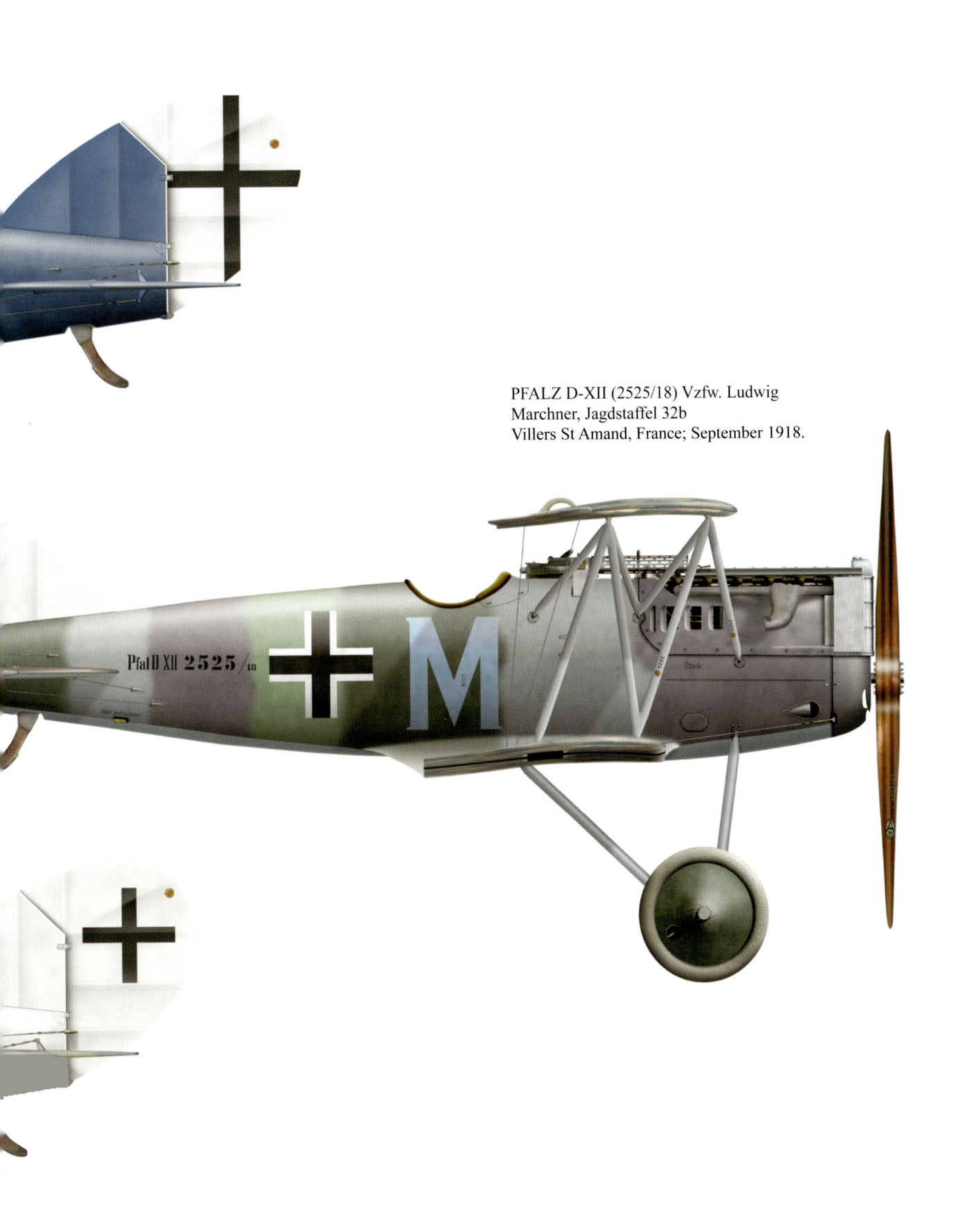

PFALZ D-XII (2525/18) Vzfw. Ludwig Marchner, Jagdstaffel 32b
Villers St Amand, France; September 1918.

FOKKER E-V

FOKKER E-V (150/18) Jagdstaffel 6
Bernes, Belgium; August 1918.

FOKKER E-V (serial unknown) Jagdstaffel 36
Chambray, France; August 1918.

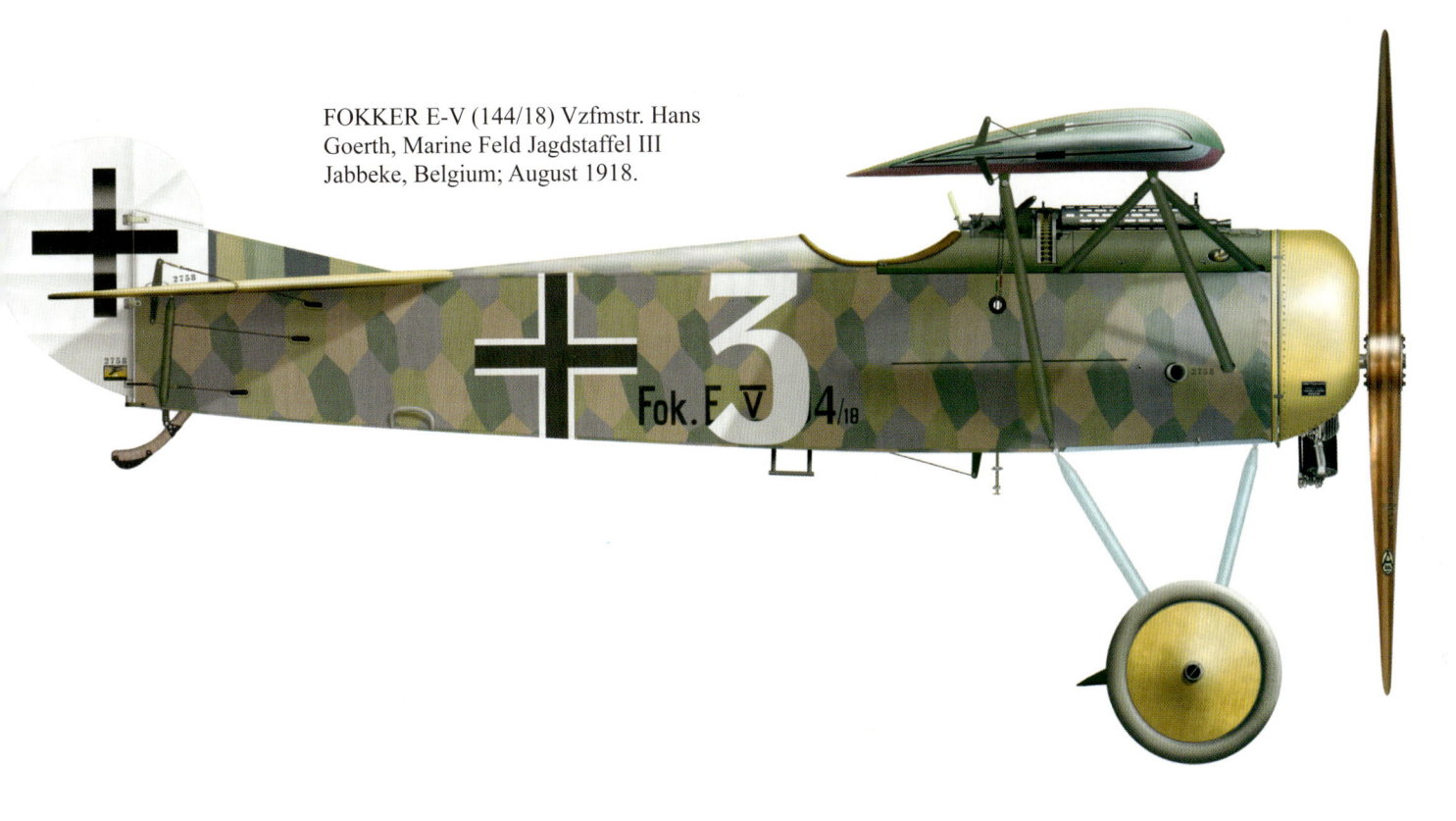

FOKKER E-V (144/18) Vzfmstr. Hans Goerth, Marine Feld Jagdstaffel III Jabbeke, Belgium; August 1918.

FOKKER E-V (160/18) Ltn z S. Gotthard Sachsenberg, Marine Feld Jagdstaffel I Jabbeke, Belgium; August 1918.

SSW D-III

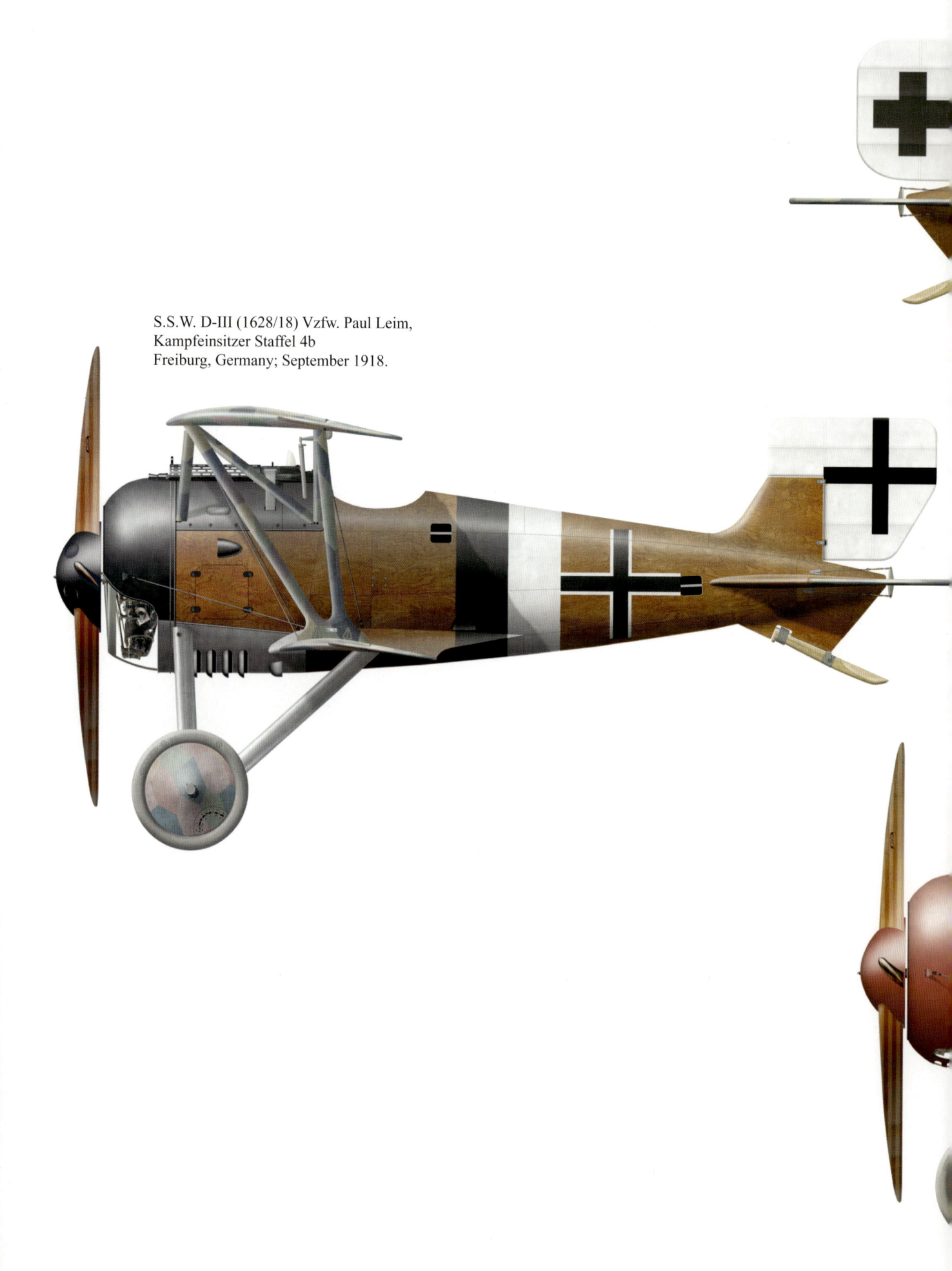

S.S.W. D-III (1628/18) Vzfw. Paul Leim,
Kampfeinsitzer Staffel 4b
Freiburg, Germany; September 1918.

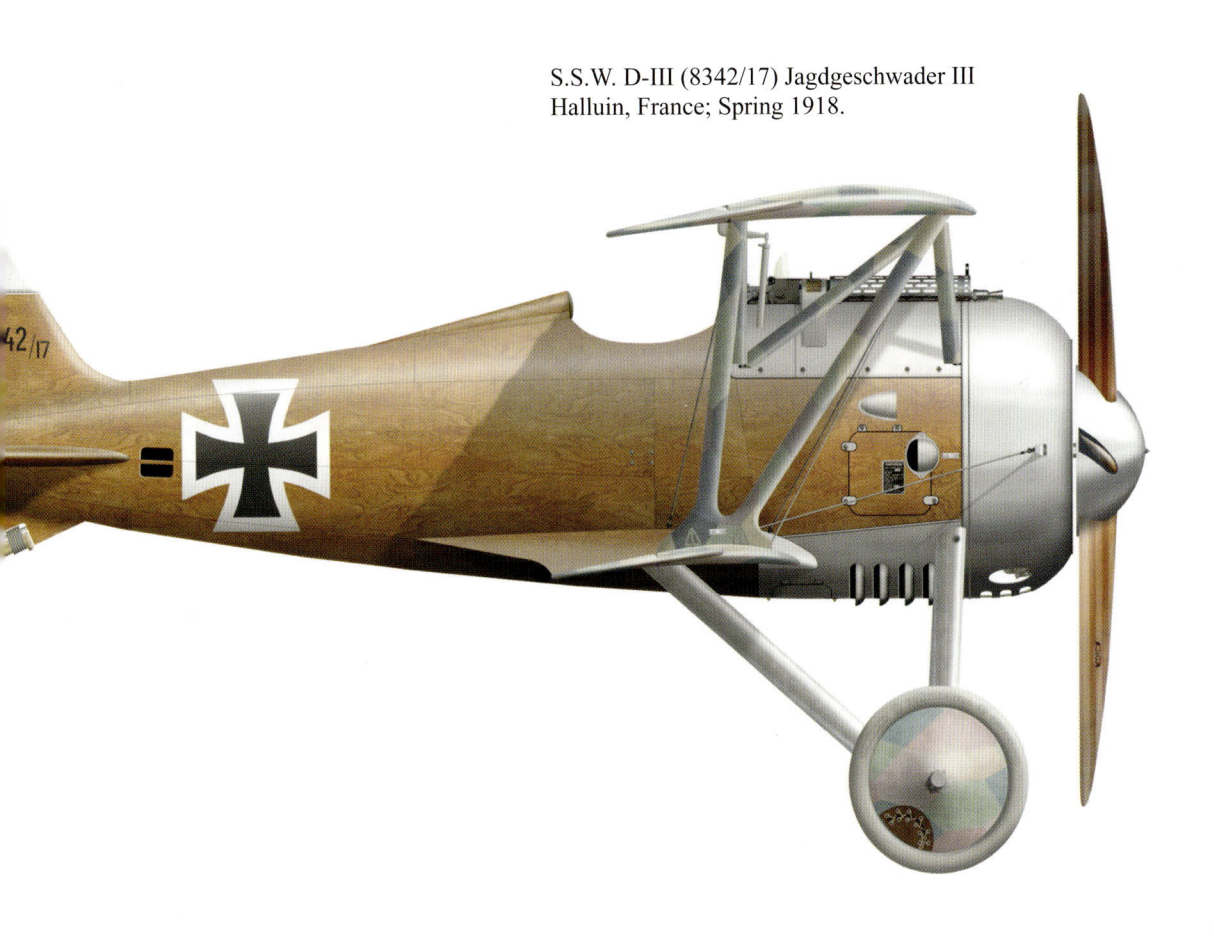

S.S.W. D-III (8342/17) Jagdgeschwader III
Halluin, France; Spring 1918.

S.S.W. D-III (serial unknown) Ltn.
Joachim von Ziegesar, Jagdstaffel 15
Le Mesnil, France; May 1918.

SSW D-IV

S.S.W. D-IV (7554/18) prototype, at the Second Fighter Competition Adlershof, Germany; May 1918.

S.S.W. D-IV (serial unknown) Ltn zu See S. Franz, Marine Feld Jagdstaffel II Jabbeke, Belgium; Summer 1918.

S.S.W. D-IV (7553/17) Jagdstaffel 12
Chéry-les-Pouilly, France; August 1918.

S.S.W. D-IV (3083/18) Ltn. Alfred Lenz, Jagdstaffel 22
Guise, France; October 1918.

127

JUNKERS D-I

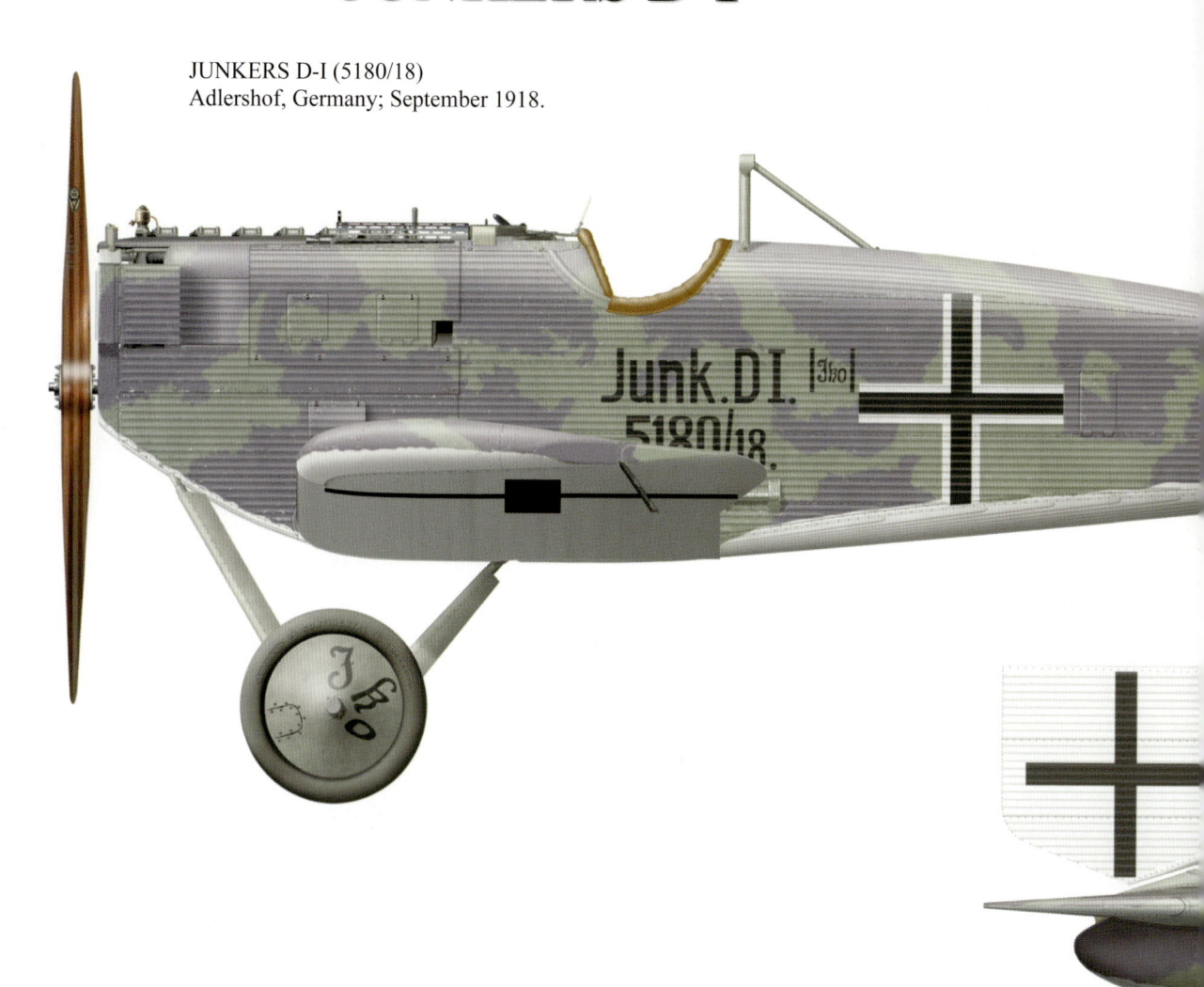

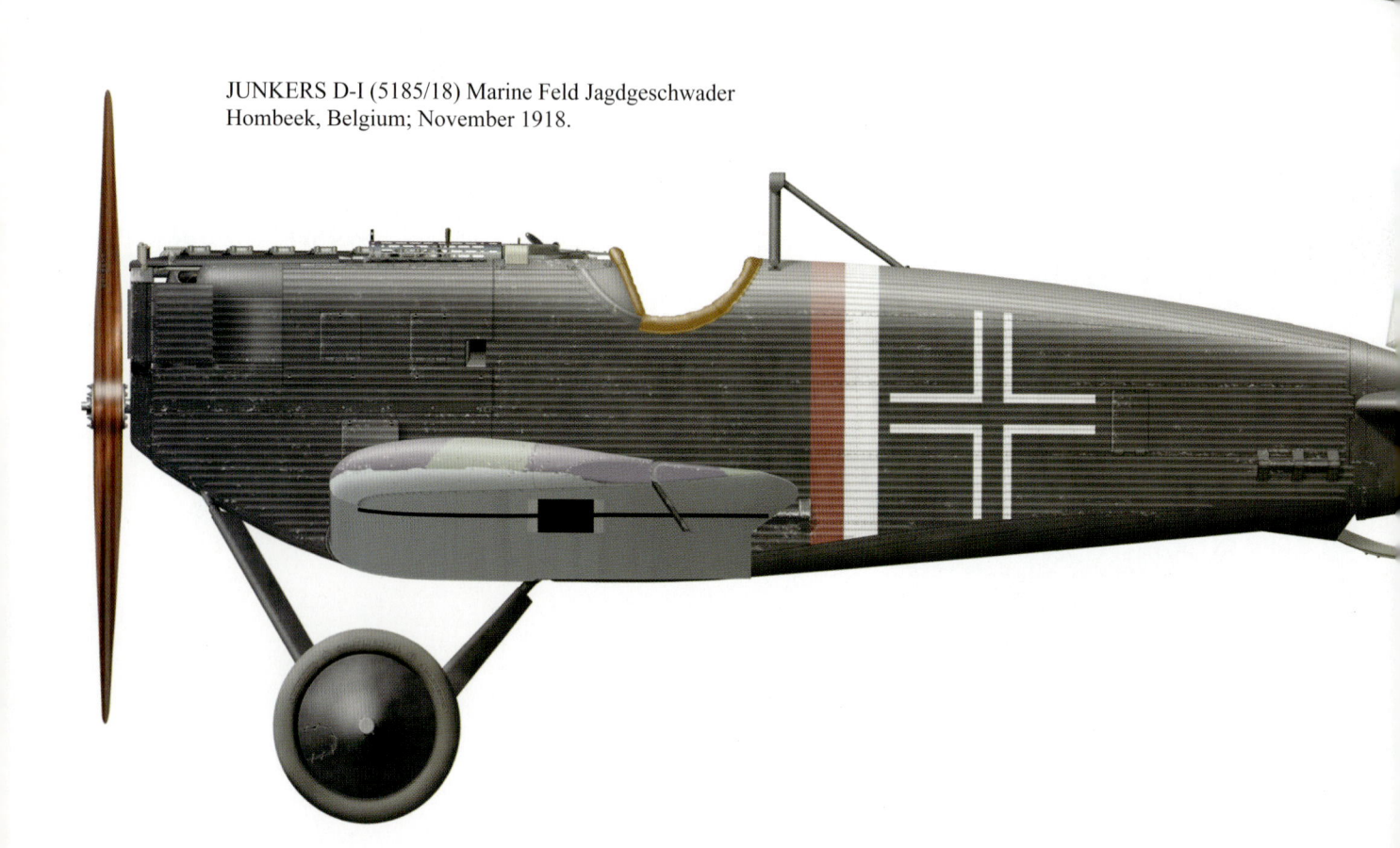

JUNKERS D-I (5180/18)
Adlershof, Germany; September 1918.

JUNKERS D-I (5185/18) Marine Feld Jagdgeschwader
Hombeek, Belgium; November 1918.

JUNKERS D-I (9166/18) Flieger Abteilung 416
Wainoden, Courland; Early 1919.

Acknowledgements

JUNKERS D-I (5185/18)
Marine Feld Jagdgeschwader
Hombeek, Belgium; November 1918.

I'll be forever grateful...

To Peter Kilduff. For choosing me to illustrate several of his wonderful books.

To Greg Van Wynngarden: For taken the time to review each profile in this book and advising and helping me make this work as accurate as possible.

To Josef Scott: For generously sharing with me his expertise on the Fokker Eindeckern.

To Sir Peter Jackson: Because working with him on his amazing Wingnut Wings project for more than 15 years was an unforgettable experience which also boosted my career in an incredible way.

To Richard Alexander, for the support and patience during all the time we worked together in the already legendary Wingnut Wings and currently in the new Kotare Models, and for the friendship we built during my times in New Zealand.

To Ray Rimell: For his enduring and generous support throughout all these years publishing my work in the iconic Windsock Datafiles.

To Ray again, and also to my good friend Colin Huston from Cross & Cockade, Jack Herris from Aeronaut Books, Aaron Weaver from Over The Front, Ruth Sheppard from Casemate Publishers, Michael Spilling from Amber Books Ltd, Nigel Dingley from Air Britain Ltd, Steve O'Hara from Mortons Books, and to many other publishers: For publishing my work and making it known by thousands of readers and enthusiasts all around the world.

To authors and writers, Greg VanWynngarden again, to my friend Colin Owers, Peter Kilduff, Alan Toelle, Josef Scott, Jim Wilberg, Bruno Schmaelling, Gregory Alegi, Paelo Varriale, Mark Wilkins, Paul Hare, JS Alcorn, Xavier Chevallier, Phillip Jarret, Edward Ward: For trusting me to illustrate their magnificent books and articles and for generously sharing their huge knowledge, expertise and advice to help me improve my work.

To my colleague artists: Juanita Franzi, Russell Smith, Robert Karr, Bob Pearson, Jim Miller, Dave Douglas, Steve Anderson, Mark Miller, Tomasz Gronczewski, Piotr Mrozoswski, Jerry Boucher: For their exquisite and always inspiring artwork, and for the good vibes I've always received from them.

To Eugene Ushakow, who whenever I asked provided me with good information.

To my good old friends: Claudio Meunier, Diego Fernetti and Hector Martin Afflitto Echagile, for encouraging and supporting me to enter this fascinating world of professional aircraft profiling.

Ronny Bar